THE TWO SICK MEN OF EUROPE?

BRITAIN AND ITALY BETWEEN CRISIS AND RENAISSANCE (1976-1983)

P.I.E. Peter Lang

Bruxelles · Bern · Berlin · New York · Oxford · Wien

EUROCLIO is a scientific and editorial project, a network of research institutions and researchers, and an ideas forum. EUROCLIO as an editorial project consists of two aspects: the first concerns studies and documents, the second concerns tools. Both are aimed at making the results of research more accessible, and also at opening up paths through the history of European construction/integration/unification.

The EUROCLIO series meets a dual objective:

- to provide reference tools for research,
- to provide a platform for this research in terms of the publication of results.

The series thus consists of two sub-series that satisfy these requirements: the Studies and Documents series and the References series. These two series are aimed at general libraries and/or university history departments, teachers and researchers, and in certain cases, specific professional circles.

The Studies and Documents series consists of monographs, collections of articles, conference proceedings, and collections of texts with notes for teaching purposes.

The References series consists of bibliographies, guides and other tools. It thus contributes to the creation of a database making up a "Permanent catalogue of sources and bibliographies on European construction".

THE TWO SICK MEN OF EUROPE?

BRITAIN AND ITALY BETWEEN CRISIS AND RENAISSANCE (1976-1983)

Giulia Bentivoglio

Euroclio
Vol. 104

Published with the contribution of the Department of Political Sciences, Law and International Studies of the University of Padua.

Linguistic supervision: Nicola Resnati.

This publication has been peer reviewed.

Éditions scientifiques internationales
Brussels, 2018
1 avenue Maurice, B-1050 Brussels, Belgium
brussels@peterlang.com; www.peterlang.com

Printed in Germany

ISSN 0944-2294
ISBN 978-2-8076-0720-0
ePDF 978-2-8076-0721-7
ePUB 978-2-8076-0722-4
MOBI 978-2-8076-0723-1
DOI 10.3726/b13687
D/2018/5678/35

CIP available at the Library of Congress and the British Library.

Bibliographic information published by "Die Deutsche Nationalbibliothek".

"Die Deutsche National Bibliothek" lists this publication in the "Deutsche Nationalbibliografie"; detailed bibliographic data is available on the Internet at <http://dnb.de>.

Table of Contents

Acknowledgements

For their help and support during the long journey out of which this research developed, I owe many people a debt of gratitude.

First, I would like to thank the Department of Political Sciences, Law and International Studies of the University of Padua for the research fellowships granted me in these years. This research took its first steps during my participation in the Project of National Interest (PRIN) *L'Italia nel contesto internazionale (1968-1981): crisi, trasformazioni, stabilizzazione*, led by Prof. Antonio Varsori. To him goes my heartfelt thanks, also for his precious advice.

I owe much to the Gerard Ford Foundation for awarding me a travel grant that has been fundamental for my research in the United States.

The months spent as Visiting Fellow at the IDEAS Centre of the London School of Economics and Political Sciences have proved to be an inexhaustible source of inspiration. I would like to thank Prof. Odd Arne Westad, then co-director of the Centre, and Dr. George Lawson for their assistance.

I also express my gratitude to the scholars who offered to share their advice and knowledge with me during the years of this research: I refer, in particular, to Prof. Piers Ludlow and Prof. Mark Gilbert. Special thanks also to my colleague and friend Prof. David Burigana, for the encouragement and support.

I would like to thank the staff of the many archives I have visited during my research, in particular Jeremy Schmidt (Gerald R. Ford Presidential Library, Ann Arbor, Michigan), Jeremy McIlwaine (Conservative Party Archive, Oxford) and Darren Treadwell (Labour History Archive and Study Centre, Manchester). I am also grateful to the staff of the library "Ettore Anchieri" of the University of Padua. Thanks to Paul for the final revision of this work.

Last but definitely not least, my final thanks go to Sebastiano, without whom this book would have never seen the light of day. Words cannot explain how much he has helped me through these long and difficult months, sharing my burden (most of the time, carrying it all by himself) and being my firm foundation in this shaky world. I hope I will be able to repay him in the life we will spend together. This book is dedicated to him.

Abbreviations

ASPR	*Archivio Storico della Presidenza della Repubblica*, Rome
BBQ	British Budgetary Question
BR	Red Brigades
CAB	Cabinet series
CAP	Common Agricultural Policy
CBI	Confederation of British Industry
CGIL	Italian General Confederation of Labour
CIA	Central Intelligence Agency
CPA	Conservative Party Archive, Oxford
CPGB	Communist Party of Great Britain
DC	Christian Democracy
ECOFIN	Economic and Financial Affairs Council
ECU	European Currency Unit
EEC	European Economic Community
EMS	European Monetary System
FCO	Foreign and Commonwealth Office
GFL	Gerald R. Ford Library, Ann Arbor, Michigan
GDP	Gross Domestic Product
IGC	Intergovernmental Conference
IMF	International Monetary Fund
INF	Intermediate-Range Nuclear Forces
IRD	Information Research Department
LHASC	Labour History Archive and Study Centre, Manchester
MFO	Multinational Force and Observers
MNF	Multinational Force in Lebanon
MP	Member of Parliament
NATO	North Atlantic Treaty Organisation
OECD	Organisation for Economic Co-operation and Development

OPEC	Organization of the Petroleum Exporting Countries
PCF	French Communist Party
PCI	Italian Communist Party
PLI	Italian Liberal Party
PREM	Prime Minister series
PRI	Italian Republican Party
PSBR	Public Sector Borrowing Requirement
PSDI	Italian Socialist Democratic Party
PSI	Italian Socialist Party
PUS	Permanent Under-Secretary
SALT	Strategic Arms Limitation Talks
SEA	Single European Act
SPD	Social Democratic Party of Germany
TNA	The National Archives of the United Kingdom, Kew
TNF	Theatre Nuclear Forces
TUC	Trades Union Congress
UNIFIL	United Nations Interim Force in Lebanon

Introduction

The Anglo-Italian relationship, whether personal or general, has always been an emotional one, quite different from feelings between any other two European countries. Anti-Italian feeling was one of the forces harnessed by Henry VIII to carry out the Reformation and make it an essential part of the modern English nation state; while pro-Italian feeling by Britain was equally essential to the process by which the Italians, a century ago, constructed their own nation state. Both are still present.[1]

It is hard to find two countries more diverse than Britain and Italy: their geography, climate, habits are almost poles apart. The former is considered one of the cradles of democracy, whose two-party system has been an example for many countries; the latter could be labelled the most unstable democracy in Europe, if we look at the records of consecutive governments – 64 in 72 years.[2] The British Parliament has been the model for most other parliamentary systems since the 13th century. Conversely, the Italian system offers no comparison with the British one, and this led to frequent misunderstandings and quite often alarm about Italian democracy. Moreover, Italy is a young country and, as a republic, still younger (although it has been underlined how by 1979, during the generation and a half since the founding of the Italian Republic, democracy had already suffered "virtually every ill that a democracy can endure").[3] Also, the two countries have very different attitudes towards Europe: Italy can be counted among the most pro-European countries, participating in the integrationist project since its very beginning and considering the European dimension as one of the pillars of her foreign policy.[4] On the other hand, Britain entered into the European Community at a later

---

1 Nichols P., "Italy: a laboratory for the ills that beset the rest of the western world", *The Times*, 20 June 1977.

2 This introduction has been written before the Italian general election of March 2018, which should lead to the installation of the 65th government in the history of the Italian Republic.

3 Tarrow S., "Italy: Crisis, Crises or Transition?", in Lange P., Tarrow S. (eds.), Special issue on "Italy in transition: conflict and consensus", *West European Politics*, Vol. 2, No. 3, October 1979. The Kingdom of Italy was established in 1861, while Italy became a republic with the referendum of 2 June 1946.

4 Varsori A., *La Cenerentola d'Europa? L'Italia e l'integrazione europea dal 1947 ad oggi*, Rubbettino, Soveria Mannelli 2010.

stage, and from the start she was considered an "awkward partner" and a "reluctant European", a reputation some British governments wanted to prove wrong, but that can no longer be denied after the *Brexit* referendum of 23 June 2016.[5]

These fundamental differences have stimulated, through the years, many stereotypes which are still rooted in both countries. On the British side, there is an attitude favourable to Italy but rather patronising: Italian intelligence, creativity, and enterprise are counterbalanced by lack of punctuality, steadiness, and reliability.[6] Italians, on the other hand, usually ascribe to the British some old-fashioned virtues such as loyalty, persistence, and pragmatism, while considering them rigid and wanting in vivacity.[7]

Yet, despite all these differences, since the mid-1970s Britain and Italy shared a common destiny of struggle against the crisis. In the general turbulence of the "long 1970s" which affected the two shores of the Atlantic, London and Rome emerged as the weakest countries: they were the two "sick men" of Europe. The present work, based on multi-archival research and mainly unpublished primary sources, is the first study on this neglected topic.

More generally, Anglo-Italian relations in the Cold War are an almost unexplored territory. Historiography has occasionally dealt with the relationship between Rome and London in the 20th century, focussing mainly on the period between the two World Wars and on relations between Britain and Fascist Italy.[8] Since the 1980s, a branch of research

---

5 The reference here is to two volumes: George S., *An awkward partner. Britain in the European Community*, Oxford University Press, Oxford 1990; Gowland D., Turner A., *Reluctant Europeans: Britain and European Integration 1945-1998*, Routledge, London 1999.

6 The perception of Italians as untrustworthy interlocutors has its roots deep in history, in Italy's "volte-faces" in 1915 (when the country joined the Triple Entente during the First World War despite having signed the Triple Alliance with Germany and Austria) and in 1943 (when the Italian Army capitulated after the Allied invasion of Sicily). British stereotypes of Italians partly derive from the warmer climate and a more relaxed, Mediterranean atmosphere, which otherwise Brits appreciate (a county in Tuscany has gained the nickname of "Chiantishire" for the number of tourists and also property owners from the UK). In the 18th century, the Grand Tour, a journey of discovery to Italy's art and landscapes, was a rite of passage for young British noblemen. See Chaney E., *The Evolution of the Grand Tour: Anglo-Italian Cultural Relations since the Renaissance*, Frank Cass, London 1998.

7 See Campbell A., *Colleagues and Friends*, Michael Russell, Salisbury 1988, pp. 128-129.

8 Micheletta L., *Italia e Gran Bretagna nel primo dopoguerra: le relazioni diplomatiche tra Roma e Londra dal 1919 al 1922*, Jouvence, Roma 1999; Fiore M., *Anglo-Italian relations in the Middle East, 1922-1940*, Ashgate, Farnham 2010; Lamb R., *Mussolini and the British*, John Murray, London 1997; Baldoli C., *Exporting fascism: Italian fascists and Britain's Italians in the 1930s*, Berg, Oxford 2003.

investigated the relations between anti-Fascism in Italy and the Anglo-Americans, particularly the British, during the Second World War: we can quote here the works by Massimo de Leonardis, Elena Aga Rossi and Antonio Varsori.[9] If we consider the few works dealing with the relations between the UK and the Republic of Italy (since 1946), most authors, like Effie Pedaliu and the above mentioned Varsori, have analysed the aftermath of the Second World War; Ilaria Favretto, though studying a wider time frame, has instead focussed on the British Labour Party and the Italian Left, investigating mainly their domestic policies.[10]

According to received opinion, Anglo-Italian relations during the Cold War were of secondary importance. In the Western bloc, both Britain and Italy had other privileged and coinciding interlocutors, namely the United States, France and the Federal Republic of Germany. The special relationship between London and Washington has been one of the pillars of British foreign policy since 1945 – and the second of the "three circles" of Britain's influence conceived by Winston Churchill in 1948.[11] In the

---

9 de Leonardis M., *La Gran Bretagna e la Resistenza italiana (1943-1945)*, Edizioni Scientifiche Italiane, Napoli 1988; Aga Rossi E., *L'Italia nella sconfitta: politica interna e situazione internazionale durante la seconda guerra mondiale*, Edizioni Scientifiche Italiane, Napoli 1985; Varsori A., *Gli alleati e l'emigrazione democratica antifascista (1940-1943)*, Sansoni, Firenze 1982; and the more recent volumes by Piffer and Berrettini: Piffer T., *Gli Alleati e la Resistenza italiana*, Il Mulino, Bologna 2010; Berrettini M., *La Gran Bretagna e l'antifascismo italiano. Diplomazia clandestina, intelligence, operazioni speciali (1940-1943)*, Le Lettere, Firenze 2010. On Anglo-Italian relations during the Second World War see also Ellwood D.W., *L'alleato nemico. La politica dell'occupazione anglo-americana in Italia (1943-1946)*, Feltrinelli, Milano 1977; Filippone Thaulero G., *La Gran Bretagna e l'Italia dalla conferenza di Mosca a Potsdam (1943-1945)*, Edizioni di Storia e Letteratura, Roma 1979.

10 Pedaliu E., *Britain, Italy and the Origins of the Cold War*, Palgrave Macmillan, Basingstoke 2003; Varsori A., *Il diverso declino di due potenze coloniali: gli eventi di Mogadiscio del gennaio 1948 e i rapporti anglo-italiani*, Elengraf, Roma 1981; *Id.*, "Great Britain and Italy 1945-1956: The Partnership between a Great Power and a Minor Power?", *Diplomacy and Statecraft*, Vol. 2, 1992, pp. 188-228; *Id.*, "La Gran Bretagna e le elezioni politiche italiane del 18 aprile 1948", *Storia Contemporanea*, Vol. XIII, No. 1, 1982, pp. 5-71; Favretto I., *The Long Search for a 'Third Way': the British Labour Party and the Italian Left since 1945*, Palgrave Macmillan, Basingstoke 2003.

11 On the Anglo-American "special relationship" see Dumbrell J., *A Special Relationship: Anglo-American Relations from the Cold War to Iraq*, Palgrave Macmillan, Basingstoke 2006; Bartlett C., *'The special relationship': a political history of Anglo-American relations since 1945*, Longman, London 1992; Bentivoglio G., *La relazione necessaria. La Gran Bretagna del Governo Heath e gli Stati Uniti (1970-74)*, FrancoAngeli, Milano 2011. On Churchill's "three circles" see Deighton A., "Britain and the Three Interlocking Circles", in Varsori A. (ed.), *Europe 1945-1990s – The end of an era?*, Palgrave

meantime, the United Kingdom tried to transform the Paris-Bonn axis inside the European Community into a "triangle" (to continue with geometric metaphors), adding London as a new "vertex". Italy too shared this ambition to create a European "triangular relation" with France and West Germany, while the alliance with the United States had been an axiomatic foundation since the creation of the Republic.[12] Moreover, while Britain's decline after the Second World War had been swift, she was one of the "big four" powers of the Western world; conversely, during the Cold War era, Italy was usually considered more as a subject rather than an active factor in foreign policy, without any pretension to exerting a significant global influence, although recent studies have proved this image wrong and limiting.[13]

The aim of this book is to show that, from the mid-1970s to the early 1980s, the relationship between London and Rome was important and strategic for both countries, just because of the similar difficulties that Britain and Italy had to deal with. Nonetheless, the relationship between London and Rome had not always been easy, especially in the aftermath of the Second World War. Britain had built her policy towards Italy on the twofold idea of punishment and de-escalation of Italy's international position, particularly with respect to the Mediterranean and African scenarios.[14] The United Kingdom had opposed Italian participation in the Atlantic Alliance, and the question of Trieste added some bitterness to the relationship, even after colonial disputes had been settled.[15]

Macmillan, London 1995, pp. 155-169. It must be noted that Churchill referred to "the English-speaking world, centring upon the United States, in which [Britain], Canada, and the other British Dominions play so important a part"; the first circle was the British Commonwealth and Empire, while the third one was a "United Europe".

12 Miller J., *The United States and Italy: the politics and diplomacy of stabilization*, University of North Carolina Press, Chapel Hill 1986; Nuti L., *Gli Stati Uniti e l'apertura a sinistra. Importanza e limiti della presenza americana in Italia*, Laterza, Roma-Bari 1999; Del Pero M., *L'alleato scomodo. Gli Usa e la DC negli anni del centrismo (1948-1955)*, Carocci, Roma 2001; Mistry K., *The United States, Italy and the Origins of the Cold War: Waging Political Warfare 1945-1950*, Cambridge University Press, Cambridge 2014.

13 Varsori A., Zaccaria B. (eds.), *Italy in the International System from Détente to the End of the Cold War*, Palgrave Macmillan, London 2017; Bentivoglio G., Varsori A. (eds.), *Realtà e immagine della politica estera italiana*, FrancoAngeli, Milano 2017.

14 Gat M., *Britain and Italy, 1943-1949: The Decline of British Influence*, Sussex Academic Press, Brighton 1996; Kelly S., *Cold War in the Desert: Britain, the US and the Italian Colonies, 1945-52*, Palgrave Macmillan, Basingstoke 2000.

15 Folly M., "Britain and the Issue of Italian Membership of NATO, 1948-49", *Review of International Studies*, Vol. 13, 1987, pp. 177-196; de Leonardis M., *La 'diplomazia atlantica' e la soluzione del problema di Trieste (1952-1954)*, Edizioni Scientifiche

Anglo-Italian relations began to improve after the Suez crisis. From London's perspective, Italy was no longer a competitor in the Mediterranean area, but rather a loyal ally within NATO, with unexpectedly fast economic growth. Conversely, Britain was perceived in Italy as a prominent element in the Western system, also due to the "special relationship" with the United States. Many among the centre-left parties also looked to the United Kingdom as a model of democracy and a point of reference, thanks to the economic and social achievements of its Welfare State.[16]

In this framework, European integration became a privileged context for consolidating Anglo-Italian relations. The possibility of creating an "alternative axis" between London and Rome as a counterpart to the Franco-German partnership has emerged on several occasions and with various aspects in the process of European integration. Italy and Britain shared a similar approach towards some Community issues, from social to regional, and both countries had a strong Atlantic commitment to try to contain any French anti-Alliance deviation, which has survived the end of the Cold War. They are also the other two large Community powers and their demographic weight makes them able to compete with France and Germany in representing European institutions. Ultimately, "the building bricks of a Rome-London axis have therefore been in existence throughout much of the last fifty years".[17]

It is therefore not surprising that the Italian government openly endorsed Britain's application for entry into the European Community in 1961, not only as a way to moderate Charles de Gaulle's hegemonic goals, but also in an attempt to please its American ally. The Kennedy administration had openly supported the candidature of the United Kingdom, and Italian politicians hoped that their endorsement could help them move closer to the major goal of Washington's recognition of the centre-left experiment.[18] The Italian delegation was very active in trying to solve the many problems affecting negotiations in Brussels, and the British government appreciated these initiatives. However, Italy was perceived as a minor actor, incapable of having a vital influence on the political aspects

Italiane, Napoli 1992; Whittam J.R., "Drawing the Line: Britain and the Emergence of the Trieste Question, January 1941-May 1945", *The English Historical Review*, Vol. 106, No. 419, 1991, pp. 346-370.

16 See Favretto I., quoted.

17 Ludlow N.P., "In search of a balance: Italy, Britain and the dream of another European axis?", in Craveri P., Varsori A. (eds.), *L'Italia nella costruzione europea. Un bilancio storico (1957-2007)*, FrancoAngeli, Milano 2009, pp. 68-69.

18 Nuti L., *Gli Stati Uniti e l'apertura a sinistra*, quoted.

of London's application, and advice from the Italian government was not taken into consideration.[19]

The second British attempt, in 1966-67, was once again supported by the Italian government, but this time Rome seemed to prefer the attitude of a "prudent wait".[20] When Britain eventually joined the European Community in 1972, the Anglo-Italian partnership failed to materialise. Ten years of Italian commitment to the British cause were laconically summarised in a note to "Signor Moro's decisive intervention about New Zealand butter". The Italians were advocates of European political construction and of UK participation within the Community, but they were too "sensible to press the point with much vigour".[21] Apart from the usual British tendency to downgrade Rome's stance in Europe and in the world, this harsh judgement was partially correct: Italy seemed unable to take the opportunity of having a new member inside the Community which shared some of her interests in the social and regional fields. Internal

[19] In the latter stages of the negotiations, the leader of the Italian Republican Party, Ugo La Malfa, proposed an Anglo-Italian cooperation treaty along the lines of the French-German one which Konrad Adenauer and Charles de Gaulle were negotiating. In London, such an initiative was quickly discarded: in the words of a Foreign Office official, "we should look rather absurd if we started at this moment to develop a special relationship with Italy. People would think that we had either lost our sense of reality or that we were at our wits ends". The National Archives of the United Kingdom (TNA), FO 371/163718, CJ1051/4, Tomkins minute, 2 January 1963. On La Malfa's initiative, see Ludlow N.P., *Dealing with Britain: the Six and the First UK Application to the EEC*, Cambridge University Press, Cambridge 1997; Nuti L., "Italy, the British application and the January debacle", in Griffiths R., Ward S. (eds.), *Courting the Common Market: the first attempt to enlarge the European Community 1960-63*, Lothian Foundation Press, London 1996, pp. 112-113. On the first British attempt, see also Camps M., *Britain and the European community: 1955-1963*, Princeton University Press, Princeton 1964; Deighton A., Milward A.S. (eds.), *Widening, Deepening and Acceleration: the European Economic Community 1957-63*, Peter Lang, Brussels 1999; Kaiser W., *Using Europe, abusing the Europeans: Britain and European integration, 1945-63*, Palgrave Macmillan, Basingstoke 1996.

[20] Varsori A., *La Cenerentola d'Europa*, quoted, pp. 207-212. On Britain's second attempt, see Daddow O., *Harold Wilson and European integration: Britain's second application to join the EEC*, Frank Cass, London 2003; Parr H., *Britain's policy towards the European Community. Harold Wilson and Britain's world role, 1964-1970*, Routledge, London 2006.

[21] TNA, FCO 33/1827, "Annual Review on Italy" by Hancock P., WRJ 1/1, 1 January 1972. On the British entry, see Poggiolini I., *Alle origini dell'Europa allargata. La Gran Bretagna e l'adesione alla CEE (1972-1973)*, Unicopli, Milano 2004; Bentivoglio G., "'Our sole commitment is to negotiate; no more, no less': the Conservative Party and Britain's entry into the EEC", in Bonfreschi L., Orsina G., Varsori A. (eds.), *European Political Parties and the European Integration Process, 1945-1992*, Peter Lang, Brussels 2015.

problems prevailed, and the lack of a defined guide in her international policy brought Italy to a certain inactivity within the EEC which was the first symptom of a profound crisis. For the following years, Italy's very democratic solidity appeared to be challenged. In the meantime, Britain also did not take advantage of her new European role, soon becoming the "awkward partner" among the other member States; the 1975 referendum for re-negotiation of the terms of entry definitely did not help the UK's reputation, while British economic weaknesses had already become a front-page international issue.

It is in this scenario that the two "1976 crises" in Italy and the United Kingdom developed. Of course, the crisis was not limited to London and Rome: by the middle of the 1970s, in times of economic downturn and after the oil shock of 1973, the United States showed relative decline, epitomised by the Watergate scandal and the fall of Saigon, while on the other shore of the Atlantic Euro-pessimism had taken the place of the impetus in EEC policy following The Hague Summit in 1969.[22] Britain's and Italy's problems, therefore, were not unique. Nevertheless, the peculiarity of the Italian and the British case alike was the inability of these two countries to cope with the difficulties faced by other economies, or at least with worse results. The "Italian case" was more blatant and concerned all the major Western powers: Italy was generally perceived as the great "sick man of Europe", and her crisis seemed to threaten the stability of the continent and the East-West balance of power. Yet, there was another "sick man" in the Old Continent: in those years, Britain was to face a severe economic and monetary crisis which weakened her international stance and forced her to play the double role of "doctor" of the Italian disease while being a "patient" herself.

Another similarity between the British and the Italian crises was the influence – and sometimes the primacy – of internal policies on their foreign policies. This national-international nexus was more apparent in Italy, because of the influence exerted by the parties' political cultures. The Cold War was also, and sometimes above all, a matter of Italian domestic policy, due to the strong divisions in the political system.[23] Yet, even in Britain in the 1970s and 1980s, foreign policy was dominated by internal matters (like politics was dominated by economic matters).

---

22 Varsori A., Migani G. (eds.), *Europe in the International Arena during the 1970s*, Peter Lang, Brussels 2011.

23 On the relations among the Italian political forces during the Cold War period, see Formigoni G., *Storia d'Italia nella guerra fredda (1943-1978)*, Il Mulino, Bologna 2016.

This research draws on a wide range of sources from several archives in Britain, Italy and the United States. For the British sources, the work is based mainly on the records from the National Archives of the United Kingdom in Kew, as well as the Labour Party Archive at the Labour History Archive and Study Centre in Manchester and the Conservative Party Archive, Oxford. As regards Italian archival sources, the papers of the Italian Ministry of Foreign Affairs concerning the 1970s and 1980s are still not available for research. However, the *Archivio storico della Presidenza della Repubblica* in Rome stores the papers of the *Ufficio per gli Affari Diplomatici*, where it is possible to find some documents from the Ministry of Foreign Affairs forwarded to the Diplomatic Advisor of the President of the Republic. Finally, for the US sources, the research focussed on the records of the Gerald R. Ford Presidential Library in Ann Arbor, Michigan. Also, the analysis of the British and Italian press made it possible to evaluate the trends in national public opinion and cast new light on reciprocal images; moreover, especially for the case of Italy, it helped to fill some gaps in primary sources.

This volume follows a chronological order. Chapter 1 is dedicated to 1976 when the two crises exploded. In Italy, the fear was that the Italian Communist Party could "overtake" the Christian Democratic Party in the general elections of June 1976; the Western powers, Britain included, tried to work out a common strategy to counter the Communist "threat" and to solve the country's economic problems. As for the United Kingdom, a dramatic economic situation forced the Callaghan government to approach the International Monetary Fund (IMF) for the largest loan ever requested. Chapter 2 deals with the first effects of these "cures" and the relationship between the Labour Party and the Italian left. Chapter 3 analyses 1978, one of the most difficult years for Britain and Italy alike, when both democracies seemed to be put on trial, although for different reasons and to diverse extents. The President of the Italian Christian Democrat Party Aldo Moro was kidnapped and killed by terrorists, while the "winter of discontent" struck Britain with the largest and most critical series of strikes since the 1920s. Negotiations for the European Monetary System (EMS) were also a moment of potential Anglo-Italian collaboration. The passage from the "long 1970s" to the 1980s is investigated in Chapter 4. In both countries, the fast and radical change in the international scenario was balanced by new internal trends and protagonists and the first signs of recovery. In the United Kingdom, the Conservative Party came back to power under the leadership of Margaret Thatcher, while in Italy the end of "national solidarity" led to a redefinition of the political scene which would culminate with the creation of the *pentapartito* coalition and full realignment with the major Western powers. Finally, Chapter 5 examines the results of internal changes and new foreign policies for Britain and Italy, to see whether there were the preludes for a "renaissance" after the long crisis. It assesses the role of the Falklands War (which also caused some tension between London and Rome) in the redefinition of the UK's international position, while continuity was granted by Thatcher's electoral success in 1983. As for Italy, the same year saw a significant change in her political history, with the election of Bettino Craxi, the first Socialist Prime Minister since the foundation of the Republic. The electoral triumph in the general election of June 1983 gave the Tory government a new impetus to pursue the most distinctive features of the Thatcherite policy in both domestic and foreign policy. As regards Italy, Craxi would mark the whole decade with his firm leadership aspirations for internal reforms and emphasis on Italy's international role. But was it the real beginning of a new Renaissance? This is what we will investigate throughout this volume.

CHAPTER 1

A tale of two crises

On 20 and 21 June 1976, the most controversial general elections in Italy since 1948 took place. In the aftermath of the Second World War, the country had been called to the polls to choose the political fate of the newly born Italian republic, in a Manichean struggle between the forming Western bloc and the Communist threat. Twenty-eight years later, the fear was that the Italian Communist Party could "overtake" the Christian Democratic Party, bringing the Communists to government in one of the major European – and NATO – countries. The Western powers tried to work out a common strategy in order to counter the Italian Communist "threat".

Two months prior to the Italian elections, after being defeated by the left wing of his own Labour Party, British Prime Minister Harold Wilson resigned. His successor, former Foreign Secretary James Callaghan, had to face a dramatic economic situation, with rising unemployment and inflation. In September 1976, Britain approached the International Monetary Fund (IMF) for the largest loan ever requested, putting an official seal on the country's decline.

The Italian crisis

The "Italian case" and its origins

Political scientist Sidney Tarrow wrote that "the 'Italian question' of the 1970s is like what one imagines the impact of the French Revolution to have been on people living in the 1790s: no one knew quite what it was, but everyone had an opinion".[1]

---

[1] Tarrow S., "Italy: Crisis, Crises or Transition?", in Lange P., Tarrow S. (eds.), Special issue on "Italy in transition", *West European Politics*, Vol. 2, No. 3, October 1979, p. 166. The issue was published the following year as a volume: Lange P., Tarrow S. (eds.), *Italy in transition. Conflict and consensus*, Frank Cass, Abingdon 1980.

Interest in the Italian situation was not limited to its politics. Academics wondered about the nature and the likely outcome of Italy's crisis, as proved by a series of publications that focused on just this subject. In particular, in October 1979 there was a special issue of *West European Politics* titled "Italy in transition: conflict and consensus". In the preface, Peter Lange stressed how the apparent inscrutability of Italian developments had brought foreign observers to resort to exceptionalism in their academic and journalistic analysis of Italy's crisis. There was a tendency to treat the country with a language all its own (often using Italian words, like *trasformismo* to describe Italian practices seen in other countries but there described as consociationalism). The application of terms drawn directly from the Italian context had tended to stress the uniqueness of the Italian case "beyond reasonable conceptual rigour". There was also the frequent search for metaphors and paradoxical catch-phrases, usually with a pejorative undertone: the Italian political system was described as a "Republic without Government", its economy as the potential "Bangladesh" of the West. These descriptions actually expressed the incapacity to come to terms with the reality of the Italian experience and to make it comprehensible within a more useful comparative framework. Italy was not unique: it was one of the advanced industrial democracies and many of the problems which had marked the Italian crisis had appeared in other of these democracies. There was, then, much which was "common" or "general" in the Italian case. What seemed peculiar was the mix of problems and crises and some response to them. Italy was peculiar like the others were peculiar, "no more and no less".[2]

Even the British press used the paradigm of exceptionalism to tell readers in the United Kingdom about the Italian scene.[3] When exceptionalism was put aside, Italy was narrated to the British via the "prism of liberalism" and it was very difficult to forget about the Westminster model to try and explain the complexity of Italy's political situation.[4] The peculiarity of the political scene was a product of the unique character of Italian politicians, as *The Times*'s Rome correspondent (and at that time recognised as a great connoisseur of the Italian society) Peter Nichols, summarised:

---

2 Lange P., "Preface", in Lange P., Tarrow S. (eds.), quoted, pp. 1-3.

3 For an analysis of British press reporting on Italy in the 1970s see Farrell-Vinay G., "Lo specchio europeo. L'Italia vista dalla stampa britannica", in Giovagnoli A., Pons S. (eds.), *L'Italia repubblicana nella crisi degli anni Settanta. Tra guerra fredda e distensione, Vol. 1,* Rubbettino, Soveria Mannelli 2003, pp. 479-498.

4 Gilbert M., "Il governo e la politica dell'Italia repubblicana", in Woolf S. (ed.), *L'Italia repubblicana vista da fuori (1945-2000)*, Il Mulino, Bologna 2007, pp. 126 ff.

> To say that Italian politicians are a class apart is like saying that Chianti is a sort of liquid: not a half of the truth and no real indication of its significance or effect. They live in a world of their own which has nothing to do with the world at large, and this they recognise. They cannot speak its language. [...] They do not share its problems though its problems are constantly being put before them for solution. Their contact with the masses is to bestow favours (usually in the form of rights denied by bureaucratic clumsiness or political discrimination) in return for which they take votes. [...] The politicians are the complete products of the system by which self-centredness from the cradle and concern with one's own affairs become a way of life.[5]

British diplomatic documents partly turned to exceptionalism in explaining the peculiar mixture of economic crisis, social unrest and political instability which characterised Italy in the 1970s, although, as we shall see, this constituted more an asset than a liability: it was just the unique attitude and history of the Italian people to work as an actual defence against irreparable drifts from democracy and the Western system.

Indeed, by the end of the 1960s, Italy's "miracle" looked like a thing of the past. In the wider context of the European and international crisis of the "golden age" of economic growth in the 1970s, the Italian malaise seemed more acute than those of other Western countries: Italy was perceived – and treated accordingly – as one of the "sick men" of Europe.[6]

The high rates of economic growth that Italy had enjoyed in the 1950s, and a slower but still healthy pace in the 1960s, had disappeared by the beginning of the 1970s. The miracle years of the 1950s and 1960s created an economy heavily dependent on small manufacturing firms, many of them

---

5 Nichols P., *Italia, Italia*, Fontana Press, New York 1975, p. 91.

6 On Italy's crisis in the 1970s and its international context and for an American interpretation of the Italian scene, see Cominelli L., *L'Italia sotto tutela. Stati Uniti, Europa e crisi italiana degli anni Settanta*, Le Monnier, Firenze 2014; Gentiloni Silveri U., *L'Italia sospesa. La crisi degli anni Settanta vista da Washington*, Einaudi, Torino 2009; Bosco V., *L'amministrazione Nixon e l'Italia. Tra distensione e crisi mediterranea*, Eurilink, Roma 2009; Fornasier R., "The DC and the PCI in the Seventies: A Complex Relationship Supervised by the United States", *Bulletin of Italian Politics*, Vol. 4, No. 2, 2012, pp. 209-229; Heurtebize F., *Le péril rouge. Washington face à l'eurocommunisme*, PUF, Paris 2014; Guarna L., *Richard Nixon e i partiti politici italiani*, Mondadori, Milano 2015. See also Gentiloni Silveri U., "Gli anni Settanta nel giudizio degli Stati Uniti: 'Un ponte verso l'ignoto'", in Giovagnoli A., Pons S. (eds.), quoted, pp. 89-122; Gualtieri R., "The Italian Political system and Détente (1963-1981)", *Journal of Modern Italian Studies*, Vol. 9, No. 4, 2004, pp. 428-449. On the West German reaction see Bernardini G., "Stability and socialist autonomy: the Spd, the Psi and the Italian political crisis of the 1970s", *Journal of European Integration History*, No. 1, 2009, pp. 95-114.

concentrated in the North of the country and in specialist areas (mainly textiles, furniture, machine-tools, etc.) which needed a low cost-base to sustain competitiveness, secured by continuing devaluations of the lira. The Italian economy suffered low investment and growth, high rates of inflation and balance of payments' difficulties, which erupted in severe crises that required exceptional policy measures, external financial assistance, and the acceptance of externally-imposed economic conditions which limited the policy authorities' scope for economic management. The crisis of the early 1970s was harshly exacerbated by the lira's floating in 1973 and OPEC's oil shock later that year. Of the major industrial countries, only Japan depended on oil for a higher share of its total energy needs.[7]

When the oil crisis broke, the Italian economy was in a phase of rapid expansion marked by a high rate of capacity utilisation and the early stages of intense rising pressure on prices and wages. In the first half of 1974, the situation was one of continuing expansion, mounting inflationary pressures and, above all, the emergence of a massive disequilibrium in the balance of payments. This led the Italian authorities to shift their economic policy to a decidedly restrictive stance, just when demand was falling in several major OECD countries. The result was a marked decline in production in the second half of the year, which continued until the autumn of 1975. 1975 saw the deepest recession in Italy since the early 1950s: a 4.5 per cent drop in the gross domestic product in real terms, with industrial output down by nearly 10 per cent. Paradoxically, the low level of activity had not caused an abrupt rise in unemployment, since agreements were reached with trade unions to reduce working hours rather than dismiss large numbers of employees. Finally, in 1975 the overall balance on current account seemed to be close to equilibrium.[8]

Beyond the economic difficulties, the underlying question was about the nature of the Italian crisis – whether it was an organic system crisis or rather a severe variation of the "governability crisis" which had been observed in the whole industrialised world since the end of the 1960s. The Italian crisis was indeed a "multiform" crisis and almost surely a long-term one, but, as seen from abroad, it had not taken on the more menacing

7 Lubitz R., *The Italian Economic Crises of the 1970s*, International Finance Discussion Papers, No. 120, June 1978.

8 *OECD Economic Surveys. Italy 1976*, Organization for Economic Co-operation and Development, Paris 1976. On the Italian economy see Felice E., *Ascesa e declino. Storia economica dell'Italia*, Il Mulino, Bologna 2015; Di Martino P., Vasta M. (eds.) *Ricchi per caso. La parabola dello sviluppo economico italiano*, Il Mulino, Bologna 2017.

form of an organic crisis, a crisis of regime.[9] Yet there was another aspect that concerned foreign observers most: instability was not limited to Italy, but seemed to threaten the future of the whole southern European area. In April 1974, after the "Carnation Revolution", in Portugal the extreme left seemed to be on the eve of coming to power; a few months later, the military regime in Greece fell and the new moderate Prime Minister Konstantinos Karamanlis withdrew from the military branch of NATO because of the pressure of public opinion; the Greek scenario was worsened by the failed coup d'état in Cyprus and by the island's Turkish invasion; finally, in 1975 Francisco Franco's illness opened a new phase of political uncertainty about Spain's future. It was feared that the whole of Southern Europe could be lost to the West.[10] In this context, Italy was considered more a subject than an active factor in foreign policy.[11]

Apart from the economic strains, two more aspects characterised the Italian crisis of the 1970s: widespread political violence, which could put the very democratic status of the country at risk; and the growing influence of the Italian Communist Party. As to the former, the *anni di piombo* ("years of lead", from the metal used to make bullets) were a period of both left-wing and right-wing incidents of political terrorism that lasted from the end of the 1960s until the early 1980s. Conventionally, they were initiated in December 1969, when a bomb exploded in Piazza Fontana in the centre of Milan. Seen from London, even Italian terrorism was a peculiar phenomenon: it had no separatist or religious basis, like that of the IRA, the PLO or the Basques in Spain. But the use of violence for political ends had long been endemic in Italy. The analysis was almost anthropological and not devoid of prejudices: British papers reported how "in the primitive societies of the south and the islands, Italians have long settled quarrels by violence rather than the law".[12]

---

9 Tarrow S., "Aspetti della crisi italiana: note introduttive", in Graziano L., Tarrow S. (eds.), *La crisi italiana*, Einaudi, Torino 1979, pp. 3-5.

10 Del Pero M., Gavìn V., Guirao F., Varsori A. (eds.), *Democrazie. L'Europa meridionale e la fine delle dittature*, Le Monnier, Firenze 2010; Del Pero M., "The United States and the crises in Southern Europe", in Varsori A., Migani G. (eds.), quoted, pp. 301-316; Rizas S., *The rise of the Left in Southern Europe: Anglo-American responses*, Pickening&Chatto, London 2012.

11 Varsori A., Zaccaria B. (eds.), quoted.

12 TNA, FCO 33/4594, "Terrorism in Italy", despatch (051/4) by Arculus R., WRJ 051/3, 8 August 1980. On British perceptions of Italian terrorism and its implications in the Cold War scenario, see Bentivoglio G., "Violenza endemica o eterodiretta? Il terrorismo italiano degli anni Settanta e Ottanta visto da Londra", in Lomellini V. (ed.), *Il mondo della guerra fredda e l'Italia degli anni di piombo. Una regia internazionale per il terrorismo?*, Le Monnier, Firenze 2017, pp. 205-224.

With regards to the second aspect, one could ask why a Communist problem existed in Italy. To try and answer this question, and to understand the Italian crisis and in particular the peculiar situation of 1976, we must take a closer look at the political scene.

The PCI was the largest Communist party in Western Europe and presented an anomaly among the parties of international Communism: it was a mass party with a significant following in all classes. The PCI was also characterised by its recurrent appeals to the Constitution, the fruit of the anti-fascist unity that existed before the Cold War. Thus, Italian Communism's strength came from the country's peculiarities in the European context: "the mass politics inherited from the fascist regime, convergence and osmosis with essential elements of the dominant Catholic culture and morality, and limitations on the national ruling class's willingness to reform, it being incapable of creating a welfare state comparable to the other large European states".[13]

Even the Italian Christian Democratic Party represented an almost unique case among Western multiparty systems. From December 1945 until June 1981, the DC supplied all the Prime Ministers – and most of the ministers – in the forty Italian governments which had succeeded, dominating all the different phases of the evolution of the political system. The DC represented the case of a continuous and successful adaptation of a complex organisational structure to environmental changes and political challenges; however, success in remaining in power was not matched by a satisfactory governmental performance.[14]

According to Sidney Tarrow, the Christian Democrat Party chose to pursue an interclass coalition rather than a narrower social bloc dominated by the middle class to maintain its ruling place; this led the PCI to expand its interclass basis, formulating programmes which appealed to local, regional and group interests and opposed to DC's patronage with a policy of gradual structural reforms. In this strategy, the Communist Party had to face some problems, like the inefficacy of its economic programme or the preference for political alliances instead of social alliances. Yet all these problems were the internal dimension of the Communist problem, which had affected and was now threatening the long Christian Democrat hegemony in Italian politics. The fact that the PCI had developed as an inter-class party and as a party of structural

---

13 Pons S., *The Global Revolution. A History of International Communism 1917-1991*, Oxford University Press, Oxford 2014, p. 197.

14 Pasquino G., "Italian Christian Democracy: a party for all season?", in Lange P., Tarrow S. (eds.), quoted, p. 88.

reform – with the ambition to be present everywhere in society and the political system alike – brought at the beginning an equilibrium between the two main blocs, later the need for new political initiatives, and lastly the likely disintegration of the DC dominant bloc, or at least its radical change, with the introduction of social groups represented by the PCI. There was indeed a Communist problem in Italy, and its causes did not lie in the widespread corruption and inefficiency of the Christian Democrat system, but in what all this evidence revealed: DC's inability, after 30 years of government, to compensate for the growing PCI's political hegemony on the left. Therefore, the Communists' problems were the logical result of the Communist problem, and the latter reflected the Christian Democrat problem: the fact that the DC was a dominant party without being a hegemonic party.[15]

In this context, the PCI was the only Communist party to increase its support after 1968. Moreover, the Italian Communist Party under the leadership of its Secretary General Enrico Berlinguer, developed its own political strategy in the first half of the 1970s. In the aftermath of the military coup of General Pinochet in Chile, who overthrew the Government of the Unidad Popular, Berlinguer proposed a "historic compromise" with the Christian Democrats, to form a coalition government with moderate forces, while rejecting the old strategies of popular fronts. The PCI also embraced European integration and tried to create a path for Western communism that was freed from the links with Moscow. This distinctive political agenda endorsed the values of democracy and pluralism, the idea of "moving beyond the blocs" and the concept of Europe as a new international actor: it was the beginning of "Eurocommunism".[16]

This new political strategy coincided with an unprecedented electoral success: in the local elections held in June 1975, the Italian Communist Party obtained 33.4 per cent of the vote. For the first time, there was the possibility that the PCI could become the leading party in Italy, overtaking the DC in the polls, and the participation of the Communists in a government seemed ineluctable. It was in this scenario that the crisis of 1976 developed.

---

15 Tarrow S., "Aspetti della crisi italiana", quoted, pp. 26-30.

16 Pons S., *The Global Revolution*, quoted, pp. 284-293. By the same author see also *Id.*, *Berlinguer e la fine del Comunismo*, Einaudi, Torino 2006; *Id.*, "The rise and fall of Eurocommunism", in Leffler M., Westad O. (eds.), *The Cambridge History of the Cold War*, Cambridge University Press, Cambridge 2010, pp. 45-65. For a more detailed analysis of the Eurocommunist policies of the PCI and how it affected relations with the Labour Party see Chapter 2.

The 1976 crisis

The political crisis began on 7 January 1976, when the Moro government resigned after the Socialists had declared their intention to withdraw from the majority on which it was based. Despite its weakness, British diplomacy described it as one of the more distinguished of recent Italian administrations, managing to "belie the reputation of Italian governments for inaction" (although it would not stand comparison with the volume of business which governments at Westminster managed to get through!). Moro led a strong team, assisted by his Deputy Prime Minister, Republican Ugo La Malfa who was in charge of economic affairs, in which he was extremely competent and experienced. The government lasted longer than average (fourteen months), mainly because there was no visible alternative to put in its place: no party was sufficiently sure of making electoral gains to wish to run the risk of early elections – the likely result of the overthrow of the government. Moro used his political skills to exploit this situation to the utmost. He was also helped by Communists, particularly in the later stages, who were giving the government tacit support. British Ambassador in Rome Guy Millard was sure that a certain amount of consultation, particularly on economic affairs, went on between the government and the PCI behind the scenes. The Moro government showed respectable achievements and encouraged the hope that if, against the odds, he succeeded in forming a new administration, there could yet be a return to moderate progress and a degree of political stability.[17]

In this scenario, all three main actors of the Italian political scene – the Christian Democrats, the Communists and the Socialists – were a cause of concern, although with different scopes and degrees, for the British government.

The Christian Democratic Party

An analysis by the British embassy in Rome of the role of the DC at the beginning of 1976 and its prospects for the future reported that the reputation of the party had become "tarnished", as was inevitable after so long a period of office. According to Millard, the relationship between the electorate and government in Italy was more complex than in northern Europe: there was a vast network of exchanged favours, personal friendships and loyalties, interests and pressure groups, and not

17 TNA, FCO 33/2940, "The fall of the Moro government", Diplomatic report No. 88/76, Millard G. to Callaghan J., WRJ 011/1, 19 January 1976.

a little corruption. The British assessment of the party's leaders, and in particular Secretary Amintore Fanfani, was harsh: the years of power had produced a complacent and patronising attitude, and Fanfani personified this "arrogance of power". Under his leadership, the Christian Democrats alienated many potential supporters among intellectuals by installing party nominees in controlling positions in cultural bodies, by neglecting governmental and party links with academic institutions, and by generally affecting to have a monopoly of political wisdom. They squandered their support among Catholic-orientated workers' organisations by failing to show understanding of, or even concern about, workers' problems. By disbanding the party's youth movement in February 1975 over a relatively minor disagreement, Fanfani at a stroke exacerbated the party's relations with the younger generation.[18]

On these premises, the British embassy in Rome considered the result of 1975 local elections as an unsurprising disaster for the DC. Fanfani fought the party's campaign on a "return to the traditional values of Christian Democracy", described as "a dish composed mainly of visceral anti-Communism, with a little power, a little Church, and a dash of law and order". Two main trends had emerged: the first "reformist" trend believed that radical changes were required in the party's structure and in its method of exercising power. It had to repair its links with a changing society at all levels, and it had to seek to establish a new political identity as a popular, democratic, reforming party of the moderate left. This trend found sympathy in the left-wing *correnti* (factions) and among the followers of outgoing Prime Minister Aldo Moro, and quickly began to attract members from the Centre and even the Right of the party as well. The other trend had found its main spokesmen in Flaminio Piccoli and Fanfani, who could be labelled "the old guard". It upheld the view that it was the dilution of the party's doctrine, caused by the necessity to accommodate its coalition partners and the views of its own diverse components, that had led to its loss of support. The party should offer more effective government, through a "moderate" (slightly right-wing) programme of social and economic reforms, and then offer this to the party's coalition partners from a position of strength. So long as the Christian Democrats remained united, the Socialists and others would have no alternative but to lend their support. According to Millard, Giulio Andreotti was somewhere on the fence between these two opposing points

18 TNA, FCO 33/2940, "The Christian Democrats and the Italian political crisis", Diplomatic report No. 143/76, Millard G. to Callaghan J., WRJ 011/1, 2 February 1976.

of view; he was described by British papers as having an ambiguous relationship with the Socialists and had recently made an attempt to "torpedo Moro".[19]

The Party Congress of July 1975 saw a demonstrable break with the past: Fanfani was duly defenestrated after an "unseemly struggle". The old guard was in the majority but was unable to agree on a candidate to succeed him. As a result, the reformists were able to slip in Benigno Zaccagnini, a friend of Moro's but without a power base of his own in the party. Zaccagnini had made some progress with improving the party's image, reforming the DC youth movement, setting up a Cultural Commission in an attempt to repair the party's links with intellectuals, and calling a series of meetings of DC members and supporters at the local level to sound opinions among the rank and file. However, he had had little success in his attempts to change the party's internal machinery. As seen from London, the present crisis could increase the Communist vote. The next elections could not be later than May 1977 and most of the DC old leaders would still be there: the electorate could simply vote for a change and by doing so bring the PCI into the government. Millard's assessment was very critical of the DC's behaviour: the crisis had been precipitated without apparent regard for its consequences for the country, and the "leisurely way" in which the Christian Democrats and the Socialists were negotiating for an unsatisfactory and inevitably short-lived compromise would increase the impatience of the electorate with the whole political system. The PSI, as the party which brought the government down, could lose votes and these would go to the Communists. Against this, the DC had hopes of picking up votes from the smaller parties: those who were scared of Communism would tend to vote for the only party capable of keeping the Communists out.[20]

At the moment, as seen from the British embassy in Rome, the most likely solution for the crisis appeared to be a one-party Christian Democrat government, supported by the Republicans and Social Democrats and dependent for its existence on PSI abstention. This prospect, however, had limited attraction for the Christian Democrats: they would be responsible, in a complicated situation, for everything which went wrong but without having the power to do much about. Their policies would be subject to the PSI veto, and it was likely that the Socialists would make large use of it since they did not want to give the DC a free hand to carry out a programme with a strong appeal to the electorate. Millard considered it the impasse of

19 *Ibidem.*
20 *Ibidem.*

Italian politics: the DC locked into an impossible position, unable to pass the hand to someone else. The Christian Democrats were the "prisoners of the system" and, in the absence of a democratic alternative, they were obliged to soldier on to avoid letting the Communists in.[21]

The Communist Party

According to David Lipsey, then political adviser of Foreign Secretary Anthony Crosland, the Foreign Office was "viscerally anti-communist" and found it difficult to take Eurocommunism as other than "a ruse".[22] This would also explain the role of the Information Research Department (IRD) as a propaganda tool, to help the Foreign Office to warn Italian public opinion on the contradictions between the new liberal image of the PCI and its real long-term objectives.[23]

In the aftermath of the fall of the Moro government, Ambassador Millard tried to analyse the sincerity of the PCI's new attitude in a report titled *Italian Communists: how different are they?*[24] According to the British diplomat, they were not very different from Communists in other countries, and it was right to be sceptical about their policies. The efforts of the PCI to present itself as a democratic political force and an alternative party of government had been increasingly successful. The domestic and foreign policies which Communist leaders had recently been advocating were considered by Millard as at first sight indistinguishable from those of genuine Social Democratic parties. It was not difficult to understand their attractions for Italians: to many people, the Communists seemed to offer a "new, heretical, western European form of Communism", committed to the continuance of democracy as understood in the West, and therefore unwelcome to the Soviet Union. Central to the PCI's domestic platform was the "historic compromise" launched by Party Secretary Berlinguer in 1973 and endorsed by the party's Congress in 1975. As defined at the Congress, this would be "an understanding, a political alliance, between Communists, Socialists, Christian Democrats and other anti-Fascist popular forces both of Catholic origin and of lay and democratic tradition, in order to give the government of the country a wider basis of consent

---

21 *Ibidem.*

22 Lipsey D., *In the Corridors of power: An Autobiography*, Biteback, London 2012, p. 92.

23 Di Donato M., Portolani R.D., "Il Foreign Office e la stampa italiana", in Taviani E., Vacca G. (eds.), *Gli intellettuali nella crisi della Repubblica (1968-1980)*, Viella, Roma 2016, pp. 345-351.

24 TNA, FCO 33/2945, "Italian Communists: how different are they?", Diplomatic report No. 94/76, Millard G. to Callaghan J., WRJ 011/2, 23 January 1976.

and the strength and authority needed to overcome the crisis and enable Italy to advance".[25] The Communists professed to believe that Italy could only be governed in alliance with the Catholic forces; that in office they would respect the institutions of the Republic, seeking to make them work better; that they would guarantee a series of rights and freedoms; and, expressing growing concern over declining law and order, that they would support increased powers for the police.

Despite his scepticism towards the PCI, Millard acknowledged that Berlinguer himself was one of the party's "greatest assets": he was an attractive figure and inspired confidence with his "unpretentious oratory and evident sincerity". The things which he said were plausible, and he said them in a very plausible way. However, the British ambassador did not think that it would be very difficult to show that most of the reassuring things which the PCI had said had been said in the past by other Communist Parties, which had then said and done quite the opposite. Even if the official policies of the PCI reflect its real intentions, and even if the mass of its supporters were to accept their continuance, the international and economic repercussions of the entry of the Communists into government would be much the same, since the Americans and perhaps the Germans would react in any case to the event; and it was hard to see that any government including the Communists, the Socialists, and maybe half of the Christian Democrats could provide a reassuring degree of stability.

So, what could Britain do to help to keep the Communists out? "Not much, I am afraid", answered Millard. The Italian voters had been admonished from various quarters, ranging from the Italian Council of Bishops to Gianni Agnelli to Henry Kissinger. These warnings were considered "salutary", but a British statement on these lines could not be helpful. Most importantly, the United Kingdom should avoid giving any legitimacy to the PCI demands:

> […] We and the other countries in the Alliance should not act and talk as though we thought the advent of the Communists in government inevitable, or as though we contemplated the prospect with equanimity. To do so would be to help to bring it about. Any apparent endorsement of the PCI's claims to democratic respectability will diminish the Socialists' and Christian Democrats' chances of resisting their advance. We should avoid it in word and deed.

[25] XIV Congresso del Partito Comunista Italiano. Atti e Risoluzioni, Editori Riuniti, Roma 1975.

Millard concluded that it was an unfortunate fact that the defence of Italy against Communism was so largely in the hands of "such an unsatisfactory instrument as the Christian Democratic Party". Within the limits of "proper discretion and without incurring the accusation of intervention in Italian politics", Italy's allies had an interest in encouraging those elements in the DC who were working for reform. But it was only the Italians who could save themselves. There was a natural anti-Marxist majority in Italy, and it was for the Italian politicians and parties to find the formula to express this. The centre-left was such a formula, but it had been eroded. The British government could only hope that the Italians found another before it was too late: indeed, the PCI's entry into government "would be an event of possibly catastrophic significance".[26]

The Socialist Party

The Italian Socialist Party had a peculiar position in Italian politics. It had managed to preserve its strategic importance in the party system despite an almost uninterrupted record of electoral decline. In the 1970s, its electorate was dwarfed by the much larger Communist Party. Yet its decline had not destroyed the PSI's pivotal role, and the relationship between the Socialists and the Christian Democrats dominated the making and unmaking of Italian governments. The fall of Moro by the hand of PSI's leader De Martino was just the last example. Nevertheless, this pivotal position proved, in the long run, to be more a liability than an asset for the Italian Socialists: as a small party, it could never hope to govern alone, and in whatever relationship the PSI had established, it was the junior partner. Moreover, the party was left with an image of a vacillating and dilatory party, uncertain of its own identity and irresponsible in the use of power. Never were these problems more apparent than in 1976.[27]

Francesco De Martino – described by Millard as "not a strong leader" – was originally against provoking a government crisis. He seemed in the end to have given way to the pressures from more powerful characters like Bettino Craxi, his deputy, and to those of leaders further to the left. No doubt he had in mind the need to preserve the unity of the party.

According to the British Ambassador, the PSI had come to think that perhaps the Christian Democrats after all were after all beginning to do too

---

26 TNA, FCO 33/2945, "Italian Communists: how different are they?", Diplomatic report No. 94/76, Millard G. to Callaghan J., WRJ 011/2, 23 January 1976.

27 Hine D., "The Italian Socialist Party under Craxi: surviving but not reviving", in Lange P., Tarrow S. (eds.), quoted, pp. 133-148.

well, despite talk about the disintegration of the party after 15 June. It was beginning to look as though the local elections, instead of being a mortal blow, had been a salutary shock for the DC which, instead of behaving like a defeated party and entering into a relationship of equality with the PSI as the pivot of the political situation, showed disturbing signs of recuperation. The Socialists saw their chances diminishing of establishing a more equal relationship with the Christian Democrats in government. Moreover, on the left of the PSI, some held the belief that early elections would be to their advantage and hoped to attract the Communists to the "alternative of the left", meaning a common front of PCI and PSI. The Socialists were also at odds with the government over economic issues and particularly over what they regarded as the inadequacy of the government's measures to protect employment. For Millard, these tensions over economic policy threaten all centre-left coalitions and in the Italian case were greatly sharpened by the severity of the economic crisis. Anyway, from a tactical point of view, the moment was ill-chosen. The fall of the government shortly after the 15 June elections could have enabled the PSI to exploit the Christian Democratic disarray. But now the Socialists could very possibly have to pay an electoral price for appearing to put party before country.[28]

The importance of the Socialists in the Italian political scene as a means to hinder the PCI's advance was acknowledged by the US administration, which tried to organise a joint action, also involving the British government.

Kissinger wrote a message to Willy Brandt in his capacity as Joint Chairman of the forthcoming meeting of Social Democratic leaders in Copenhagen on 18-19 January. The Secretary of State assessed very positively the degree of consultation between Europe and the United States, unique in the history of international relations and leading to a remarkable policy harmonisation. But this could not endure if Communist parties were occupying governmental positions. As for the United States, they understood very clearly the difference between Socialists and Communists: "Indeed, relations with [the German] government and with other governments which [were] dominated by Social Democrats were better than they had ever been before". Both in Britain and elsewhere "Social democrats represent[ed] many of the staunchest friends and most effective political leaders in the Western world". It was just to these Social Democrat leaders that the US Secretary of State addressed his appeal to

28 TNA, FCO 33/2940, "The fall of the Moro government", Diplomatic report No. 88/76, Millard G. to Callaghan J., WRJ 011/1, 19 January 1976.

successfully challenge Communist expansion. At the same time, Kissinger instructed the American Ambassador in London to show Wilson and Callaghan the text of the letter to Brandt and to "amplify certain points orally". These points were related to the situation in Southern Europe – Italy, Spain and Portugal. As for Italy, Kissinger said that it was clear that there could be no viable democratic majority in the Italian government without the participation of the Italian Socialists. The PSI's ambivalence as to its political allegiance reflected, in his view, the party's doubts about the strength and the will of the DC to resist Communism, and its fears that the Communists would take over the non-Communist left in Italy. The Italian Parliamentary elections of early 1977 would be a crucial test of stability in Italy, and the Christian Democrats needed the support of the PSI to get through. Kissinger hoped that Brandt – and of course Wilson – would encourage De Martino to return to a policy of co-operation with the Christian Democrats.[29]

The British government had watched "with some amazement" the development of the movement in the PSI towards the withdrawal of support from the government. The Socialists' dilemma since the 1975 elections had been that if they moved too close to the PCI, they ran the risk of being totally overshadowed by the Communists; if they returned to a "special relationship" with the DC, they would probably share in the latter's unpopularity and lose votes this way. Anyway, the decision to make Moro fall was considered by British diplomacy as an "act of political suicide"; this view was shared with French newspaper *Le Monde* when it said that the PSI, which should be able to act as a pivot between the two main parties, had never produced the political wherewithal, the internal cohesion or the strategy to achieve this position.[30]

The Italian scene darkens

Despite the confused situation, in February 1976 the Christian Democrats formed a new government, this time only with DC ministers: the President of the Council – for the fifth time – was still Aldo Moro. In the meantime, the Christian Democrats had to face two scandals, in addition to the difficult political situation. The first happened in January, when American

[29] TNA, FCO 33/2940, "Message from Dr Kissinger to the Prime Minister and the Foreign and Commonwealth Secretary", WRJ 011/1, 14 January 1976.

[30] TNA, FCO 33/2940, "Behaviour of the Italian Socialist Party", Layden A. to Hulse C., 6 January 1976; "Les socialistes italiens entre le marteau et l'enclume", *Le Monde*, 6 January 1976.

newspapers wrote about the CIA financing non-Communist Italian parties. The second, which had much more emphasis, was the Lockheed scandal: it was an international affair including a series of bribes and contributions made by officials of American aerospace company Lockheed to obtain the exclusive right to sell aircrafts to the Italian Air Force.[31] The allegations of bribery were endorsed by political left-wing magazine *L'Espresso* and targeted former Cabinet ministers and two former Prime Ministers, Mariano Rumor and then-President of the Republic Giovanni Leone.

The political and economic scene had deteriorated sharply, and the title of a long despatch from the British embassy in Rome left no room for positive interpretations: "the Italian scene darkens".[32] The new government was "of the weakest kind conceivable", while the CIA and Lockheed scandals had been producing a flood of stories tending to discredit further the political establishment, particularly the DC. Although Italy was used to scandals, the present ones were more serious than most, and had strengthened the widespread belief in the country that the system and its leaders were corrupt "through and through". Moreover, the scandals had created a strong mood of anti-Americanism, which the Communists were exploiting.

According to Millard, the PCI had made a considerable psychological advance in the two previous months, and the number of people who believed that the Communists could be kept out of government for much longer was decreasing. It was a short step from believing that their continued advance was inevitable, to persuading oneself, and trying to persuade foreign opinion, that their entry into government would not be dangerous, domestically or internationally. The British Ambassador reported with dismay that even Guido Carli, ex-Governor of the Banca d'Italia, and Ugo La Malfa, leader of the Republican Party and Deputy Prime Minister in the last Moro government, had accepted that only the PCI could help Italy to overcome her present difficulties. The bandwagon effect was growing and "the basic Italian political instinct to avoid confrontation, to come to a compromise somehow", was exercising an increasingly powerful effect. Millard went as far as to say that Moro and

31 The Lockheed scandal involved, apart from Italy, also West Germany, the Netherlands, and Japan. It started in 1976, following revelations by the US Senate Committee chaired by the Democrat Frank Church. The Church Committee revealed a chain of corruption linked to the Lockheed Corporation, paying large sums of money into the account of "shadow" companies in Italy, for bribes to Italian officials and ministers. See TNA, FCO 33/2941, "The Lockheed scandal in Italy", Layden A. to Hulse C., WRJ 011/1, 2 March 1976.

32 TNA, FCO 33/2941, "The Italian scene darkens", Millard G. to Callaghan J., WRJ 011/1, 8 March 1976.

Zaccagnini could not only prove unable to stop the bandwagon rolling but could also climb on it themselves.

There could yet be some change in political sentiment before the elections, resulting in the DC being able to hold most of its vote: it could be that the Italian voters would "turn back from the brink", if they come to realise that the international consequences of PCI participation in government could affect them "in their pocket and in their spirit", through the withdrawal of international financial support and their detachment from the Western alliance. But the recent developments had diminished the reasons for confidence in such an outcome.[33]

Further reasons for concern for the British came from the press. On 10 February, an article in *The Times* dealt with the Communist question in Western Europe, reporting that "not since the immediate aftermath of the Second World War ha[d] West European Communist parties been infected with such a veritable epidemic of moderation". As for the Italian case, the article said that since a Christian Democrat/Communist coalition could prove unsatisfactory, it could be better to give the PCI a spell of office at the head of a left-wing alliance, if it can convince the world – as it almost had – that its acceptance of the democratic rules of the game was genuine. The Communists were the one Italian party which still had "some identity of its own and some moral credibility".[34] Millard was upset by the article, which he thought was a much more favourable judgement of the Italian Communists than seen before, at least in *The Times*, and confirmed "the extent to which the Communist thesis ha[d] become accepted abroad".[35]

By the end of March, the Western European Department of the Foreign Office produced a memorandum on the prospects for PCI participation in the Italian government. Three were the questions of immediate British concern:

- Was PCI participation in the government of Italy at that point inevitable?
- Given the "democratic" professions of the PCI, how seriously need the British government be concerned at this prospect?
- If the answer to the first question was no, what policies should the British government be pursuing to make the PCI's advent to power less likely?

33 *Ibidem.*

34 "West Europe's Communists", *The Times*, 10 February 1976.

35 TNA, FCO 33/2945, "The Italian Communists", Millard G. to Campbell A., WRJ 011/2, 12 February 1976.

Despite the omens, the entry of the Communists into an Italian government was still not inevitable. There were various barriers in the path of PCI ambitions; whether these proved impassable would depend entirely on the Italians themselves. The DC retained a good deal of its strength and, potentially, much of its influence. Although the Italians were well used to political crises and had a considerable ability to manage without a strong central government, a continuation of the present economic crisis would make it necessary to appoint a government capable of producing strong remedies, and this was likely to work to the PCI's advantage.

For the Foreign Office, Communist participation in the Italian government could have implications on four different levels: internal, bilateral, NATO and EEC. As for the first level, such a situation would present manifold dangers for Italy: the process could be irreversible, since the PCI would stand a good chance of consolidating its position and accustoming public opinion to its presence; the stresses and strains of cooperation with the PCI could well lead to the fragmentation of the DC and the PSI, thus further strengthening the Communist electoral base; international confidence in Italy's economic and financial position would be undermined, possibly precipitating an economic collapse; the stress of power would expose the PCI to strains which it did not experience in opposition, and could alter the internal balance in favour of the "hard liners"; finally, the PCI showed no signs of abandoning its allegiance to Marxist thought. Bilateral relations would depend upon the degree of influence exercised by the Communists over the government as a whole: the greater the influence, the less likely it was that the present easy bilateral cooperation between governments and officials would continue as smoothly as in the past. The implications for the Atlantic Alliance would be serious: the arrival in power in a major NATO country of a Communist party with declared anti-American policies would be likely to cause a strong reaction in the United States, eventually leading Washington to reconsider US military commitment to the defence of Europe. More generally, the accession of Communists to power in Italy, the heartland of West European culture, would inevitably be a great psychological blow to the West, and to Western Europe in particular. Finally, the European Community was very different from NATO: there were already Communist deputies in the European Parliament, and the EEC did not deal with sensitive politico-military issues. Communist involvement could, however, cause difficulties for political cooperation.

The final recommendations for the British government were to favour action taken in conjunction with the principal allies: although only Italian could save themselves, they were conscious of external opinion and to some extent responsive to it. It was recommended that the British government should seek suitable opportunities to discuss the Italian situation privately with the Americans, the Germans and the French in order to reach a coordinated view and, if possible, agreement on the policies to be followed. The British government should make it clear that Italy's partners did not take at face value the PCI professions of democratic respectability – governments should decline to receive prominent members of the PCI at ministerial level, or to give them any other form of special treatment of favourable publicity – and it should be careful to do or say nothing to suggest that Italy's partners regarded the PCI accession to power as inevitable. Conversely, the British government should encourage maximum contact between allied ministers and ministers in the present Italian government to boost the DC's confidence by demonstrating publicly that it was regarded as an *interlocuteur valable*.[36]

Under mounting pressure, the new Moro government resigned on 30 April, and the President of the Republic dissolved the Parliament and called for early elections to be held on 20 and 21 June. The weakness of the government stimulated a series of proposals for inter-party agreement on an emergency programme, which confronted the DC with an awkward political dilemma. In the end, the Socialists' insistence that the Communists should be associated with governmental responsibility brought about Moro's resignation. The motivation of the PSI seemed illogical for the British: their principal aim was to prevent the Communists exploiting the advantages of remaining in opposition, while in practice enjoying a considerable influence on policy through the trade unions and informal consultation with the government.[37]

With the benefit of hindsight, one could wonder whether the DC did not make a mistake when it decided in January to form a single-party government, rather than going to the country immediately on the fairly creditable record of Moro's fourth government. The intervening three months had brought a further decline in the position of the DC owing to the scandals and the inability of the government to control events. Not only were they powerless to arrest the alarming fall in the value of the lira, but the economy in general performed badly. Italy was almost alone

36 TNA, FCO 33/2945, "How near to power is the PCI?", by Western European Department, 24 March 1976.

37 TNA, FCO 33/2942, "The fall of the fifth Moro government: Italy approaches elections", Diplomatic report No. 222/76, Millard G. to Crosland A., WRJ 011/1, 12 May 1976.

among Western industrialised countries in failing to show any sign of emerging from the recession during the spring of 1976.

The elections held greater uncertainties and were more heavily charged with potentially serious consequences for Italy, for Europe and for the West generally than any which had been held in this country since the war. Italians of all political persuasions were approaching the poll in a sombre and anxious mood. There was caution in the air and a realisation that a vote for the PCI this time would not just be a protest vote against the DC, but could possibly contribute to a drastic and perhaps irreversible change in Italy's political institutions and international alignment.[38]

With the Italian situation precipitating, the option of a multilateral solution to Italy's question became more pressing. At the end of April, Kissinger proposed a quadripartite meeting on the "Italian case", but the British government was quite reluctant in accepting the American proposal since it seemed to arise from US internal considerations: it was an election year, and the Ford Administration showed many signs of weakness. After much hesitation, also to evaluate the attitude of the other European countries involved – France and West Germany – the Foreign Secretaries of the "Big Four" met on 21 May and fixed the date of 27 and 28 of June for a summit of the seven most industrialised countries in Puerto Rico.[39]

In the meantime, a memorandum by the Foreign Office considered "possible courses" open to the British and other Western governments in order to try to stem the decline of the non-Communist forces in Italy. The document examined the actions designed to help prevent the PCI from acquiring a share of power, like public and private warnings, undermining the Communist party, bolstering the democratic parties and warning the Russians to refrain from interference, and the actions after PCI entry into government (mainly quadripartite consultations and the likely "freezing" of Italy's role in both NATO and the EEC). There was also a third part, dedicated to the implications of a coup in Italy: "by its nature, a coup d'état could lead to unpredictable developments", but, in theory at least, "it could be promoted. In one way or another, the force of the right could

38 *Ibidem.*

39 Varsori A., "Puerto Rico (1976): le potenze occidentali e il problema comunista in Italia", *Ventunesimo Secolo*, 2008, pp. 93-104. On the creation and evolution of institutionalised summits, see Mourlon-Druol E., Romero F. (eds.), *International Summitry and Global Governance. The Rise of the G7 and the European Council, 1974-1991*, Routledge, London 2014. For Italy's role see Neri Gualdesi M., "Under a Multinational Mantle: Italy's Participation in the G7 (1975-76)", in Varsori A., Zaccaria B., quoted, pp. 69-94.

be counted on, with the support of the police and the army". However, the idea of a coup to remove the PCI or stop it coming to power in Italian circumstances was "unrealistic".[40]

The Italian situation was the subject of a meeting on 18 May in Anthony Crosland's office, who replaced James Callaghan at the Foreign Office when the latter became Prime Minister in April 1976. According to the Foreign Secretary, there seemed to be no clear collective view among Ministers about the way in which the British government would react to possible Communist participation in the Italian government. He assumed that the present Prime Minister shared the view of his predecessor. He had seen the Minister of State for Foreign and Commonwealth Affairs Roy Hattersley, and he was strongly of the view that the UK should "keep its head well down"; from a brief discussion with the Chancellor of the Exchequer Denis Healey, Crosland knew that this was his view. For Foreign Office Permanent Under-Secretary (PUS) Michael Palliser, there were two main strands. He accepted that one important aspect was what reaction would be politically feasible within the Labour Party. The second aspect was to assess what was the UK's overall interest, taking this in the widest sense. It was important to make the best calculation of what was likely to happen. The underlying risk was that, in the end, Italy would pass through not just Communist participation in government, but to a Communist majority leading to its becoming a Communist country. No doubt it would not become the same sort of Communist country as the Soviet Union or China, but Yugoslavia could be a possible model. It was hard to judge what were the implications of this to Britain, recognising that Italy was on her own backdoor and developments in Italy were liable to affect her own security and economic development. Kissinger's remarks were all in all right: if a key country in the NATO and EEC context became Communist, this would create an uncertain situation in France, Spain and Portugal at the least. The British government had, therefore, to consider whether there were any actions which could be undertaken collectively, not to deprive the Italians of their right to choose, but to point out to them the consequences of Communist entry into government. Such actions could be counter-productive in countries like France and the United Kingdom, but they would not necessarily be so in Italy.[41] As

40 TNA, FCO 33/2948, "Italy and the Communists: options for the West", WRJ 011/2, 6 May 1976. This document caused a considerable stir in the Italian press after being made available by the National Archives of the United Kingdom under the 30-year rule: after a superficial reading, some journalists speculated on a British coup in Italy. See Ceccarelli F., "Il golpe inglese", *La Repubblica*, 13 January 2008.

41 TNA, FCO 33/2942, "Italy", by Fergusson E., WRJ 011/1, 19 May 1976.

Political Adviser David Lipsey wrote, "if we give the Communists enough rope, they may prove themselves innocent; or they may hang themselves. If we embark on a lynching operation, it will be our democratic credibility which is damaged, not theirs".[42]

The dreaded overtaking and Italian economy

Despite the growing concern, the British government tried to avoid making any statement on the Italian elections. However, other Labour politicians without ministerial responsibility were willing to speak out about Italy's situation. The main example was former Foreign Secretary Lord Chalfont, who firstly published an article in *The Times* with the headline "Communists in Italy are the same as any others",[43] then wrote an article for the Italian daily *La Stampa*,[44] and finally was interviewed by the weekly *L'Espresso*.[45] The essence of Chalfont's interventions was that the emergence of a new Communist country in the heart of the Mediterranean could lead to a domino effect in the area; that Italy would have to accept a special "second-class" status within NATO (should the PCI decide not to withdraw from the Alliance); that the Europeism of the Italian Communists was not sincere and that they could not have the best of both worlds. They could not be Communists and at the same time pluralist and allies of the West in its resistance against international Communism. The last governments had performed so poorly that Italians would make any electoral choice for a change, but a Communist victory would be the worst damage for the country.

As for the opinion of the Labour Party, its International Department delivered a paper on the PCI just before the June elections. According to the document, the possibility of Communist participation in an Italian government should not be exaggerated: whatever the precise results of the elections, the DC would remain a major party, and they had "set their face firmly against a coalition with the Communists". Moreover, as long

---

42 TNA, FCO 49/610, "Italy", by Lipsey D., RS 011/510/1, 18 May 1976.

43 Chalfont A., "Communists in Italy are the same as any others", *The Times*, 24 May 1976.

44 *Id.*, "L'Italia via dalla NATO", *La Stampa Sera*, 24 May 1976. A week later the member of the Central Committee of the PCI, Sergio Segre, and General Nino Pasti, former NATO Vice-Commander and then independent candidate for the Italian Communist Party, refuted Chalfont's accusations: "Certo, la NATO e il PCI possono stare insieme", *La Stampa Sera*, 31 May 1976.

45 Russo F., "A quei compagni non ci credo. Colloquio con Lord Chalfont", *L'Espresso*, 13 June 1976.

as the majority of the Christian Democrats were opposed to co-operating with the Communists in government, it was unlikely that the PCI itself would be willing to enter government. Nonetheless, it seemed likely that the elections of June 1976 would make the future direct participation of the Communist Party in Italian government inevitable. It was difficult for the Labour Party, at this geographical and cultural remove, to arrive at an absolute judgement of the character and policies of the PCI, and impossible for any outside observer to judge the party's ultimate intentions. However, it was entirely appropriate for the Labour Party to lean heavily on the views of its fraternal parties in Southern Europe, which quite clearly favoured the PCI. On the evidence which should be most persuasive for the Labour, the Party could wish to re-affirm in the case of Italy the opposition it expressed in the *Labour's Programme 1976* to "any interference, in the context of either NATO or the European Community, with the formation of governments resulting from free and democratic political processes".[46]

The Italian case was a major concern not only for the British government but also for the opposition. An example can be found in the pamphlet *A Conservative interpretation of the Italian crisis*, by the Monday Club – the largest Tory political group. The portrait made by the pamphlet was not optimistic at all: it stated that Italian politics had been the scene of continual political crisis since 1943 when King Victor Emmanuel III dismissed Mussolini. The main problem was that, since the fall of Mussolini, the Italian political scene had been characterised by various kinds of coalitions. The dependency of the Christian Democrats on the Socialists in order to stay in office not surprisingly entailed concessions to the left generally. The decline of the Socialists and the rise of the PCI, together with the deep economic problems facing Italy, had led to what in effect was a coalition between the Christian Democrats and the PCI, although the smaller parties were also involved nominally. The Communist Party was therefore exercising great influence, despite being formally excluded from office. Another form of coalition in Italian politics lay in the nature of Christian Democracy in Italy. The DC was not ideologically homogeneous: the Christian Democrats were a coalition of various threads of opinion ranging from those prepared to accommodate the Neo-Fascists to those prepared to accommodate the PCI. The left-wing of the Christian Democrats had steadily gained ground since the 1972 election. Another element to be taken into consideration was the state

---

46 Labour History Archive and Study Centre (LHASC), Labour Party (LP), International Department, National Executive Committee (NEC) Minutes, "The Italian Communist Party and the Italian general election", ID/1975-76/146, June 1976.

apparatus. The significance of the DC since the end of the Second World War had not been merely because of their role as the party of government, but also the vast influence they had wielded outside of government. This power was exerted through state-run organisations and the vast network of patronage known as *sottogoverno*. Were the PCI to become the governing party of Italy, it would presumably stand to inherit the power of the Christian Democrats in all respects. This was highly alarming, especially considering the power of the Communist Party in the regions, where it was either the majority or strongest single party in a number of areas. Since Italian unity was a recent phenomenon, while the regional governments were rooted deep in the past, local government had an added importance and individual loyalty was often to the city or the province rather than the central government. The most striking element of the Tory pamphlet was the stress on similarities between the current climate in Italian politics and the situation in 1922, when the Fascist Party came to power. "Big business" was backing Berlinguer, as it had backed Mussolini in the early 1920s, because it saw the PCI as the best guarantee of economic stability, whatever the cost in other spheres. Another similarity was that one of the most pernicious argument put forward in favour of the Communist Party was "the same as that which brought Mussolini to power in 1922 – namely that 'the trains will run on time'". The PCI had tried to portray itself as being more moderate than it used to be in economic affairs, in a strategy to gain votes by exploiting corruption and inefficiency in Italian public services generally. In the short term, the situation in Italy was pessimistic, and there could well be a PCI government in the near future. However, there were some hopeful signs, like the reported revival of Catholic activists in the political arena and the threat which the Communist Party was facing from the extreme left, which reflected the overall difficulties it was now encountering as a de facto party of government. There were no easy answers to the problems facing Christian Democracy in Italy. For the most part, these would have to be solved by the DC itself. Nevertheless, the gradual evolution of EEC institutions offered greater scope of co-operation among parties of a similar ideological basis, and the Conservative Party should do "everything possible in the case of Italy".[47]

The Italian political scene was also carefully observed by British finance. A month before the elections, the weekly *L'Espresso* published an interview to Rupert Hambro of the Hambros Bank, reporting that the City was carefully following the evolution of the Italian political

---

47 Young J., *A Conservative interpretation of the Italian crisis*, The Monday Club, London 1979.

situation. Nevertheless, the turnover with Italian banks did not decrease and, in the event of a Communist victory, the British financial world could adopt a "wait and see" strategy. PCI's economists were "smart enough to understand that restrictive measures do not produce the desired effects", at least in that sector. Hambro believed that Communism in Italy would not take the unpleasant form of the Soviet experience: the Italian Communists were "responsible people", able to create a new way of governing. He would be much more concerned about the coming to power of Communists in France, because the PCF was too "rigid and dogmatic".[48]

In the end, the dreaded "overtaking" did not happen: the Christian Democrats came out of the elections still as the most important party, with 38 per cent of votes. However, the PCI confirmed its strength, reaching 34.3 per cent of preferences, its best electoral result ever – and never repeated.[49]

In the first comments by the Foreign Office, the Italian elections appeared to have produced a virtual stalemate. The DC had improved on its performance in comparison with both the 1975 local elections and 1972 general elections. But the Communists, although they had not succeeded in taking the lead, had continued their advance and established themselves beyond challenge as the second major political force in Italy. The main losers were the smaller parties, including the Socialists. The effect therefore was to polarise the Italian political situation still further and make it extremely difficult to form an effective government. Because of their electoral success, the Christian Democrats were unlikely to be in a mood to go back on their electoral pledges by inviting the PCI to join them in government. But, for the Foreign Office, the success of the PCI and the extent of its influence over the trade unions, at a time when stringent and unpopular measures needed to be taken to restore the Italian economy, meant that Italy could hardly be governed without Communist consent. Although therefore it looked unlikely that the PCI would be in the next government, there would probably have to be arrangements by which they would be regularly consulted on the formation of economic policy. There was therefore no need for Italy's allies to take decisions in a hurry. The immediate problem was to decide what allied governments should say if asked to comment on the Italian election results.[50]

---

48 Modolo G., "La City non scappa davanti al rosso", *L'Espresso*, 9 May 1976.

49 On Italy's internal policy in that period see Craveri P., *La Repubblica dal 1958 al 1992*, TEA, Torino 1996, pp. 635-678. British journalist Peter Nichols wrote a book about the 1976 elections: Nichols P., *La scelta italiana*, Garzanti, Milano 1977.

50 TNA, FCO 33/2943, "Note for Cabinet on 24 June: Italian election results".

The view from the Embassy in Rome showed greater concern. Millard was relieved by the results: the natural anti-Communist majority in Italy had spoken, although the confessional basis of the DC was going to make it very difficult to give it effective expression in government. However, the Ambassador stressed how the elections did not solve any of the problems affecting Italian policy and, above all, the economy. In particular, the elections did not provide the answer to the problem of running the economy without a broader basis of consent than the DC and its potential allies could command. It was hard to see how the measures necessary to deal with inflations, primarily the restraint of wages and the reduction of the state deficit, could be achieved without trade union cooperation and therefore some basis of understanding with the Communists.[51]

On the eve of the Puerto Rico economic summit, British documents stressed how the restoration of the Italian economy was of paramount importance and went hand in hand with political stability. The Foreign Office was inviting the British government and its allies to caution: external pressure on the new government, if too abruptly applied, could have seriously adverse political consequences in Italy. The economy needed drastic measures, including firmer control of public expenditure and more effective tax collection, as well as a new approach to incomes policy. At the same time, if the new government were under visible external pressure to apply abruptly and without due steps to secure popular consent measures of the severity which economic considerations taken alone demanded, this could bring about its collapse and lead to a further strengthening of the Communists. For the United Kingdom and the other Western powers, it was a question of "balance, timing and presentation".[52]

After the elections, a document of the Labour Party International Department stated that "as long as foreign powers arrogate[d] themselves the right to dictate the course of Italian politics, democracy in Italy would remain under the threat of 'destabilization'".[53] This view seemed not to be shared by the Labour British government: in a separate informal meeting during the Puerto Rico G7, the leaders of the four major Western powers confirmed their determination to prevent the direct involvement of the

---

51 TNA, FCO 33/2943, Rome Tel. No. 405, "Italian election results", by Millard G., 22 June 1976.

52 TNA, FCO 33/2943, Economic Summit meeting – 27-28 June, "The political implications of the Italian economic situation", brief by the FCO, WRJ 011/1, 24 June 1976.

53 LHASC, LP, International Department, NEC Minutes, "Italian elections of June 1976", ID/1975-76/161, July 1976.

PCI in any future Italian government. It was also clear that financial support to the Italian economy would be affected by the exclusion of the Communists from governmental responsibilities. However, the Callaghan government maintained a lower profile in comparison with its allies: the actual proposal of linking the Communist question and the financial assistance programme came from German Chancellor Helmut Schmidt, although the idea had already been expressed by the US.[54] Italy obtained an International Monetary Fund (IMF) loan, the first to include heavy structural conditions. Two weeks later, Schmidt himself "leaked" about the restricted meeting in Puerto Rico, causing the disdain of large sectors of the European non-Communist left and a massive campaign in the Italian press.[55]

The summer of 1976 also marked a watershed for the PSI. The election was a profound psychological trauma felt throughout the party. Unless some drastic change occurred, the Communist expansion seemed destined to absorb all but a fraction of the Socialist electorate: a renewal was necessary. In this scenario was forged the so-called *rivolta dei quarantenni* ("forty-year-old men's revolt"), which brought to power a new generation of Socialist leaders in their forties who had been impatient to overturn the gerontocracy of the party. On 16 July, in an extraordinary meeting of the PSI Central Committee at the Midas Hotel in Rome, Bettino Craxi, a 42-year-old Milanese deputy, was elected Party Secretary.[56] Craxi was himself one of the leaders of a small faction inside the party, the "autonomists", who traditionally emphasised the distance which separated the PSI from the Communists as well as from the DC. As viewed from London, he was personally "a libertarian, European and Atlanticist who proclaims himself closer to the Social Democracy of Palme or Brandt than to the popular frontism of Mitterrand". His election should be "an improvement on De Martino as a leader". Although Craxi's personal position in the PSI was not as strong as that of some other leaders and his first task would be to heal the wound inflicted on the party by this

---

54 See Bernardini G., "The Federal Republic of Germany and the resistible rise of the 'historic compromise' in Italy (1974-1978)", in Varsori A., Migani G., quoted, pp. 317-338.

55 Varsori A., "Puerto Rico (1976)", quoted; Basosi D., Bernardini G., "The Puerto Rico Summit of 1976 and the End of Eurocommunism", in Nuti L. (ed.), *The Crisis of Détente in Europe. From Helsinki to Gorbachev, 1975-1985*, Routledge, London 2009, pp. 256-267; Margiocco M., *Stati Uniti e PCI 1943-1980*, Laterza, Roma-Bari 1981, pp. 211-240.

56 Hine D., quoted, pp. 133-148. See Colarizi S., Gervasoni M., *La cruna dell'ago. Craxi, il partito socialista e la crisi della Repubblica*, Laterza, Roma-Bari 2005, pp. 18-75.

traumatic Central Committee meeting, British diplomats thought that the new Secretary should at least marginally improve the chances of forming a new centre-left government in the course of the parliament.[57]

For the moment, however, that was not the case. On 11 August 1976, Giulio Andreotti formed a new DC government, known as *governo della non sfiducia* (not no-confidence government), since it was based on the abstention of the opposition parties. The PCI and the PSI were not part of the majority coalition, but they agreed not to cause its downfall: it was the era of "national solidarity". Nevertheless, according to the FCO, the British should not let down their guard. In his valedictory despatch, Ambassador Millard warned about the nature of Italian Communism. Although not all PCI voters were Communists or even Marxists ("very many of them vote Communist for personal or local reasons, because they want to be on the winning side, or because they dislike the DC"), the present leaders were "perfectly orthodox Communists". The PCI's success in penetrating schools, universities, intellectual circles and the media – by Gramsci's doctrine of the peaceful road to Communism through domination of the organs of the "civil society" – had laid the foundations for its electoral advance. However, a government with Communist participation was not inevitable, and it was in the British interest to discourage the belief in its inevitability. This reflected the nature of Italian society: Italy was a country in rapid evolution, yet likely to remain a basically conservative society and not ripe for Marxist revolution, whether by violent or parliamentary means.[58]

Also for the new British Ambassador in Rome, Alan Campbell, the Communist problem in Italy was far from being solved: the PCI's policies had to be looked at in the long term rather than the short term. The Communists' behaviour suggested that this was how they themselves calculated their prospects, trying gradually to penetrate all strata of Italian society with a view to building up their reputation here and abroad as a respectable partner of the DC and to represent themselves as a respectable party who could also one day constitute an acceptable and indeed desirable alternative. In the event of a change of government after the Communists' entry into the cabinet, Campbell believed that the most likely scenario would be "Yugoslavia-like" – certainly not more liberal and not providing for an alternative. However, the year was closing with some faintly encouraging signs that the Christian Democrats and the smaller

57 TNA, FCO 33/2943, Rome Tel. No. 466, "Italian political situation", 16 July 1976.

58 TNA, FCO 33/2954, "Valedictory despatch – The Italian situation", by Millard G., WRJ 014/2, 25 September 1976.

democratic parties were addressing themselves more effectively to the problems facing Italy. Andreotti was "probably the most effective Prime Minister for the last decade", and paradoxically the political and economic crisis actually gave him a better chance of achieving some reforms, which in easier times would be blocked by one vested interest of another. There had been a significant increase in industrial production and there were the beginnings of a dialogue between the *Confindustria* and the Unions: "amid all the gloom and frustration and evidence of incompetence and corruption, the Italians remain[ed] a resilient and for the most part hard-working people" and they were not "ripe for revolution".[59]

According to British diplomats, the prospects for the following months were of cautious optimism, although all the political parties were in an unsettled state. The Christian Democrats went through a very bad crisis earlier in the year as the result of the economic and political problems of the government and for the involvement of some of their best-known leaders in the Lockheed scandal. They emerged from the election triumphant but shaken and it took them some time to come to terms with the new political situation, although they seemed to have adjusted to it quickly. As for the Communists, Campbell thought that their troubles derived from the developing implications of their new policy of posing as respectable non-revolutionaries and advocating a coalition or "historic compromise". The main difficulty for them was that they had to continue to use language and advocate policies entirely at variance with the views of their supporters at the grass-roots without any visible benefit, even after the elections. But there was no alternative for them unless they were willing (which apparently they were not) to bring down the government and force fresh elections. As for the Socialists, they admitted ruefully that they had made mistakes and lost ground during the year, but by the end of it they had not decided on the best way of recovering their fortunes. For Campbell, some large question marks hung over Italy at the end of 1976, of which the main one was: would the Andreotti government get parliamentary and union acquiescence for an adequate package of economic measures so that an IMF loan would be forthcoming? The general expectation among observers in Rome was that they would get it and that thereafter the government should be able to survive at least until the summer, if not a good deal longer. Anyway, the government had so far done surprisingly well, better than many recent governments with strong parliamentary majorities. In the view of the British Ambassador, the outlook was rather more promising than it had seemed even a few months before: "a cynic

59 TNA, FCO 33/2944, Campbell A. to Crosland A., WRJ 011/1, 14 December 1976.

once observed that in Italy the situation is always hopeless, never serious. The true position at the end of 1976 is that the situation is serious, yet not without hope".[60]

The British crisis

"Sunny Jim" and the ghost of devaluation

A popular adage says that "in the Britain of the 1950s we managed decline, in the 1960s we mismanaged decline and in the 1970s we declined to manage".[61] The growth and productivity performance of the British economy was disappointing in the post-war period: Britain experienced no "economic miracle" after the Second World War. In fact, Britain has been in relative economic decline since the latter part of the 19th century. Since the 1970s, the UK growth rate has been consistently less (approximately two-thirds) than that achieved by the other major capitalist countries. Britain's fastest period of sustained growth was from the end of the Second World War up until the early 1970s – the so-called "golden age of capitalism". Yet even during the golden age, the UK's growth rate of 3.0 per cent compared with an average growth rate of 4.6 per cent achieved by the other leading capitalist countries. The leader of the industrial revolution was falling behind.[62]

In political terms, economic growth involved the commitment to "a high and stable" level of employment and full employment gradually came to be thought of as a fact of life.[63] There was therefore also a "British exceptionalism", like in the case of Italy, although with different origins and in diverse sectors. As in the case of Italy, Britain's crisis also originated from a mixture of international contingencies and trends and internal elements.

---

60 TNA, FCO 33/3207, "Italy: annual review for 1976", Campbell A. to Crosland A., WRJ 014/1, 4 January 1977.

61 Quoted in Gowland D., *Britain and the European Union*, Taylor & Francis, Abingdon 2016, p. 69.

62 Kitson M., "Failure followed by success or success followed by failure? A re-examination of British economic growth since 1949", in Floud R., Johnson P., *The Cambridge Economic History of Modern Britain, Vol. III: Structural Change and Growth, 1939-2000*, Cambridge University Press, Cambridge 2004, pp. 30-31.

63 *White Paper on Employment Policy*, Cmd. 6527, 1944; Alford B.W.E., *British Economic Performance, 1945-1975*, Macmillan, Basingstoke 1988, p. 13.

The 1970s marked the end of the "golden age of capitalism", and relative economic stability. In Britain, this resulted in unemployment on a scale unknown since the 1940s, the highest inflation since the aftermath of the First World War, the biggest setback in output since the beginning of the 1930s, an exorbitant deficit on the current account and industrial unrest and crises in particular industries and firms that drove Labour and Conservative governments alike to use public ownership as a remedy. At the beginning of the decade, the economic signals for Britain were mixed. 1973 was the peak of a spectacular boom, a year in which output grew by 7.3 per cent, more than in any other year since 1945. Yet as a result of the oil crisis after the Yom Kippur war in the autumn of 1973, the United Kingdom experienced an increase in import prices of 55 per cent, retail price increases that peaked in August 1975 at an annual rate of 27 per cent, and a sharp downturn in economic activity, with GDP falling by 3.9 per cent in 1974 and 2.1 per cent in 1975. These conditions, together with other perceived weaknesses in the British economy, led to the loss of confidence in sterling.[64]

In April 1975, British decline was epitomised by an article in the *Wall Street Journal* headlined "Goodbye, Great Britain", advising investors to get out of sterling. In the well-known article, the British economy was portrayed as a sinking boat. Britain's contribution to the world was to reveal the ultimate result of economic and social policies rapidly gaining ascendancy in the United States. The United Kingdom always seemed to somehow "muddle through" despite the best efforts of its government. One reason was that, in their imperfect understanding of economics, the income redistributors had always overlooked a few opportunities to confiscate wealth. Now, the British government was so clearly headed toward a policy of total confiscation that "anyone who has any wealth left [was] discounting furiously at any chance to get it out of the country". The result of all this was to bring investment to a screeching halt by drying up both available funds and potential returns. The price could only be still slower economic growth and would lower living standards for all the British, rich and poor. The conclusion of the article left few hopes for the future: "Good-bye, Great Britain. It was nice knowing you". The only cold comfort was that the United States were following the same path to crisis.[65]

As for the political scene, the Labour Party had regained office in 1974 under Harold Wilson, although without an overall majority, which made

---

[64] Pope R., *The British economy since 1914: a study in decline?*, Longman, London 1998, pp. 52-54.

[65] "Good-bye, Great Britain", *Wall Street Journal*, 29 April 1975.

it dependent on support from minor parties. The widening gap between British inflation and the rest of the world was to affect the exchange rate, which began to fall sharply. In July 1975, the Wilson government published a White Paper entitled *The attack on inflation*, stating its determination to bring the rate of domestic inflation to 10 per cent by the end of 1976.[66] As soon as inflation began to decrease, the focus of attention shifted to the alarming rise in the level of unemployment. However, there was a profound chasm between the Labour Party and the Treasury. Labour's left was anxious to press an alternative economic strategy on the government which involved increases in expenditure on industrial investment, as well as import controls. On the other hand, the Treasury's view was that things were out of hand and it was necessary to reduce Public Sector Borrowing Requirement (PSBR) and take into consideration the reaction of the international markets.

In November 1975, the Chancellor of the Exchequer Denis Healey, backed by the Prime Minister, had presented a package of cuts totalling 3 billion pounds, which was settled in the February 1976 Public Expenditure White Paper. This led to a storm in the left-wing of the Labour Party and the government's defeat at the hand of its own backbenchers on Wilson's sixtieth birthday, 11 March: the government had to recourse to a vote of confidence. Five days later, Harold Wilson unexpectedly announced his resignation as Prime Minister.

The Labour Party held an election to replace the leader of the Party (and therefore Prime Minister) for the first time while in office. In the first ballot, six candidates competed for the leadership, covering different trends inside the Party: the left-wing was represented by Secretary of State for Energy Tony Benn and Secretary of State for Employment Michael Foot; James Callaghan, the Foreign Secretary, Denis Healey, Chancellor of the Exchequer and Anthony Crosland, Secretary of State for the Environment could be described as centre-right; while Home Secretary Roy Jenkins was at the furthest right of the spectrum. The last ballot between Foot and Callaghan saw the latter winning with a majority of 176 votes, against the 137 votes of Foot.

Callaghan's experience was paramount: he was the only twentieth-century British Prime Minister to have held all four major offices of state – Chancellor of the Exchequer, Home Secretary, Foreign Secretary and Prime Minister. At 64, Callaghan was also the oldest person to become Prime Minister at time of appointment since Winston Churchill. On the

66 *The attack on inflation*, Cmnd. 6151, 11 July 1975.

same day that he became Prime Minister, he also lost the government's overall majority.[67]

Callaghan's first job was to create his own cabinet, trying to put his mark on it. Healey was confirmed as Chancellor, but the replacement of the new Prime Minister at the Foreign Office was not so simple. Roy Jenkins would have wanted the position, but Callaghan considered him too pro-European; he therefore opted for Anthony Crosland, while Jenkins requested and obtained that the Prime Minister nominate him for the position of the President of the European Commission.[68]

The Italian press followed with interest the leadership election, and the comparisons between the economic situation in London and Rome had slowly become a recurrent theme.[69] As stressed by *L'Espresso*, for the first time since 1945 life conditions in Britain were falling. The only comfort for the pound was the comparison with the lira. London, once the "capital of capitals", was now borrowing more money than any other capital in the world. The country that only a quarter of a century earlier was the greatest exporter of cars now could barely defend its internal automotive market from foreign competitors. Britain's ungovernability seemed to be caused by her irresponsible rulers, who were downgrading the political struggle to mere advertising technique. At least Italy still had the primate of ungovernability.[70]

For the daily *La Stampa*, although Callaghan had no university education and was accused by the Labour left of having no ideology, he was able to understand the masses better than ideologists. Callaghan's socialism was "instinctive", born as a protest against injustice and matured in the tradition of British reformism. He was a simple man, being at ease with simple people, and he had a small farm in Sussex. Yet Callaghan should not be underrated: he knew like no other the machinery of the Labour Party and of Whitehall and how to use it. Was he going to be a good premier? Probably yes, not exciting, but an efficient one. He could

67 On 6 April the Labour MP Brian O'Malley died; however, in reality, through the support of the two Irish Nationalist MPs, the government's parliamentary position remained relatively secure. In the following months, the majority was eroded further because of defections, poor intra- and inter-party relations and by-election defeat. Kirkup J., *The Lib-Lab Pact: A Parliamentary Agreement, 1977-78*, Springer, New York 2016, pp. 29-30.

68 Conroy H., *Callaghan*, Haus Publishing, London 2006, pp. 90-91.

69 See Russo F., "Wilson divora i resti dell'impero", *L'Espresso*, 25 January 1976; *Id.*, "La sterlina guardò la lira e vomitò" (The pound looked at the lira and vomited), *L'Espresso*, 27 June 1976, reporting that Callaghan stated: "We don't want to end up like Italy".

70 Russo F., "Chi salirà sulla zattera di Wilson", *L'Espresso*, 28 March 1976.

be too political for a Europe in need of imagination, but not for a Britain in need of a "sharp and strong helmsman".[71]

The *Corriere della Sera* focused more on the precarious conditions in Britain. Since the Labour Party had come to power more than a decade earlier (with the four-year parenthesis of the Heath government), British decline continued to grow inexorably. The pound now was worth 1.85 dollars; ten years earlier, it was 2.80 dollars. The inflation rate in the United Kingdom had beaten Italy's negative primate, corroding welfare funds and sowing the seeds of maybe uncontrollable social tensions. In these circumstances, Britain's experience in the struggle against inflation and unemployment became emblematic for all of Europe, and particularly for the most fragile economies. The Callaghan government, although it was defined as a "caretaker government", had to take emergency measures, elaborating a strategy that had to be aggressive, not passive. Because of his limited majority, Callaghan should invest more in his political skills, rather than behaving like a "technician", and he had the first result when the Labour maximalist wing accepted his call to order, urging it to overcome currents and pressure groups inside the party. Sometimes, concluded the article, "intuition is worth more than academic knowledge and is more effective than the excess of intellectual arrogance".[72]

London correspondent for PSI press, Gino Bianco – who worked at the Research Department of the Socialist International – made an appraisal of Wilson's 30-year-long political career on the monthly *Mondoperaio*. The "Wilson era", characterised by his famous pragmatism (which sometimes could verge on irresponsibility), had lights and shadows. Among his failures, there were the unsuccessful technological miracle which lay at the basis of the programme of 1964 Labour administration; the persistent economic decline; the European question; and the policy on Northern Ireland. Wilson's main successes had been the voluntary income policy, some social reforms and, most importantly, the maintenance of the unity of the Labour Party. His leadership was the expression of the centre of the party, but it was open to the Labour left, whose support had been fundamental for his political longevity. Wilson's mediating skills won him the favour of the party's left-wing and also of the majority of the trade unions, which considered him the "best option", a defensive choice against the danger of an "alternative to the right" giving the leadership to Roy Jenkins' moderates. This made the resignation of Wilson even more

71 Ciriello M., "Londra: l'ora di Sunny Jim", *La Stampa*, 6 April 1976.

72 Cianfanelli R., "Callaghan prepara un governo anti-crisi", *Corriere della Sera*, 7 April 1976.

striking, just while his position seemed more secure and unchallenged than ever. The real challenge for his successor Jim Callaghan would be not only to keep unity inside the Labour Party, but most importantly to govern the country at such a critical moment. Callaghan inherited an uneasy situation: should he fail to cope with the major problems affecting Britain or be too tentative in adopting unpopular yet urgent measures, an early general election would be inevitable.[73]

According to the Italian Ministry of Foreign Affairs, Callaghan's premiership did not bring about fundamental changes to British internal and foreign policy. Economic problems had totally absorbed the new Prime Minister; he also had to try to limit the Tories' success in local elections in May, which could be interpreted as a protest vote against the severe measures taken by the Labour administration.[74]

However, in the first months of 1976, the Italian Ministry of Foreign Affairs portrayed a British economy seemingly on its way to recovery. There had been a steady growth in industrial production, due to increasing internal demand and the rising number of orders from abroad. Even inflation seemed to slow down, thanks to the agreement between the government and the trade unions on the income policy.[75] The Italian figures were right: the economic recovery which began in the latter half of 1975 continued through 1976. Stock building became positive during the year and exports increased; the rise in output was enough to hold back the increase in unemployment, but not to reverse its trend. The rate of inflation was still very high, but falling significantly each month: from 23.4 per cent in June it came down to 12.9 per cent in July. Another encouraging sign was the reduction in PSBR.[76]

Despite these positive trends, sterling was under severe pressure. Devaluation was a ghost haunting the new Prime Minister's stay at 10 Downing Street from the very early days. In fact, Callaghan was Chancellor of the Exchequer in 1967, when the worsening economic situation ended in the forced devaluation of the pound. Nine years later, investors became

73 Bianco G., "I laburisti dopo Wilson", *Mondoperaio*, April 1976, pp. 99-101.

74 ASPR, busta 697 B/3, Visita in Italia del ministro degli Interni di Gran Bretagna Roy Jenkins, 11-12 agosto 1976, Ministero degli Affari esteri, Segreteria Generale, "Situazione politica interna", August 1976.

75 ASPR, busta 757, Signor Alan Hugh Campbell, Ambasciatore di Gran Bretagna, Presentazione lettere credenziali, Ministero degli Affari esteri, Segreteria Generale, "Situazione economica della Gran Bretagna e relazioni con l'Italia", October 1976.

76 Britton A., *Macroeconomic Policy in Britain, 1974-1987*, Cambridge University Press, Cambridge 1994, pp. 28-29.

convinced that the pound was overvalued, and a large-scale sale of sterling began: the pound rapidly lost value against the dollar, reaching a record low in June. From March to September 1976, massive sales of sterling reduced its value by 26 per cent. A first relief came in June, with a £45.3 billion standby credit. Two billion dollars came from the US, the rest from the central banks of the Group of Ten, from Switzerland, and from the Bank of International Settlements. It was impressive, but it was also a failure: the conditions were short term. If it was not enough, there would be no alternative but to go to the IMF.[77]

The greatest loan

Two images have become iconic of the second half of the 1970s in Britain: that of Healey driving to Heathrow airport on 28 September 1976 and then rushing back to the Treasury on hearing news of a further fall in the value of sterling, and the pavements full of rubbish during the "winter of discontent" of 1978-1979.[78] The IMF crisis has become part of British political memory. As Vernon Bogdanor has pointed out, the loan from the IMF was less of a turning point than a confirmation of a turning point that had already occurred, a shift in economic policy legitimated by the loan itself, but which nonetheless highlighted the difficulties of applying the doctrines of social democracy in a globalised economy. This crisis was "as much a crisis of social democracy as it was one on the British economy".[79]

In 1944, Britain had been instrumental in the establishment of the IMF at the Bretton Woods conference; few could then have imagined that its biggest rescue, overseen and heavily influenced by the US Treasury, would be of Britain. The government had already made two applications to the IMF at the end of 1975, with far less publicity. Healey later claimed that the Treasury had grossly overestimated the public sector borrowing requirement, the key figure used during the IMF crisis, and that if he had been given accurate figures he would not have had to ask for the loan.

The government debated proposals for further cuts in expenditure and tax increases to reduce the budget deficit in July 1976. By September, Britain had already drawn heavily on the short-term loan: an IMF loan

---

77 Whitehead P., *The writing on the wall*, Michael Joseph, London 1985, p. 184.

78 See Burk K., Cairncross A., *Goodbye, Great Britain: The 1976 IMF Crisis*, Yale University Press, New Haven 1992; Roberts R., *When Britain went bust. The 1976 IMF crisis*, OMFIF Press, London 2016. On the winter of discontent see Chapter 3.

79 See Vernon Bogdanor's Gresham College lectures: https://www.gresham.ac.uk/lectures-and-events/the-imf-crisis-1976.

was apparently necessary. As pressure on it continued, the government approached the IMF for a loan of 3.9 billion dollars, the largest amount ever requested, with the prerequisite of tough deflationary measures. The government had an intense debate on Denis Healey's proposals for a cut of 20 per cent in the budget deficit, but they eventually came to an agreement in order to avoid a disastrous run on the pound.

The Labour Party conference in September 1976 epitomised the confusion and dismay of that time. On the second day, 28 September, Healey was due to fly to Hong Kong for a conference of Commonwealth finance ministers, and then on to Manila for the IMF's annual summit, but he instead went back to London for an emergency meeting with Treasury advisers. Every quarter of an hour, the pound dropped another cent: "it seemed like the end of the world", Healey said later. His decision attracted many critics for its appearance of panic; in addition, Britain would not be represented by any Minister at the IMF meeting, precisely when she was going to be a heavy debtor, with no favourable effect on world opinion.[80] On the very same day of Healey's "turn-around", in Blackpool, Callaghan was giving his maiden speech as party leader and Prime Minister, leaving the audience bewildered:

> The cosy world we were told would go on forever, where full employment would be guaranteed by a stroke of the chancellor's pen, cutting taxes, deficit spending, that cosy world is gone.
> When we reject unemployment as an economic instrument – as we do – and when we reject also superficial remedies, as socialists must, then we must ask ourselves unflinchingly what is the cause of high unemployment. Quite simply and unequivocally, it is caused by paying ourselves more than the value of what we produce [...].
> We have just escaped from the highest rate of inflation this country has known; we have not yet escaped from the consequences: high unemployment. Now we must get back to fundamentals. First, overcoming unemployment now unambiguously depends on our labour costs being at least comparable with those of our major competitors. Second, we can only become competitive by having the right kind of investment at the right kind of level, and by significantly improving the productivity of both labour and capital.[81]

80 Wass D., *Decline to Fall: The Making of British Macro-Economic Policy and the 1976 IMF Crisis*, Oxford University Press, Oxford 2008, p. 229.

81 Report of the Seventy-Fifth Annual Conference of the Labour Party, Labour Party, London 1976, pp. 188-189.

Callaghan's Blackpool speech is usually regarded as the moment when Keynesianism was rejected in favour of monetarism, although there is still much controversy regarding it.[82]

The *Corriere della Sera* commented that the loan would not change the British situation. It would only be used to pay back the former loan from June, which was due in December; moreover, the IMF loan would put new constraints on an already strained economy. An over-devaluated pound could help some industrial sectors (mainly automotive and electrotechnical), while others would be seriously damaged, like chemicals, textiles, oil and most of all food production.[83]

The IMF delegation arrived on 1 November; after extenuating negotiations, Johannes Witteveen, managing director of the Fund, eventually proposed cuts in the PSBR of 2.5 billion pounds over the two years 1977-1979. Callaghan then had the difficult job of persuading the government to accept the proposed cuts.

Following the agreement with the IMF, the overall economic and financial scene improved. The pound quickly appreciated in value, and by the end of 1977 there were improvements in the balance of trade: Britain did not need to draw the full loan. Nevertheless, the IMF crisis reinforced a change in policy orientation away from full employment and social welfare towards the control of inflation and expenditure. The 1976 IMF crisis may be considered Britain's economic Suez: if 1956 had rapidly diminished London's global political role, twenty years later the United Kingdom experienced the weakening of its economic stance, with the coup de grace to sterling as a reserve currency.[84]

Despite the first signs of recovery started after the IMF loan, the theme of Britain's decline was a front-page, eye-catching topic at home and abroad. US economist Milton Friedman went so far to predict that if Britain continued on her present course, it would mean "the end of Britain's democracy". In a show on American TV channel CBS, he suggested that the United Kingdom was on the road to disaster: what had happened in recent years in Chile, where communist dictatorship was followed by a military coup, served as an "extremely pertinent example" of what could well happen in Britain. The country was on the brink of economic and

---

82 Hickson K., *The IMF Crisis of 1976 and British Politics*, I.B. Tauris, London 2005, pp. 102-106; Needham D., *UK Monetary Policy from Devaluation to Thatcher, 1967-82*, Palgrave Macmillan, London 2014, pp. 78-108.

83 Cianfanelli R., "Londra a caccia di nuovi prestiti", *Corriere della Sera*, 30 September 1976.

84 See Hirowatari K., *Britain and European Monetary Cooperation, 1964-1979*, AIAA, Reston 2015, p. 176.

political collapse. Britain's difficulties stemmed from its huge social welfare system and the massive involvement of the government in industry. As a result, Britain borrowed more money than any other country, and it was in industrial decay. However, if the country swiftly adopted a course of drastic cuts to the social service system and the British government quickly reduced its role in industry, then – according to Freidman – there was still a chance that within ten years the United Kingdom could enjoy the sort of economic miracle that Japan and West Germany had experienced. The programme concluded denying that the CBS was hostile to Britain: the Americans were dear friends of the British but "it was best for the truth to be told by a friend".[85]

Reactions in Italy were mixed. British decline was apparent, and it was indeed a cause of concern, but it was accompanied by a subtle relief in sharing with another country – more precisely, with one of the Big Four – the status of "sick man": a trouble shared was a trouble halved. Italy was "Europe's other Britain", as *The Economist* labelled it:

> Not long ago, the image of the stiff-lipped British sinking in the same boat as undisciplined Italians was funny. It is now deadly serious; Italy appears to be following Britain's example as much as the other way around. Both countries have tried to keep up employment by pumping money into economy. The result has been rates of price inflation higher than those of other major trading nations [...], and deflating currencies [...].

For political reasons, politicians in both countries allowed wage inflation to soar out of hand as the world relapsed into recession in 1974. They tried to buy relative social stability at an inflationary price that was now proving socially more damaging that if they had not. Both in Italy and in Britain the hope now was that the shock of inflation would allow the delayed adjustments to be made. Each country recognised the structural changes that were necessary – a higher rate of investment and the more productive use of it, a better-trained labour force, more productive and less profligate public services. But in each the crisis of the moment grew wider.[86]

The British IMF loan could also be considered a victory for London over Rome. It could be a defeat for Italy because it stressed in an unflattering way how the Italian situation was perceived abroad. Loans such as the one to Britain could not be improvised: the more money was granted to London, the greater would be the difficulty to find the same resources

85 "Friedman warning on 'UK road to disaster'", *The Times*, 30 November 1976.

86 "Italy: Europe's other Britain", *The Economist*, 30 October 1976.

for Italy. The Labour Party had been able to make the country accept an austerity policy and this played in its favour, just when the Italian trade unions seemed to become entrenched in their position. The British loan left Italy even lonelier, with the risk of becoming the only "black sheep" of the European family.[87]

This sense of a "common fate" was strengthened in November 1976, when Italian Foreign Minister Arnaldo Forlani went to London to meet Callaghan and Crosland. On that occasion, Crosland gave an interview to the *Corriere della Sera*. Without solidarity, firstly in Europe, Italy and Britain, that is to say the EEC countries most hit by the crisis, had no prospect of extricating themselves without devastating social, economic and political consequences. On the prospects of emerging from the tunnel of the economic crisis by means of increased European collaboration, the British view was guarded, but cautiously favourable: first the United Kingdom had to succeed in the struggle against inflation. Britain's problems, albeit complex, could not be arbitrarily exaggerated; one should also consider the encouraging aspects, such as the dramatic drop in the number of strikes, which had fallen to their lowest level for twenty years, and were now at barely a fifth of their 1974 level. In short, for the two ailing countries of Europe, Crosland proposed the search for a common therapy: "the Italians, faced with the problems which we are up against, will have no difficulty in understanding us. We know we can rely on their support, just as they can rely on ours".[88]

Yet the Italian press did not prove to be so supportive of the UK situation. Curiously, it was precisely the left-oriented press that stressed the link between Britain's economic crisis and the crisis of Labour most and indicated that it also reflected a crisis of values. *L'Espresso* portrayed a Labour government almost in agony: the Cabinet "was at loggerheads with the left of the party", while its parliamentary majority was now limited to one seat. Reading British newspapers, one could have thought that in Britain there was a new French Revolution underway and that a new Terror had begun: there were debates about the pros and the cons of the elimination of nobility and the introduction of the guillotine. Actually, there were just debates about the abolition of the House of Lords, while the allocation of time or "guillotine" motions were used to limit the amount of time that MPs could spend debating a particular stage of a Bill in the

87 Deaglio M., "Perché l'Inghilterra ha vinto la corsa ai miliardi del Fmi", *La Stampa*, 6 January 1977.

88 Cianfanelli R., "Per l'Italia e Inghilterra malate cerchiamo una terapia comune", *Corriere della Sera*, 26 November 1976.

House of Commons. Conversely, the climate in those days was rather "counter-revolutionary" and it was reminiscent more of 1814 than 1789: before Labour's defeat, the Tories were hastening restoration. Without popular approval for the government's measures, Britain, like Italy, would not be able to cope with the inexorable worsening of the economic crisis. Yet since there was no approval, political crisis and economic crisis were intertwined and were exacerbating one another. Britain was "no land of milk and honey": since Labour's victory in 1974, the price of foodstuffs had increased by 68 per cent and consumer goods by 55.9 per cent, while the average increase in OECD countries had been 27.8 per cent. Reading the British press, one could think that it wished that the IMF had set out conditions so hard as to break the power of the unions and the Labour left for decades. According to some UK newspapers, Britain was a land of "unrepentant sybarites", condemned by a deserved nemesis to "dig Ho Ci Minh channels with teaspoons: from Sodom to Peking".[89]

In a similar tone, in the PSI monthly *Mondoperaio* Barbara Spinelli, journalist and daughter of Altiero (one of the founding fathers of European federalism), wrote that the profound crisis of the Labour Party was a mirror of all the faults and flaws of Britain's standing in Europe in the aftermath of the Second World War. The loss of the empire, the "City" no longer all-powerful, the unhealthy development of industry, the rigidity of a labour market still fragmented in static corporations, were all "distortions" which British socialism had inherited without being able to straighten them out in time. It was not the case that this crisis coincided with a more general decay of values and with a widespread sense of defeat that permeated British political class as a whole. The Labour Party was facing the economic crisis totally scattered, like during the Great Depression of the 1930s. At a first glance, the situation seemed hopeless: it was as if Labour still had not learnt how to stay in government and was preparing for a slow political suicide.[90]

These were just two examples of the growing international apprehension about the state of Britain. By the end of the 1970s, concern at what was conceived as a peculiarly British problem led to real pessimism as to whether a democratic government, ruling by consent, could take the actions necessary to turn the economy around.[91]

---

89 Russo F., "Non parlatemi dei laboristi, *please*", *L'Espresso*, 28 November 1976.

90 Spinelli B., "La crisi del laburismo britannico", *Mondoperaio*, December 1976, pp. 87-89.

91 Pope R., quoted, p. 61.

All sick men together[92]

As we have seen, the idea of an Anglo-Italian "common fate" was a theme well exploited by the Italian press, while it was, predictably, less popular in the United Kingdom. Although the British had an acute self-awareness of the state of their economy, it was not easy to accept being compared and related to a "minor" country like Italy. It would, therefore, be a probable blow to Britain's pride knowing that London's "special partner" began to officially discuss the problems concerning Italy and Britain as one issue. In fact, in many documents of the Ford Administration, British and Italian economic strains were dealt with together.

Concern about the British economy increased in the United States in the first months of 1976. According to US Undersecretary for Monetary Affairs Edwin Yeo, "to our great dismay, we realised we were going to have a major UK experience ahead". Yeo's concerns went beyond Britain itself: "we feared that if a country like Britain blew up, defaulted on its loans, introduced foreign exchange controls and froze convertibility, we could have a real-world depression".[93] As for the Italian situation, concern about economic strains went hand in hand with the "red scare" of Communist strengthening: Italy had been on the list of significant borrowers made by the Comptroller of the Currency since late 1974, reflecting the sharp deterioration in the country's condition. One of the country's biggest economic problems throughout the year would be finding adequate financial support to cover the current account deficit, repayment of past debt, and sporadic bursts of capital flight. Because of the vagaries of capital outflows, it was difficult to gauge Italy's exact 1976 borrowing needs: foreign indebtedness totalled roughly 14 billion dollars.[94]

Already in mid-March 1976, the National Security Council was warned about "major storm warnings" in both the monetary and trade areas: volatility in currency markets, reflecting a severe internal problem in Britain and Italy, had contributed to a deteriorating psychological

---

92 The reference here is to the article "All sick men together", *The Economist*, 17 May 1975.

93 Quoted in Fay S., Young H., "The day the £ nearly died", *The Sunday Times*, 14 May 1978. See also Harmon M., *The British Labour Government and the 1976 IMF Crisis*, Macmillan, Basingstoke 1997, pp. 141-142.

94 Gerard Ford Library (GFL), Arthur Burns Papers, 1969-78, Federal Reserve Board, Subject File: International Monetary Reform, box B75, "Examiner classification of country risk: status of Italy", 29 January 1976; GFL, Office of Economic Affairs, L. William Seidman, box 134, "Italy: the political economic scene in early 1976", 26 March 1976. See also Cominelli L., quoted, pp. 219-224.

and political climate in Europe.[95] Chairman of the Council of Economic Advisers Alan Greenspan discussed with President Ford his concern over growing economic instability in Italy and the UK. Since the Rambouillet summit in 1975, Italy's economic deterioration was reflected in heavy foreign borrowing and a 20 per cent reduction in the value of the lira, while Britain's persistent double-digit inflation and low productivity had forced abandonment of serious Bank of England efforts to defend the pound, causing its value to decline 7 per cent in the past few weeks. Devaluation in Italy and Britain had also put severe pressure on the French franc. According to Greenspan, these developments raised crucial questions as to whether or not the industrial countries had yet faced up to the basic problems of establishing economic stability to assure economic growth throughout the free world. Domestic policies of over-consumption in Italy and Britain had driven them to maintain expansionary fiscal and monetary policies, resulting in excessive budget deficits and mounting foreign debts. Labour had demanded and been granted inflationary wage increases. The inevitable result was a declining value of the currency which could not be resisted for long by central bank intervention in exchange markets. Greenspan suggested that the United States and West Germany should cooperate in providing financial aid to Rome and London on condition that they undertake stipulated economic-political policy reforms designed to restore sound and sustainable financial stability.[96]

In preparation for the Puerto Rico summit, the US Treasury indicated that there were three policy options in the UK and Italian case. First, do nothing. Namely, in the case of Italy, refusing to extend credit, and insisting on an exclusively internal solution which would involve some further depreciation of the lira and draconian economic policies. A reluctance on the part of the Italian people to support a total austerity effort could result in a "siege economy", a series of controls on imports and foreign exchange transactions which, however, probably would not work: the ultimate result could be the financial collapse of Italy. This, in turn, could prompt countermeasures from other countries. The second option was providing official credit – country to country loans and/or multilateral credit – on a "no conditions" basis. This could involve a need for 3-4 billion dollars every 18-24 months for Italy and a larger amount of

95 GFL, National Security Adviser, International economic affairs staff, 1975-6, Presidential subject file: Energy, box 5, Memorandum from Hormats R. to Scowcroft B., "Economic storm warnings", 17 March 1976.

96 GFL, Council of Economic Adviser Records, 1974-77, RG 459, Alan Greenspan Files, Economic Summit Puerto Rico, box 39, Memorandum for the Secretary, "Greenspan Europe Support Discussion", 29 March 1976.

4-5 billion dollars for Britain. The third approach provided official credit but with meaningful conditions – an economic programme that geared the extension of credit to the accomplishment of a gradual program of domestic economic and financial stabilisation. This third approach had the advantage of tying limited amounts of official financing to corrective policies; it did not run the risks inherent in the "do nothing" option and if successfully supplemented did not involve the almost unlimited amounts implicit in the second option. The US Treasury focused its efforts on the last option. There were, however, two obstacles, namely the reluctance of countries like Britain and Italy to accept this approach, and the limited availability of money of a conditional nature for Italy. The best institutional arrangement for producing conditional financing was the IMF: it did not involve Congress, did not impact the US budget and cloaked the conditionality in a multinational mantle that diluted opposition within a borrowing country to conditions imposed by the United States or other outsiders.[97]

The British and Italian crises could have severe implications in Europe and the West as a whole. The US were "at the end of the road" with respect to their relations with certain countries in the developed world. The economic and social disequilibria that had characterised the UK for decades, Italy in an acute sense since the riots of 1969, and in varying degrees several of the smaller European countries, had resulted in financial circumstances of such magnitude and severity that they could no longer be financed. The tripping mechanism, although not the cause, had been the inability of Italy, and to a degree the UK, to borrow in international capital markets in sufficient size to finance their fundamental disequilibrium. The British and Italian situations posed several threats to the US: they had the potential, if each situation followed its worst possible track, to "badly cripple" the international monetary system and the US financial system (and in a very real sense already had); the financial and economic instability contributed to an intensification of social and political tensions, which in turn resulted in fragile middle-of-the-road governments which could be replaced by leftist dominated administrations; they could lead to "beggar-thy-neighbour policies", particularly in foreign exchange markets; these difficulties could eventually hurt, perhaps destroy, worldwide economic recovery. Under these circumstances, it was essential that the US did everything in their power "to facilitate, even force in a subtle sense",

---

97 GFL, Arthur Burns Papers, 1969-78, Federal Reserve Board Subject File: International Economic Developments: Briefing Book, 6/6/78 (3), box B62, "Memorandum for the President", by Yeo E., 24 June 1976.

the adjustment of economic and financial policies in Italy and the UK. Even in the short run, substantive and visible progress would be required if the US were to avoid the further adverse impact of these situations on their vital interests.[98]

By the beginning of July, it appeared that Puerto Rico had given added impetus to the British government's efforts to deal with their economic and financial problems. Secretary of the Treasury William E. Simon was so optimistic as to write that if the budget cuts that Healey was going to announce were viewed as genuine and if they were complemented by a firm monetary policy, "the UK [could] be able to avoid a large drawing from the IMF".[99] Simon proved to be wrong; moreover, the tendency to consider the British and Italian problems together continued even after Puerto Rico, although both sterling and the lira had strengthened considerably since the summit. As for the pound, this in part reflected a growing conviction that British authorities were prepared to tighten up on public expenditure before the end of the year. The lira, which had already been firming before Puerto Rico, was given further support by reports that financing aid had been discussed at the summit. Despite the period of tranquillity, there remained the potential for a resurgence of volatility in the exchange markets. It would be all too easy for the British and the Italians to argue that reduced pressure on their currencies meant less urgency about decreasing their domestic budget imbalances. It was neither in their interest nor that of America to let this idea gain currency. For this purpose, the US Treasury wanted to block as soon as possible an initiative of the European Commission for an "interim financial package" for Italy, even before the country had a stabilisation programme. If Italian politicians came to believe that they could receive assistance without implementing necessary corrective measures, they would take this easy way out.[100]

As the months went by, the British and Italian situation continued to be treated jointly, although the focus of the US Administration was more on the United Kingdom. In November, after the arrival of the

---

98 GFL, Arthur Burns Papers, 1969-78, Federal Reserve Board Subject File: International Economic Developments: Briefing Book, 6/6/78 (3), box B62, "International monetary problems re Italy", without date (presumably mid-June 1976).

99 GFL, National Security Adviser, NSC Europe Canada and Ocean affairs staff, Files 1974-77, box 76, Memorandum for the President by Simon W., 13 July 1976.

100 GFL, National Security Adviser, International economic affairs staff, 1975-6, Presidential subject file, Country file: United Kingdom, box 3, Memorandum from Hormats R. to Scowcroft B., "International financial developments affecting sterling and the lira following Puerto Rico", 8 July 1976.

IMF delegation in London, Robert Hormats, senior economic adviser, asked in a memorandum for White House National Security Adviser Brent Scowcroft how likely it was that the pound could collapse before completion of the Fund negotiations. With regards to Italy, there was a relative optimism about the success of Andreotti's programme.[101]

On the other hand, in late 1976, both the British and the Italian governments turned to the United States for further reassurances on their economies. At the end of November, Callaghan sent Harold Lever, Chancellor of the Duchy of Lancaster to Washington to convey a message for President Ford on Britain's economic difficulties and talk to the American Treasury, the IMF and the Federal Reserve Bank.[102] The letter from Callaghan indicated that "the orthodox approach of the bankers and monetarists to solve the UK's problems through deflation would be catastrophic", reducing employment, forcing a move to protectionism, and dangerously straining social cohesion. Callaghan wanted help from the major contributors to the IMF to ensure that the Fund did not try to push Britain too hard.[103] Simon pointed out that the "sterling balances" were not the main problem facing Britain, but merely symptomatic of the problem – which was the UK's inability to stabilise its domestic economy. In the US view, if Britain adopted firm stabilisation measures, confidence would be regained, and sterling holders would not feel uneasy about maintaining their balances. The Treasury Secretary was very critical of the actions of the two Labour governments:

> One of the tragedies in the present situation has been the time and energy devoted to finding ways of borrowing more money. If that same time and energy had been devoted to creating the political basis for the policies that ultimately must come, the outlook would be different. [...] The Government has not been dealing with the real problems.

Any further financial support could only be gauged after the successful conclusion of the negotiations with the Fund, and was dependent on the

[101] GFL, National Security Adviser, International economic affairs staff, 1975-6, Presidential subject file, Country file: United Kingdom, box 3, Memorandum from Hormats R. to Scowcroft B., "Your meeting with Yeo, Greenspan, Rogers, *et al.*", 2 November 1976.

[102] See Harmon M., quoted, pp. 177-181.

[103] GFL, National Security Adviser, International economic affairs staff, 1975-6, Presidential subject file, Country file: United Kingdom, box 3, Letter from Callaghan J. to Ford G., 12 November 1976.

emergence of strong political leadership directed at fostering support for policy changes.[104]

In the meeting in the Oval Office, Lever told the President that there would be more than a 50-50 chance that the British government would fall if it tried to respond to the IMF's harsh conditions. Ford said that the stability of Britain was important from an international military, political, and economic point of view and added that, on a personal basis, he would "bend over backwards" in enabling the UK to play the vital world role economically and militarily.[105] But three days later, American officials held a meeting at the White House to discuss the British economic situation, where the prevailing view was that the US should not exert pressure on the IMF to alter its views. American intervention would probably reduce the credibility of the agreement between Britain and the Fund; moreover, providing the United Kingdom with IMF money without its taking adequate stabilisation measures would set a "bad precedent" for such countries as Italy, convincing them that they too could receive international financial help without undertaking necessary corrective action.[106]

A few weeks later, Andreotti himself went to Washington.[107] The visit came "at the most critical moment in Italy's history since 1948".[108] According to the Treasury, the primary purpose of Andreotti's visit was to demonstrate to the Italian people continued American support for his government and his efforts to stabilise the Italian economy. It was the US view that the survival of Italian democracy depended on bringing inflation under control and that any further financial assistance to Italy should be multilateral and – as in the British case – linked to the adoption and implementation of an adequate economic stabilisation programme. The US were staying strictly in the background during the

104 GFL, National Security Adviser, International economic affairs staff, 1975-6, Presidential subject file, Country file: United Kingdom, box 3, "Memorandum for the President", by Simon W., 15 November 1976.

105 GFL, National Security Adviser, International economic affairs staff, 1975-6, Presidential subject file, Country file: United Kingdom, box 3, "Memorandum of conversation" between President Ford and Harold Lever, 16 November 1976.

106 GFL, National Security Adviser, International economic affairs staff, 1975-6, Presidential subject file, Country file: United Kingdom, box 3, "Meeting on the UK economic situation", by Scowcroft B., 19 November 1976.

107 See Gentiloni Silveri U., *L'Italia sospesa*, quoted, pp. 188-190.

108 GFL, National Security Adviser, NSC Europe Canada and Ocean affairs staff, Files 1974-77, box 77, Memorandum for the President, "Official Visit of Italian Prime Minister Giulio Andreotti", by Robinson C., 29 November 1976.

negotiations between the IMF and the Italians, and no further short-term assistance could be offered. If Andreotti should finally be able to produce an "exceptionally good, effective programme, for two years instead of one", it could be possible to improve the chances for the preservation of democratic government in Italy by offering greater IMF credits.[109] On the political side, the Department of State stressed the importance of a twofold strategy. In private meetings, it should be made clear that the participation of Communists in the Italian government "would inevitably have repercussions on Italy's present role in the Western system": it was not "a threat, but [...] a simple fact of life". Conversely, "courageous leadership, competent government, sound economics and a new image for the Christian Democrats" would, in the long run, prove to be the only alternative to further concessions to the PCI. Public statements, on the other hand, should emphasise US general agreement with the policy initiatives Andreotti had taken while making clear there was still concern at any signs of further concessions to "undemocratic forces.[110]

Therefore, from a US point of view, British and Italian economic problems, although originating from different situations and political scenes, showed many points in common and could be treated with a single strategy. This had greater implications for Britain: it meant that, while the United Kingdom consulted with the other "big powers" to try to find a multilateral solution for the Italian crisis, its economic strains were carefully assessed in Washington in the same context of the Italian one. It was as if Britain was one "doctor" of the medical team trying to cure the Italian disease and at the same time a "patient" herself, almost without her knowledge.

109 GFL, National Security Adviser, NSC Europe Canada and Ocean affairs staff, Files 1974-77, box 77, Memorandum for the President, "Visit of Italian Prime Minister Andreotti", by Simon W., December 1976.

110 GFL, National Security Adviser, NSC Europe Canada and Ocean affairs staff, Files 1974-77, box 77, Memorandum for the President, "Official Visit of Italian Prime Minister Giulio Andreotti", by Robinson C., 29 November 1976.

Chapter 2

After the cure

Italy under special surveillance

The outlook for Italy

In 1977, Peter Nichols celebrated his 20-year anniversary as Rome correspondent of *The Times*. The occasion was ripe for an evaluation of Italy's international role and how much it had evolved in just two decades, which in Italian history had been as long as "two centuries". Yet Italy was normally thought to be of rather superficial interest, "unless the Italians [were] seen to be threatening to play one of their two cards of obvious newsworthiness: voting themselves into communism, or sliding into national bankruptcy or, preferably, both at the same time". According to Nichols, Italy was in fact the country in Europe which should be most closely watched. It had the obvious elements of the biggest Communist party and the seat of by far the biggest part of Christendom; off its shores, there was the biggest daily confrontation between East and West "in the shape of the American Sixth Fleet and the Russian naval squadron". The country was a laboratory of many of the problems of the West, but in a particularly acute form, and it could produce some indications for the future – "if the Italians [did] not, it [would] be surprising if anyone else did".[1]

The British government did indeed watch the Italian situation most closely. In the autumn of 1976, the Foreign Office began to work on a paper to examine Italy's political and economic prospects over the following 6-12 months and, against this background, "to consider possible contingencies in which the Italian government [could] be forced to appeal to their allies for financial assistance on a massive scale". Some months later, in February 1977, the results of this extensive study appeared in a document entitled "The outlook for Italy", whose complexity and assessments require a detailed analysis.[2]

---

1 Nichols P., "Italy: a laboratory for the ills that beset the rest of the western world", *The Times*, 20 June 1977.

2 TNA, FCO 33/3212, "The outlook for Italy", 14 February 1977.

The duration of the uneasy political equilibrium that emerged from the latest general elections would depend crucially on what would happen in the Italian economy. Since autumn 1976, the Italian authorities had taken a series of measures designed to strengthen the lira, improve a deteriorating balance of payments and counter inflation. In the first phase of measures, implemented in October-November, the bank rate had been raised by 3 per cent to 15 per cent; selective limits had been placed on bank credit expansion; and various austerity measures had been introduced, including higher taxes and higher prices, together with a modification to the system of indexed wage increases (the so-called *scala mobile*) to freeze for 19 months cost of living increases for higher income earners.

By the end of January 1977, the government had been able to negotiate with the unions limited measures to reduce the cost of labour, covering such areas as redundancy payments, labour mobility, absenteeism, higher productivity and a reduction in the number of public holidays. In return, Andreotti had promised the unions that there would be no further interference with the *scala mobile*. The government subsequently announced additional austerity measures, the most important of which involved raising indirect taxes by 1.6 billion dollars to finance the takeover by the government of part of the manufacturing industry's social welfare contributions. The pact between the unions and employers and the government's fiscalisation of employers' social welfare contributions were intended to moderate the growth of labour costs. But the effectiveness of these measures, which left the *scala mobile* system largely untouched, had to be questioned.

There were also doubts as to whether the measures taken so far would satisfy the IMF, with whom the Italians had been negotiating a loan of 530 million dollars. The IMF had been insisting on a radical reform of the *scala mobile* system as a condition for a loan to Italy and were known to be worried about the prospects for public spending. The example set by the IMF was likely to be followed by the EEC, from whom the Italians were also hoping to obtain a loan of around 500 million dollars. Such loans were important not only for the boost which they would give to Italian reserves but also because they would be taken as a sign of international confidence in the future of the Italian economy. Failure to secure the loans would imply the opposite and would be likely to have an adverse effect on the lira. The indications were that, although some accommodation with the IMF could be reached, progress towards this would continue to be slow.

The document concluded by envisaging three possible scenarios of how the politico-economic situation in Italy could develop. The first likely development was called "the mixture as before": the current political arrangements would hold for the next 12 months and, despite continuing uncertainty and underlying political instability, the austerity measures would begin to take effect without creating uncontrollable socio-political strains. With major political and economic crises averted, both the DC and the PCI would be able to contain internal pressures; the Christian Democrats would retain the initiative vis-a-vis the PCI, but the PCI should hold to the historic compromise strategy and "responsible" behaviour. The PSI would edge back towards the centre-left option. Foreign confidence should be maintained at a sufficient level to preserve Italian access to external financial support.

The second scenario was an early politico-economic crisis, where pressure from organised labour and the base of the party would force the Communist Party to move towards confrontation rather than collaboration with the DC, encouraging widespread popular opposition to the government's austerity measures. Labour unrest and obstruction in Parliament by the PCI would, therefore, bring the Andreotti government to a standstill. Continuing failure to moderate inflationary pressures or to secure an IMF loan would contribute to the loss of domestic and foreign confidence, bringing about a fresh collapse of the lira. Faced with the choice of resignation or acquiescence in the formation of a broadly-based "government of national salvation" (including strong Communist representation), the DC would split. After a more or less prolonged period in which Italy would have no effective government, a sizeable faction of the DC could decide to support a broadly-based emergency coalition. This new government would appeal to the Western community for massive and urgent economic support.

The third and final scenario was a delayed crisis, with the government averting an immediate challenge to its authority. But its programme of economic stabilisation, although severe enough to cause popular hardship and discontent, would be insufficient to have a significant impact on the budgetary deficit, inflation and the balance of payments. Investments would remain stagnant and external factors (higher oil prices, further slowing down of the international trade recovery) would worsen the situation. The internal political effects would be similar to those in the second scenario but in slower time. In these circumstances, the government could seek large-scale external financial support as a means of averting a crisis, and to restore domestic confidence in its capacity to continue governing by demonstrating that it retained foreign confidence, but it would come at a price.

The Foreign Office considered the first scenario – a continuation of the status quo – as the most likely, followed by the third of a delayed crisis; the second option (the early politico-economic crisis) was the least probable.[3] This prediction proved to be correct.

Loans and riots

On 6 April 1977, an IMF loan of 430 million dollars was agreed. The Italian government produced a letter of intent against the IMF loan, stating five points: firstly, it rehearsed the measures taken to reduce the inflationary impact of the *scala mobile*, principally by enforced savings on indexed wage increases on high salaries, productivity agreements and the exclusion of certain items from the basket used to calculate the indexation; it promised a reduction in inflation to 13 % over the next twelve months; it promised a ceiling on domestic credit of 30,000 billion lire in the twelve months to March 1978; it aimed at reducing estimated public expenditure (from 18,000 billion lire to 14,450 billion lire in 1978); finally, it pointed to a balance of payments surplus of 1,000 billion lire in 1978 as a whole. Then there was a consequential agreement by the EEC Finance Ministers to authorise Italy to draw 500 million dollars under the Community borrowing scheme. According to the British view, although the amounts were quite small, the two agreements gave an important psychological boost to the Italian economy.[4] *The Economist* commented that the IMF was letting Italy off more lightly than it let off Britain: the reason was that "sick Italy was much frailer and […] strong medicine could do more harm than good".[5]

Some positive trends were also noted by the new British Ambassador, Alan Campbell, who had returned to serve in Italy after 25 years in October 1976, his last assignment before retiring from the diplomatic service due to age limits. He had already served at the Embassy in Rome in the early 1950s, and this allowed him to develop an uncommon understanding of the Italian events.[6]

Having been a witness of post-war Italian society in the 1950s, Campbell now noted that after a miraculous economic leap forward, and despite increased labour and raw materials' costs, Italians were enjoying a strikingly higher standard of living. Observers of Italy asked themselves

3 *Ibidem*.

4 TNA, FCO 33/3215, "Briefing Mrs Thatcher", Richardson T. to Goodall D., WRJ 026/7, 22 June 1977.

5 "Tough *ma non troppo*", *The Economist*, 2 April 1977.

6 For his memoirs see Campbell A., *Colleagues and Friends*, quoted.

two obvious questions – whether the Communists would come into the government and whether the country would solve her economic problems. As regards the first point, the Italian Communists were not so different from Communists elsewhere as to make them acceptable partners for Italy's friends and allies. The PCI policy about NATO was basically the same as the Soviet policy; as for the EEC, the Communist doctrine was incompatible with the economic and political assumptions on which the Community was based. According to the Ambassador, the idea of Italian Communists in a coalition with Christian Democrats "happily playing a co-operative role in NATO and EEC" was not to be taken at all seriously:

> What the Italian Communists want is power. To get power, they must defeat or split the Christian Democrats. If they succeed they will possibly behave with a degree of moderation to start with and will certainly be glad of the collaboration of the smaller parties [...]. But we must have no delusions about what they really want. They will work for an Italy which is only a nominal member of NATO and which within the EEC seeks to modify or block any economic or political action disagreeable to Communist countries.

However, it was quite likely that the PCI had reached the peak of its electoral support in June 1976, and would, therefore, be unable to enter government – unless a further deterioration in law and order or in the economy could still drive more Italians to vote for the Communists.

The second question about Italian economic prospects was the most serious, although "it would not be at all reasonable to talk of the Italian economy in the South American terms". Most of the signs were "ominous if not actually alarming" – inflation over 20 per cent, serious unemployment, a continuing very high cost of labour compared with competitors and government expenditure virtually out of control. There were some good signs too, like a strong revival of exports, some moderation in wage demands, evidence of resilience and prospects of renewed prosperity in the medium and smaller enterprises. A recent OECD survey suggested that the economic prospects in Italy were not at all bad if only the government could in time take quite simple measures. Campbell, however, was sceptical about the ability of the Italians to get back on the road to prosperity unless they were helped by external factors, in particular the EEC. Despite the disquieting features of the Italian situation, the Ambassador considered that one should not be too gloomy, and hazarded the guess that the Italian political and economic scene in five years' time would look much as it did at the time.[7]

---

7 TNA, FCO 33/3204, "First impression of Italy in 1977", Diplomatic Report No. 208/77 by Campbell A., WRJ 011/1, 27 May 1977.

The despatch raised some doubts in the Foreign Office for the prediction that the Communists' electoral popularity had passed its peak. Many officials did not agree, considering that it would be "complacent" and "risky" for the British to assume that the PCI's prospects were unlikely to advance – and to relax about it: "the Italian Communists [could] even seem to be not such bad fellows after all, if we did not have to worry about coping with them inside the Italian Government".[8] There were also different views inside the British Embassy in Rome, where not everyone shared Campbell's more relaxed attitude toward the PCI. For instance, Minister Alan Goodison thought that it would indeed be bad for Britain if the PCI got in, and that it could turn out to be possible to use British influence to stop the Communists: statements by other western leaders, if made at the right time and in the right tone, did influence the Italian electorate, for good or ill.[9] However, British Ministers were extremely doubtful about such an option, and they surely would be opposed to any public statement *à la* Kissinger about the dangers of Communist participation in Allied governments.[10] As stated on several occasions, Britain's policy was one of "strict non-interference in Italian domestic affairs", while developing good relations with the Italian Government and contacts with other moderate non-Communist politicians.[11]

Nevertheless, there was a widespread agreement about the first year of Andreotti's government being "cliff-hanging", but the Prime Minister had shown considerable skill in holding the PCI to their policy of benevolent abstention, without which no measures could be carried in Parliament. At the end of June, an agreement was concluded between the "constitutional" parties to put before the Parliament a common programme of legislation in the fields of public order, education and the economy. Although couched in vague terms, the agreement could offer a firmer basis than hitherto for the stabilisation of the Italian economy and an attack on the country's growing social problems, especially law and order. According to the Foreign Office, the new agreement brought the Communists a step closer to power but still fell short of giving them a formal share in the government, which would split the DC. Berlinguer did not achieve all that he could have wished in the 29 June agreement. Most commentators

8 TNA, FCO 33/3204, "Sir Campbell's first impressions on Italy", 21 June 1977.

9 TNA, FCO 33/3205, "Politics and the parties in Italy", Goodison A. to Goodall D., WRJ 011/2, 31 May 1977.

10 TNA, FCO 33/3205, "The Italian Communist Party", Goodall D. to Goodison A., WRJ 011/2, 28 June 1977.

11 TNA, FCO 33/3212, "The Italian political scene", by Western European Department, 15 April 1977.

had expected a government re-shuffle which would have involved the introduction of some Communist-backed technocrat ministers. The DC should be congratulating themselves on having given so little away, despite the strains within the party; however, the tensions within the PCI had been almost as great. There was mounting discontent with Berlinguer and the PCI leadership on the part of party functionaries and workers who thought that the party was getting too little in return for its policy of collaboration with a Christian Democrat government. Moreover, the current preoccupation with law and order – exacerbated by student riots in Rome and Bologna – did not favour the Communists, even though they had been "*plus royaliste que le roi*" in opposing violence in the streets. The deteriorating climate of political violence was the major preoccupation of the Italian government and society at the moment.[12]

Indeed, in addition to the economic malaise and a still unstable political scene, Italy in 1977 suffered a massive wave of public disorders. Young people became the protagonists of new forms of urban conflict in all major cities. Rome and Bologna were the two major centres of this movement, which involved tens of thousands of young people in mass protest and battles with the police. There were radical differences with the 1968 movement, which was more idealistic and ideological: in 1977, proletarian youth groups were formed, squatting in buildings, setting up free radio stations and calling for self-fixed prices (*autoriduzione*) of transport fares and cinema tickets. If one part of the "movement of 1977" was more spontaneous and creative, irreverent and seeking to create alternative structures, epitomised by the "Metropolitan Indians", the other strand was autonomist and militarist, aiming at a new battle against the state. The leftist movement *Autonomia Operaia* ("Workers' Autonomy") sought to lead this tendency, with Toni Negri and Oreste Scalzone, former founder of *Potere Operaio* ("Workers' Power" – another radical left-wing political group active in big factories in Northern Italy between 1968 and 1973) at its forefront.[13]

---

12 TNA, FCO 33/3216, "Mr Judd's visit to Italy: 20-21 July. Brief: Italian political scene", by Western European Department, 18 July 1977.

13 Ginsborg P., *A History of Contemporary Italy. Society and Politics, 1943-1988*, Penguin, London 1990, pp. 381-382. On the movement of 1977: Falciola L., *Il Movimento del 1977 in Italia*, Carocci, Roma 2015; Hajek A., "Memories on the Move: The Italian Student Movement of 1977 between Local, National and Global Memories of Protest", in Beyen M., Deseure B. (eds.), *Local Memories in a Nationalizing and Globalizing World*, Palgrave Macmillan, London 2015, pp. 258-276. See also "Italian Youth Movement turns to violence for cultural change", *Rolling Stones*, 17 November 1977.

The "movement of 1977" was the expression of an open cleavage between the PCI and some sections of the Italian youth, which were highly disappointed by the policy of the Communists and their strategy to overcome the crisis. Unemployment affected young people most, despite the growing number of people going into higher education. In February 1977, the protest started precisely in the universities when the Minister of Education Franco Maria Malfatti circulated his reform proposals, which included a quota system. The students considered the proposals irrelevant to solve the real problems – gross overcrowding and no jobs after graduation. The portrait of Italian universities made by *The Economist* was very unforgiving: they had become "parking places for jobless young people". There was no selection and standards had fallen over the years under pressure from large numbers of school leavers:

> A university degree no longer confers the prestige which once went with title of *dottore*. So the students tend to make common cause with the mass of unemployed or under-employed workers who do not belong to a union and feel themselves victims of a system which discriminates between the "protected" and the "unprotected".[14]

Students occupied Rome University under the control of *Autonomia Operaia*. On 19 February, Luciano Lama, head of the CGIL (the Italian General Confederation of Labour, based on a Communist majority), came to deliver a speech but was shouted down, and violent clashes broke out between the *Autonomi* and Lama's supporters. From Rome, in March the movement spread to Bologna, with tanks patrolling the city to halt the riots following the killing by the police of Francesco Lo Russo, a militant of the far-left extra-parliamentary organisation *Lotta Continua* (Continual Struggle). *The Times* defined the riots "Italy's worst disorders since the war", while *The Economist* portrayed a South-American-like situation, quoting the words of PCI leader Giorgio Amendola: "We are in Chile before we [the Communists] have even got into government".[15] The use of armed forces by a Communist administration in the "red" capital of Italy made the protest increasingly anti-Communist, culminating in a three-day conference in September when Bologna was "invaded" by the protagonists of the youth movement from all over the country.[16]

14 "Get lost, comrades", *The Economist*, 26 February 1977.

15 "Battles on streets of Rome bring night of terror to capital in Italy's worst disorders since war", *The Times*, 14 March 1977; "Or is it Chile?", *The Economist*, 19 March 1977.

16 Ginsborg P., *A History of Contemporary Italy*, quoted, pp. 382-383.

Callaghan visited Rome in September 1977, precisely during the days of the Bologna conference, yet public order was not on the agenda of the meeting with Andreotti (although the British embassy did not welcome how the Italian public had so far "shown itself tolerant of the present level of urban violence").[17] The visit, considered both timely and useful from the British side, showed that Italy and the United Kingdom had very close views on all the international issues discussed. According to Ambassador Campbell, the visit served above all to create a closer personal relationship between Callaghan and Andreotti, and it helped to remove "the suspicion, never far from Italian minds", that her major European partners were too willing to exclude Italy from a Paris-Bonn-London axis of European consultation.[18]

In preparation for the meeting, the Foreign Office stressed how Italy's partners had greatly admired the skill with which Andreotti had steered his government through a difficult year. Italy and the UK faced similar problems, especially in the economic field, and it was "heartening" to see the improvement which was taking place in the Italian economy under Andreotti's administration. Political developments in Italy were followed in London with great interest, and it would be valuable to have Andreotti's assessment of both the present situation and the future. The Foreign Office indicated some fundamental questions about the Italian political scene. How durable was the arrangement of the PCI's and PSI's "benevolent abstention" in Parliament likely to prove? How did Andreotti see the political balance in Italy developing in relation to the "historic compromise"? At what point could the PCI be expected to move back into opposition? What was the future role of the Socialists likely to be? Was there any prospect of Italy, through a change in the PSI attitude, returning to the centre-left formula under some other name? How did Andreotti see the future of the DC and was progress being made in the direction of the much-needed renewal of the party?

As to the PCI itself, there was keen interest throughout Europe in the degree to which it had apparently adapted itself to the requirements of parliamentary democracy and had thus become a valid interlocutor in the parliamentary process. The same question arose regarding the French and Spanish Communist parties: but in France the Communist Party was only the junior partner in the Union of the Left, and in Spain it had no real

17 TNA, FCO 33/3565, "Italy: Annual Review for 1977", by Campbell A., Diplomatic Report No. 13/78, WRJ 014/1, 3 January 1978.

18 TNA, FCO 33/3210, Rome Tel. No. 542, "Prime Minister's visit to Italy", by Campbell A., 26 September 1977.

prospect of achieving a share of power in the foreseeable future. In Italy, on the other hand, it was the main party of the left with an important popular vote. This made the nature of the PCI a subject of keen interest to Italy's partners and allies. In the view of the British government, questions relating to the role of the PCI in Italian politics were for the Italian people themselves to solve. It would nevertheless be interesting to know what part, if any, Andreotti thought Italy's allies could play in helping Italy to achieve a stable evolution in its political balance.

On the economic side, the austerity programme which Andreotti managed to sell the trade unions, with PCI support, involved stricter monetary policies, tighter exchange controls and certain amendments to the inflationary *scala mobile* system of automatic index-linked wage increases. Italy's successful negotiation of loans from the IMF and EEC helped to improve her credit rating on international exchanges and offered a breathing space for a measure of economic recovery. Andreotti was to be given credit for being more robust in his efforts to get a grip on economic problems than was expected would be feasible a year earlier. At the end of the summer of 1977, there were signs of an improvement in the economic situation. The balance of payments had also been in surplus and inflation was slowing down, although it remained the highest in Europe. The forecasts were nonetheless uncertain, due to the difficulty of estimating how successful the restrictive fiscal policy measures would be – both in implementation and effect – and the future trend of wages.[19]

As seen from London, 1977 was not considered a bad year for Italy, "by the standards of recent years": the political scene was relatively untroubled, although, below the surface, the calm was only illusory. All major parties were facing strains and contrasts. The DC was divided over its attitude towards the Communists, while Aldo Moro was increasingly regarded as the most important politician on the scene and the most likely to be the next President of the Republic in the forthcoming presidential election in December 1978. The climate inside the PCI was tense too: as Campbell described it, "to have achieved 34 per cent of the vote and thereafter condemned apparently to support or at least acquiesce in the policies of an exclusively Christian Democrat Government, without any decisive influence, brought about a self-questioning uneasiness which even the disciplined Communist Party found it impossible to hide". Moreover, the PCI's potential electoral strength seemed actually diminished. As for

19 TNA, FCO 33/3211, Prime Minister's visit to Rome 21-23 September 1977, "Italian internal political and economic scene", brief by Foreign and Commonwealth Office, 15 September 1977.

the Socialist Party, its "able and energetic" Secretary Bettino Craxi exerted himself to achieve a separate identity for his party and a unity so tragically lacking for the last 30 years; but for all his efforts, at the end of the year the party was as split as ever, and Craxi seemed unsure about the right path to take. At the root of the political malaise was the basic structural weakness of the economy. Although the headlines more often featured incidents affecting law and order, the British embassy indicated that the fundamental weakness of Italy in 1977 was economic. Campbell was not optimistic about the near future, and much would depend on world economic trends: the Italians had a "well-deserved reputation for getting themselves out of tight corners", but it seemed unlikely that they could get out of their troubles in 1978 without "serious damage to themselves or their friends or both".[20]

Britain: on the verge of falling

Was Britain healing?

1977 opened with some positive economic trends for Britain. The Italian Ministry of Foreign Affairs reported that, in the first months of 1977, the balance of payments improved massively, due to a more favourable trend in trade exchanges and the unexpected capital flows. The predictions for the whole year, however, called for prudence: the government esteemed a 1.5 per cent growth in national income. Much would depend on the recovery of industrial production, the currency situation, the successful outcome of Labour's economic programme and the survival of the "social pact". As for commercial links between Italy and the United Kingdom, there would be many pressures from the trade unions and economic milieus to adopt restrictions in imports: should the British government give in to these pressures, Anglo-Italian trade would be affected, particularly the automotive industry.[21]

With regards to the internal political scene, the Callaghan government seemed to gain new strength with the so-called "Lib-Lab pact", an alliance between the Labour Party and the Liberals, which guaranteed the Cabinet a working majority and averted the threat of early elections.

---

20 TNA, FCO 33/3565, "Italy: Annual Review for 1977", by Campbell A., Diplomatic Report No. 13/78, WRJ 014/1, 3 January 1978.

21 ASPR, busta 697 B/3, Visita a Roma del Capo del Partito conservatore Margaret Thatcher, 24-25 giugno 1977, Ministero degli Affari esteri, Segreteria Generale, "Gran Bretagna. Situazione economica", June 1977.

In February 1977, the sudden death of Foreign Secretary Anthony Crosland was a serious personal blow to Callaghan; he was replaced by his young deputy, David Owen. This also meant that the government faced the prospect of fighting a by-election in Crosland's constituency. By March 1977, the number of seats held by Labour had declined from 319 to 310: this left the government vulnerable to defeat on a motion of confidence. As noted by Jonathan Kirkup, "if the need for financial support from the IMF was the economic nadir of the 1974-1979 Labour Government, then spring 1977 was the political equivalent" (before the arrival of the "winter of discontent").[22]

The Conservative leader, Margaret Thatcher, had already given notice that the opposition would move a vote of no confidence on 23 March. On that same day, Callaghan negotiated an agreement with the Liberal Party led by David Steel. The Liberals agreed to work with the government "in the pursuit of economic recovery", and a joint consultative committee was formed to meet regularly, although it did not commit either party to accept the views of the other or to grant support. Despite strong opposition to the pact from some ministers, including Tony Benn, the cabinet agreed, and Labour won the no-confidence motion by 322 votes to 298. The Lib-Lab pact was renewed in July 1977 and was to last until August 1978.[23]

The *Corriere della Sera* compared British Liberals to the Italian Communists: both parties tried to gain votes in a "fluctuating electorate", presenting themselves as an effective third force in the political scene, an alternative between the "thaumaturgic value of free enterprise" endorsed by the Tories and the cure proposed by the Labour, made of "radical injections of socialism".[24]

Italian Ambassador Roberto Ducci described the Lib-Lab pact as the "result of a mutual survival instinct".[25] The Italian Ministry of Foreign Affairs stressed the importance of the pact as a precedent in British political practice: apart from the war years, in the past, the party in government had always been able to lead the country without further help since it had the majority – albeit narrow – in Parliament. The agreement between Labour and the Liberals warded off the threat of early elections, which would have penalised

22 Kirkup J., quoted, pp. 30-31.

23 See Conroy H., quoted, pp. 101-108.

24 Cianfanelli R., "Callaghan si salva con i voti dei liberali", *Corriere della Sera*, 24 March 1977.

25 Telespresso da Ducci al Ministro degli Esteri Forlani, "Visita a Roma del Primo ministro britannico", 2 September 1977, in *Collana di testi diplomatici, Vol. 13 Roberto Ducci*, Ministero degli Affari Esteri – Ufficio Studi, Roma 1989, p. 205.

Callaghan's party, yet it did not seem to stop the rise of the Conservatives, who could now exploit the difficulties of a government without a majority. The local elections in May 1977 had been a major setback for the Labour government, and the Conservatives were now holding 42 out of 54 county councils in England and Wales and had regained control of the Greater London Council. The government's unpopularity could not be ignored, but it was partly inevitable as long as austerity measures did not bring concrete results. The most striking result was that this unpopularity also showed in local government, which were a traditional part of British democracy: under their jurisdiction came the decentralised management of services most close to people's needs – schools, police, social services and council housing. "The feeling of dissatisfaction of the man on the street" swept Labour away from local government and it would not be easy even for the Tories to gain a more committed popular involvement.[26]

"Crisis? What crisis?", asked the *Corriere della Sera* on its front page in July 1977. "England was healing", and those who arrived in London could find anything but a country under economic siege: crowded restaurants (despite the expensive bills), well-kept parks and museums, the usual display of Rolls Royce in smart areas. There was a crisis, but it was invisible: it could be found only by carefully looking up statistics, although growing inflation, chronic unemployment and the label of "other sick man of Europe" (the first one being Italy) seemed less worrying under a sunny summer sky. It was not only a matter of weather: a report by the European Commission stated that the British economy was coming out of the crisis thanks to the discovery of North Sea oil. The United Kingdom had reached a form of balance which could seem stable if seen from the outside. In fact, it was not: the "miracle" of submarine oil was a "gift from geology", but it was to be consumed in a generation and could only offer the chance to update the balance of a system that "since the beginning of the 20th century got used to consuming too much while producing too little".[27]

In the autumn of 1977, the assessment of Ambassador Ducci of Callaghan's first eighteen months in power described the lights and shadows of British politics in those months. The inheritance that Callaghan received from Wilson was so difficult that Ducci wondered whether the real cause for Sir Harold's resignation was the desire not to take the historical responsibility

26 ASPR, busta 697 B/3, "Ultimi sviluppi della situazione politica in Gran Bretagna. Avanzata dei Conservatori e parabola discendente del partito al governo", Ministero degli Affari Esteri, Segreteria Generale, Appunti di documentazione per la visita a Roma di Mrs Thatcher, 24-25 June 1977.

27 Cianfanelli R., "L'Inghilterra sta guarendo", *Corriere della Sera*, 7 July 1977.

for it. The new Prime Minister was reluctant to call for early elections until the economy had shown a radical change of direction. The main concerns for Italy were not only about economic strains, but also the political scene and in particular the divisions inside the Labour Party, which reflected on the government's performance. The moderate wing had been progressively impoverished by either death (as in the case of Anthony Crosland) or the temptation to other responsibilities, as happened to Roy Jenkins when he was appointed President of the European Commission that year. The maximalist wing had its standard-bearer in Tony Benn and defended an "intransigent socialism" which could not adapt to the economic pressure of the moment – and, according to the Italian ambassador, also to the "petty-bourgeois mentality of British people". Benn wanted to run for the premiership, trying to exploit the temporary radicalisation of the party. On these premises, Callaghan was playing for time, postponing issues of wider scope that would only with difficulty win a majority in the Parliament (like the Scotland and Wales Bill).

As for the economy, despite some positive monetary signs, the Italian Embassy in London reported that the production of goods and services was still stagnating, inflation did not seem to decrease, while the "social contract" proved not to live up to expectations: there was no price containment (in the previous year, salaries had risen an average 9.7 per cent, while the cost of living rose 17.7 per cent) and the remunerative gap between skilled and unskilled workers almost vanished. While the Labour left wanted a "siege economy", basically autarkic and protectionist, there was growing pressure from the trade unions for a wage adjustment, tax cuts and the resumption of public investments to create new jobs. In Ducci view, the government seemed tempted to fulfil at least part of these demands, adopting deflationary measures to develop internal demand and the offer of consumer goods, which should also reduce unemployment. In Callaghan's strategy, these measures would help him to win the favour of the electorate and to face early elections "light-heartedly". Ducci envisaged three likely scenarios, in order of decreasing probability: general elections in the autumn of 1978; elections in the late spring of 1978; and the fall of the government before this last date, due to a "sudden speed bump". Nevertheless, Callaghan had plenty of clarity of ideas, pragmatism, firmness and mediating skills and had therefore great personal prestige in Britain.[28]

[28] Telespresso da Ducci al Ministro degli Esteri Forlani, in *Collana di testi diplomatici*, quoted, pp. 205-208.

The Labour Party and the Italian Left

Despite internal strains, the Callaghan government followed with great interest – and a certain apprehension – the evolution of the Italian left. As we have seen in the previous chapter, since 1973 the PCI had started a more distinctive political agenda, which led to the adoption of the formula of the "historic compromise" and the creation of Eurocommunism.

The word "Eurocommunism" was first used by the Yugoslav journalist Frane Barbieri, in an article in the daily *Giornale nuovo* of 26 June 1975.[29] The newspaper was set up in the previous year by Indro Montanelli, one of the leading figures of Italian journalism, who dissented from the new leftish line of the *Corriere della Sera* where he had been working and wanted to create a new daily to check the growing strength of the Italian left. Barbieri later explained that he decided to use the expression Eurocommunism because it was geographically precise, but "ideologically imprecise". Eurocommunism was an "ideologically fluid, imprecise phenomenon", and it was not clear what it actually was; what seemed clear, however, was that a Eurocommunist Europe would "definitely mean the Sovietisation of Europe".[30] In its origins, therefore, the concept of "Eurocommunism" was intended to indicate opposition to and scepticism about current trends in some of the major Western Communist parties.[31] The term was used for the first time officially by Enrico Berlinguer in January 1976, in a meeting held in Paris with PCF Secretary Georges Marchais.[32]

The Labour Party's reaction to Eurocommunism, and more generally to the PCI, in the second half of the 1970s was peculiar.[33] Although the Labour Party established some relations with the Italian Communists, official contacts between Britain and the PCI had been relegated to a low level. Giorgio Napolitano, the Italian Communist leader, held in the highest esteem in the West, met privately with Roy Jenkins and Tony Benn in March 1976, but it was against Callaghan's will.

---

29 Levi A., "Eurocommunism: myth or reality?", in Filo della Torre P., Mortimer E., Story J. (eds.), *Eurocommunism: myth or reality?*, Penguin Books, London 1979, p. 9.

30 Elliott P., Schlesinger P., "Studying 'Eurocommunism', on unfolding ideology", *The Sociological Review*, No. 27, 1979, pp. 58-59.

31 *Id.*, "Eurocommunism: their word or ours?", in Childs D. (ed.), *The Changing Face of Western Communism*, Routledge, London 1980, p. 41.

32 Rizzo A., *La frontiera dell'Eurocomunismo*, Laterza, Roma-Bari 1977, p. 3.

33 See Di Donato M., *I comunisti italiani e la sinistra europea*, Carocci, Roma 2015, pp. 195-200.

In February 1977, the International Department of the Labour Party produced a paper titled "The Italian Communist Party and Italian Politics".[34] According to the document, the vulnerability of the European left to centrifugal tendencies had increased in the last decade, and it was no longer possible to divide the left into two simple categories – the Communists and the Social Democrats. Actually, there were five currents within the European left. Firstly, the revolutionary left, which sought to achieve a radical social transformation by revolutionary methods, and was divided into numerous, often fiercely opposed groups, none of which were of numerical importance. Secondly, the old style, hard-line Communists, a diminishing and discredited force, still subservient to the Kremlin, "by necessity or perverse choice". Thirdly, the Social Democrats, the major voice in most Labour and Socialist parties in the West. They no longer sought to effect radical changes in the socio-economic systems of Western Europe and were content with mild reforming measures. Fourthly, the Democratic Socialists, who aspired to basic structural changes in Western capitalism, to be achieved by peaceful means. Finally, the so-called Eurocommunists, who insisted upon autonomy from Moscow and believed that Socialism could be established in the West by constitutional methods. The most powerful and vigorous exponent of Eurocommunism was the PCI, "the largest Communist Party in Western Europe, easily the strongest force in the Italian Left and, after the recent elections, supported by over one-third of the Italian electorate".

Although it accepted the basic principles and institutions of political democracy, the PCI regarded the dominant conception and practice of democracy in the West as inadequate, no more than a form of democratic elitism. They opposed to it the concept of participatory democracy. Here lay the distinctive contribution of the PCI to the Italian political scene. The paper's conclusion stated that the sincerity of the Italian Communists' attachment to democratic principles and institutions could no longer be doubted. The PCI accepted "a peaceful, parliamentary route to socialism, on the basis of securing as wide a measure of agreement as possible". Its activities in support of human rights and political freedom in the Soviet bloc underlined its adhesion to democratic values and its willingness to face up to Soviet disapproval. As it asserted its independence from Soviet political control and loosened its ties with the Soviet bloc parties, the PCI had affirmed its desire for closer collaboration with Socialist parties; the

34 LHASC, LP, International Department, NEC, ID/1976-77/61, "The Italian Communist Party and Italian Politics", 23 February 1977.

Labour Party should develop relations much further, on a par with the extensive contacts that existed with other Socialist parties.[35]

The conclusive points of the paper raised many criticisms in the Foreign Office, which, as we have seen, had a strong anti-Communist view.[36] The FCO agreed that the mainstream of the present PCI leadership was "genuine" in the sense that they wished to put into effect a political vision which they were convinced would increase "the sum total of human happiness in Italy". Also, they attached importance to the preservation of individual liberties and of Italy's constitutional machinery. But the FCO did not agree that the PCI rejected Marxist-Leninism. David Lipsey could "have been moved by enthusiasm for the intellectually exciting ideas put forward by Segre" into accepting what he said as a representative of the political thought of the PCI as a whole. Segre and Napolitano were in fact "the PCI's ambassadors", charged with cultivating the party's image in the West, and "allowed a great measure of freedom in saying things calculated to appeal to western listeners, particularly Socialists", not all of which reflected accurately the views of the party leadership as a whole, still less of the party faithful. One could interpret the fact that PCI leaders said different things to different audiences as indicating that they were seeking to dissemble as far as possible to the electorate merely to attract votes, while reassuring the party rank and file that their line had not really changed. Officials in the Foreign Office considered that, taken in conjunction with the undemocratic nature of the party's own organisation, the sort of "democracy" aimed at by the PCI would probably turn out to be indistinguishable from Communism as it was known in Eastern Europe. Above all, the FCO did not agree either with the suggestion that Britain's allies should be discouraged from "doing anything which would appear to bolt the door against the PCI", or with the proposal to cultivate the Communists to make it easier to deal with them if they did come to power – in that event, the PCI would need the British government more than the other way around, and there would be no difficulty about contact.[37]

Moreover, officials in the Foreign Office thought that the PCI had had consistently good notices in the Western press in general and in the British press in particular. This was particularly evident during the 1976 election campaigns. An important element in their success had been the

---

35 *Ibidem.*

36 See Chapter 1.

37 TNA, FCO 33/3205, "Politics and the parties in Italy", Goodison A. to Goodall D., WRJ 011/2, 31 May 1977.

high calibre of the PCI spokesmen who had travelled abroad. The anti-PCI case had, on the other hand, gone largely by default – partly because neither the DC nor the PSI seemed to be able to find convincing and presentable spokesmen capable of impressing foreign audiences. One of the most effective propagandists for the PCI was Giorgio Napolitano, who was a long-standing member of the Royal Institute of International Affairs or Chatham House and who had twice lectured there within the past 18 months. The Embassy in Rome suggested that Chatham House should be "tactfully" told that it was about time they balance Napolitano with some non-Communist speaker from Italy. They should also give forewarning on the next occasion on which Napolitano or some other PCI spokesman was going to address them so that the Embassy could be able to stimulate the DC into some counterstrategy and have its own speakers at Chatham House.[38]

Despite the Foreign Office's scepticism, the first contacts between the Labour Party and PCI started in mid-1977. In June, some members of the National Executive Committee of the Labour Party met with members of the Central Committee of the Italian Communist Party (Napolitano, Gian Carlo Pajetta and Sergio Segre) in Rome, on the occasion of a meeting of the Bureau of the Socialist International. The British report stressed how the PCI group repeatedly said what a historic occasion it was; they also spoke at great length about "how respectable they were and how they were now an established part of the Italian political and governmental scene".[39]

Still in 1977, the book-interview of historian Eric Hobsbawm with Giorgio Napolitano, *The Italian Road to Socialism*, had widespread success.[40] Napolitano also participated in the annual Labour Party Conference in October that year: it was the first time that members of Communist parties (there were invitations also to the PCF and the Spanish Communist Party) took part in the conference. Napolitano's participation was widely reported in the Communist and left-wing press in Italy. Interviewed by *L'Espresso*, the Communist leader stressed the important political meaning of that invitation: apparently, the Labour Party thought that the political ideas and action of the major Communist parties in Western Europe were a reality which could be ignored no longer.

---

38 TNA, FCO 33/3205, "Chatham House and the Italians", Goodall D. to Richardson T., WRJ 011/2, 29 June 1977.

39 TNA, FCO 33/3205, "Contacts between the Labour Party and the PCI", WRJ 011/2, 22 June 1977.

40 Napolitano G., *The Italian Road to Socialism. An interview by Eric Hobsbawm with Giorgio Napolitano of the Italian Communist Party*, Journeyman Press, London 1977.

Napolitano was not able to make any prediction for future developments in the cooperation between the Labour Party and the PCI; nevertheless, there seemed to be a common interest in searching the best occasion and formula for an exchange of opinions on the problems that both Britain and Italy had to face at a European level.[41]

Yet the main problem in the relation with the PCI was the Eurocommunist issue. Since late 1977, a lively debate started inside the Labour Party on this topic. Former Prime Minister Harold Wilson attacked Eurocommunism harshly at the end of 1977, urging that democratic socialists should treat it with scepticism and vigilance. His main warning was about what he labelled "Mitterrandisme" – i.e. the proposals and plans for electoral alliances between Social Democrats and Communists, aiming at the formation of Socialist-Communist governments. Socialists throughout Europe, he wrote, should avoid Mitterrandisme "like the plague – for its infection would recognise no international boundaries, the Channel not excepted". Wilson's assessment of Italian Communists was equally critical: they were the most confident among the Eurocommunist parties, held "the Christian Democrat government in fief" and could afford "to make monkeys out of the ineffective and divided Social Democratic parties". The PCI was confident that time was on its side, as long as it could continue to show that it had no connection with the USSR. In that age of "Communism schism", European Social Democracy should try to investigate how far national Communism had actually broken with Moscow.[42] For this public attack on Mitterrand, the leader of a member party of the Socialist International, Wilson was criticised by Willy Brandt.[43]

In December 1977, Foreign Secretary David Owen warned the party about the real nature of some European Communist parties in an interview in *The Guardian*. Amplifying an analysis he had made in a Cambridge lecture the month before, Owen took a different line to both those on the left who advocated unquestioned cooperation with the Eurocommunists and Wilson's advice. For the Foreign Secretary, if the Italian Communists won a majority – a possibility he did not rule out – the verdict of the ballot box would have to be respected. "You can't pick and choose": if they came

41 Russo F., "Un bel gemellaggio Napolitano-Brighton", *L'Espresso*, 16 October 1977.

42 Wilson H., "The impact of Eurocommunism on the Western alliance", *Labour & Trade Union Press Service of the Labour Committee for Transatlantic Understanding*, Vol. 11, No. 9, November 1977, reprinted with the title "Euro-communism and the Western Alliance", *Socialist Commentary*, December 1977.

43 Di Donato M., "The Cold War and Socialist Identity: The Socialist International and the Italian 'Communist Question' in the 1970s", *Contemporary European History*, Vol. 24, No. 2, 2015, pp. 193-211.

to power legitimately, the British had to accept the verdict of the Italian electors. It would be "intolerable" if the outside world sought to invoke a crisis of confidence in Italy, although Communist participation in an Italian government would pose some difficult questions for NATO. Owen saw no virtue in a policy of "total ostracism where you never talk with Western Communists": that would be trying to pretend that a "serious, interesting phenomenon" did not exist. The Foreign Secretary found that the PCI could increase its support because of its "law and order appeal". Owen was also very critical towards Europe's social democrats, whose failures made Eurocommunism grow.[44] As for the term "Eurocommunism", the Socialists should give it "no currency":

> I reject the term because I am not convinced that the phenomenon which it is supposed to describe exists as a separate entity. I reject the term because I do not wish to give communism anywhere, particularly in Europe, a coherent entity. I reject the term because it can easily mean lowering the guard of democratic socialists.[45]

There was a widespread mixture of fear and curiosity in the Labour Party towards Eurocommunism, insomuch that in 1978 a Western Europe Sub-committee of the International Department was created with the aim of monitoring developments in Europe Western and examining the concept of Eurocommunism.[46]

In the meantime, the debate continued in the press. Michael Stewart, Labour MP and former Secretary of State for Foreign Affairs, proposed to adopt a more concrete approach to the issue of Eurocommunism. "Academics work towards a conclusion; politicians work towards a decision". Therefore the immediate task for the Labour Party was not to write a historical and philosophic study of Eurocommunism, but to decide what attitude Socialist parties should adopt towards Western Communists in their "new dress". Stewart identified three test questions. First, what was the real attitude of Eurocommunists towards the USSR? Second, what about defence? Did the professed acceptance of NATO include a readiness to argue in favour of – and, if in government, to assist in – the maintenance of the effective defence of the West? Third, how genuine was the professed conversion to a belief in the right of non-Communist

44 "Dr Owen plays a waiting game", *The Guardian*, 8 December 1977.

45 Owen D., "Communism, Socialism, and Democracy", *The Washington Quarterly*, Vol. 1, No. 2, 1978, pp. 4-15.

46 Its first meeting in LHASC, LP, International Department, NEC, ID/1977-78/166, "Western Europe Sub-committee", 28 April 1978.

parties to exist and, more generally, to democracy? If the answers to these questions were such as democratic Socialists could accept, then a great deal of what Western Communist parties had been saying for the last thirty years was nonsense; and one could ask, if they were so fully converted, what was the point of the continued existence of Communist parties, as distinct from democratic Socialist parties, in the West.[47] According to historian Donald Sassoon, what was striking in much of the reaction of British labour to Eurocommunism was the lack of critical analysis and the refusal to examine new processes. Instead, it was necessary to locate the Eurocommunist phenomenon in the wider perspective of the changes which had occurred in the international system.[48]

Eric Heffer proposed to analyse the issue with objectivity. If one was concerned with socialist and democratic development in Europe, then the Eurocommunists could not be ignored. The first question was about the sincerity of these Communist parties – how far they gained independence from Moscow and how far they "jettisoned much of their old intellectual baggage which ha[d] naturally stopped genuine co-operation between the Communists and the Socialists in the past". If the Communist parties did declare that they accepted the democratic process, if they declared independence – albeit limited – from the Soviet Union, if they were prepared to accept pluralism, it was obvious that agreement should be discussed, and if necessary entered into. This was a correct tactic for the French Socialist Party to adopt, as it was for the PSI to enter an agreement to administer the large cities and municipalities of Italy. In the process, further discussion could take place.[49]

As for the relation with the Socialist Party, Bettino Craxi was invited to the 1976 Labour Party Conference, but the focus on that occasion was almost entirely on the internal scene and the economic problems.[50] Callaghan met Craxi during his visit in Rome in September 1977, when they were able to discuss the Italian situation. The Socialist Secretary said that the present political truce could last until the next fixed point of political reference, namely the next presidential elections in 1978. Although Italy was not a presidential republic, the President had considerable

---

47 Stewart M., "Western Communists – in new dress?", *Socialist Commentary*, May 1978, p. 12.

48 See Sassoon D., "Eurocommunism, the Labour Party and EEC", *Political Quarterly*, Vol. 50, No. 1, 1979, pp. 86-99.

49 LHASC, LP, Eric Heffer papers, ESH/10/42, "Eurocommunism and the Labour Party", c. 1977.

50 See Chapter 1.

powers, and the identity of the next incumbent would be important for the future political balance. The PSI's interest, according to Craxi, was that the existing situation should continue so that the Socialists could endeavour to renew themselves and gauge how the PCI was evolving. Time was not on the side of the Communists, who had many internal difficulties which were not always visible to the outsider. The PCI had been subject to strong Soviet pressure ever since Eurocommunism had become the subject of controversy. This Soviet activity caused unrest within the PCI, as in other Communist parties. There was a connection with the recent resurgence of extreme leftist terrorism, in which some people discerned the hand of Eastern intelligence services. The theory was that the Eastern block was deliberately creating disturbances which themselves exerted pressure on the PCI. Most importantly, the PSI did not wish to leave the Communists with a monopoly of opposition; they would like to compete with the PCI electorally and thus change the political balance of power.[51]

The most important element, however – and what influenced the relations between the Labour Party and the Italian Socialists – was that the PSI policy seemed incomprehensible by British standards. It was another aspect of the Italian "exceptionalism", probably too difficult to understand for a party moving in an (almost) perfect two-party system. This Labour bewilderment towards the PSI was well resumed in the report of the 1978 Italian Socialist Party Conference: the Italian Socialists' backing of the "historic compromise" was, for a British socialist, difficult to understand. It seemed "almost like asking the Labour Party to enter into a coalition with the Conservatives".[52]

---

51 TNA, FCO 33/3210, "Prime Minister's visit to Italy, 21-23 September 1977: conversations with Italian Socialist leaders", 26 September 1977.

52 LHASC, LP, International Department, NEC, ID/1977-78/159, "The Italian Socialist Party Congress", April 1978.

Chapter 3

Democracies on trial?

1978 was a pivotal year for Italy, one of the most difficult moments in her history as a republic. The year opened with a governmental crisis which was only resolved in March, a few days before the kidnapping of Aldo Moro and the resulting extraordinary new crisis culminating in a most tragic epilogue – the murder of the leader of Italy's Christian Democrats. With an underlying economic crisis, the weakness of the lira and high inflation rates, 1978 was also a pivotal year for some decisions in international politics which were to mark the future of the country, one example being the decision to join the European Monetary System (EMS). Negotiations for the EMS were also a moment of potential Anglo-Italian collaboration, although the Callaghan government eventually decided not to join. By the end of the year, Britain was struck by the largest and most critical series of strikes since the 1920s, and the "winter of discontent" proved to be a fatal test for Labour.

The "annus horribilis" of the Italian Republic

"The comedy is over": the (new) Italian crisis and Anglo-American relations

1978 had an inauspicious start for the Italian political scene, with the end of the third Andreotti government and a crisis which was to last for almost two months. The reasons for this lay partly in the worsening economic situation at the end of 1977, and partly in the political factor of internal pressures within the Italian Communist Party.[1]

According to British diplomacy, disillusionment with Italy's governmental policy was growing. It began with the presentation of the 1978 budget law in September and the failure of the government's attempt

[1] See Scoppola P., "Una crisi politica e istituzionale", in De Rosa G., Monina G. (eds.), *L'Italia Repubblicana nella crisi degli anni Settanta, Vol. 4 Sistema politico e istituzioni*, Rubbettino, Soveria Mannelli 2003, pp. 17-40.

to introduce a measure of control into the unplanned rise in public expenditure. This situation first led the Republican leader, Ugo La Malfa, and then the Socialists, to start calling for an emergency government which would include the Communists. At that stage, the PCI appeared to be content to let others make the running.[2]

The British press followed the evolution of political events in Italy with apprehension. *The Economist* devoted its cover to the crisis of the Andreotti government, with the title in Italian *La commedia è finita* ("the comedy is over"): the former Prime Minister and Berlinguer, like two Harlequin puppets, were trying – unsuccessfully – to straighten the Leaning Tower of Pisa. The Communist leader wore a knife with the hammer and sickle, ready to stab Andreotti in the back. According to the weekly, at the heart of Italy's political crisis lay the fact that, for 30 years, it had been governed by the same party, because the main opposition party (i.e. the PCI) was not trusted by enough Italian voters to behave democratically. Each of Italy's three major parties bore some of the responsibility for this:

> The Christian Democrats for trying to preserve their power by claiming that the voters' only real choice lay between them and the unthinkable Communists. The now dispirited Socialists for being such ineffectual partners in government to the Christian Democrats during the 1960s that they let the Communists become the main party of the left indisputably. And the Communists themselves for failing to end suspicions about their good democratic intentions by not breaking with their Stalinist rump.

At least Italy's lack of a credible alternative had spared the country the two-party competition which "bedevilled" Britain.[3]

Articles in the *Financial Times* and *The Guardian* stressed the climate of violence which was afflicting Rome, while the Communists were moving in the direction of securing a direct role in the government.[4] *The Times* reported the details of the "worst wave of violence for more than a year", with extremist groups fighting with police in the capital, wounding a FIAT official in Turin and threatening to assassinate Berlinguer, in revenge for the death of three rightists.[5] The Foreign Office offered a less worrying interpretation. The Republican Party called for participation by the PCI

---

2 TNA, FCO 33/3568, "The Italian political crisis (January to March 1978)", Campbell A. to Owen D., WRJ 014/2, 23 March 1978.

3 "La commedia è finita?", *The Economist*, 21 January 1978.

4 "Risky time for Berlinguer to raise the stakes", *Financial Times*, 10 January 1978; "Andreotti prepares to go quietly", *The Guardian*, 10 January 1978.

5 "US envoy to report on Italian crisis", *The Times*, 11 January 1978.

in the government, the Socialists called for a new political formula which would bring the PCI into the majority – voting with affirmative votes in Parliament but without Ministers – while the other small parties added to the confusion. The position of the Communists was ambivalent. In public, they reiterated their call for a government of national emergency and remained committed to the establishment of the historic compromise. But "secret sources" revealed to the Foreign Office that the leadership of the party was, in fact, not yet anxious to participate directly in the Italian government. They feared both internal and external consequences of such a move forward and would rather continue to let the situation mature more slowly to a point where their entry into the government could be achieved "without drama". A further threat had arisen from the economic difficulties of the country. Actually, none of the parties wanted early elections, while continuity was needed to grapple with Italy's considerable problems (including the high level of political violence, although it did not affect government business or daily life). It was therefore likely that any solution to the present political crisis would be limited to a reshuffle of the government, with or without the inclusion of some "technocrats" acceptable to the PCI, and with Andreotti continuing as Prime Minister.[6]

Andreotti's attempts to establish a minimum agreement about a new political framework with the other five parties of the Agreement Programme ran into the ground during the second week of January. When he resigned on 16 January, the crisis was therefore technically "in the dark" ("uncontrolled" in Italian political jargon), since the terms on which it would be resolved had not been agreed in advance. But it was clear to all concerned that Andreotti himself would be asked by the President of the Republic to try to form a new government – as he duly was on 19 January. It was also clear that if Andreotti failed, there was no one else who was likely to succeed, and that the consequence of such a failure would almost certainly be early elections, which no one wanted, least of all the Communists.

At 54 days, it was the longest crisis in recent Italian history, except on the two occasions when there were anticipated elections in 1972 and 1976. In the first phase of the crisis, the PCI was firm in its request for entry into a "Government of Democratic Unity", while the DC's refusal was equally firm, though less coordinated. British observers considered it unlikely that the Communists could achieve this objective. On 7 February, Berlinguer announced that the Communists would be prepared to consider entering

---

6 TNA, FCO 33/3566, "US Ambassador's call on the PUS: Italy", by Goodall D., 11 January 1978.

a "clear and recognised Parliamentary majority" in support of an agreed programme.

When the threat of Communist participation in government receded, an "extended process of soul-searching" began within the Christian Democrat Party about whether they could accept a majority with the Communists, and if so what sort of majority, now that the Communists had withdrawn their original demands. A group of back-bench DC Deputies calling themselves "The Hundred" emerged in January with the specific aim of resisting Communist inclusion in any majority. It looked for a time as if they could mount a serious challenge to the authority of the Christian Democrat leadership. Indeed, as viewed from London, one of the features of this crisis was the conflict between leadership and rank and file in both major parties: "one often had the feeling that it was easier for Zaccagnini (the DC Secretary) to talk to Berlinguer than to his own back-benchers". These internal party difficulties were eventually resolved at the beginning of March, after a three-day meeting of the assembly of Christian Democrat Parliamentarians, when Moro was said to have played the decisive part in bringing the dissenters into line.[7]

Once the Christian Democrats had accepted the inclusion of the Communists, it did not take Andreotti long to finalise an agreement with the other parties on the arrangements for the majority, except the small Liberal Party which preferred not to join a majority with the Communists. On 11 March, the period of crisis formally ended, with the formation of a new Andreotti government.

Although almost indistinguishable from its predecessor, the fourth government led by Andreotti had a new significant feature: for the first time in thirty years, the Communists would form part of the majority in Parliament voting in support of the government's programme. The PCI claimed it as a step forward, while the Christian Democrats also argued that it was a tiny one: it was only a formalisation of a previously existing arrangement and the DC successfully resisted the Communists' main demand, which was to have Ministers in the government. The PCI did not even secure any significant Cabinet changes such as the introduction of "technicians" sympathetic to their interests. Indeed, British sources noted that the Communists would find the result of the "crisis" somewhat disappointing.[8]

---

[7] TNA, FCO 33/3568, "The Italian political crisis (January to March 1978)", Campbell A. to Owen D., WRJ 014/2, 23 March 1978.

[8] TNA, FCO 33/3567, FCO Tel. No. 151, WRJ 014/2, 13 March 1978.

The Italian situation also affected Anglo-American relations, in particular at the beginning of 1978, in the days before Andreotti's resignation. There was an evident chasm between London and Washington about the way to solve the Italian crisis, which reflected the different evaluations of the two Ambassadors in Rome.[9]

The British government learned that the Americans intended to make an official statement against the PCI's participation in the government on 11 January, when the British Ambassador in Washington Peter Jay met Zbigniew Brzezinski. The National Security Advisor said that the Administration was becoming increasingly worried by the deteriorating situation and was examining what – if any – action they could take to assist Andreotti. On the one hand, President Carter wished to avoid being seen to interfere in Italian internal affairs, but on the other hand, he did not want to give the appearance of being indifferent to the prospect of Communist participation in the Italian government and thereby to let the situation go by default. In these circumstances, the Americans were thinking in terms of "some statements" by the US, Britain, and Germany (Brzezinski did not mention the French) which should not be joint, but broadly in similar terms to strengthen Andreotti's resolve. The Ambassador pointed out that the British government were equally worried at the prospect of Communists in the Italian government, but they feared that the American strategy would be counter-productive, bearing in mind the criticism of Kissinger's intervention in that field.[10]

The Labour government did not comply with the American request; nonetheless, the US seemed to accept this choice, on condition that they should not seem to stand alone. As long as there was no negative comment on Carter's statement, the Americans "would be content".[11] British reasons were clear: from Rome, Campbell assured that the American concern was "exaggerated". He did not consider that there was at present any likelihood of members of the PCI entering the Italian government, though there was the possibility that the next Cabinet would depend on the positive votes of the Communists, rather than their abstention. The DC, however, would make no concessions to the PCI beyond the absolute minimum necessary; yet, some small concessions would be inevitable and could not be prevented by international pressure. Moreover, statements by the US ambassador and other American spokesmen against an influential or

9 For an American evaluation of the Italian situation in the 1970s see Gentiloni Silveri U., "Gli anni Settanta nel giudizio degli Stati Uniti", quoted.

10 TNA, FCO 33/3566, Washington Tel. No. 131 by Jay P., WRJ 014/2, 11 January 1978.

11 TNA, FCO 33/3566, Washington Tel. No. 140 by Jay P., WRJ 014/2, 12 January 1978.

dominant role of Communist parties in Western Europe had been front pages news throughout the Italian press for weeks. Such a media storm meant that there was no possibility of a new US statement being regarded by the Italians as "reasonably casual". According to the British Ambassador, the American attitude was fully known to all shades of political opinion and was already being considered by Andreotti, insofar as his actions could be influenced by external pressures. Equally, Andreotti – as well as political and public opinion – was aware that his principal European partners would regret any advance of the PCI towards power in Italy. Therefore, in Campbell's view, no further statement, whether by the Americans, the British, or another European country, would be crucial in resolving the Italian situation (which could be settled primarily by calculations of an internal political character).[12]

The following day, the State Department spokesman issued a statement about the Administration's attitude toward Western European Communist parties. Recent developments in Italy increased the level of American concern for Communist participation in West European governments. The Administration did not favour such participation and would like to see the Communist influence in any Western European country reduced.[13]

Campbell was extremely critical of the US strategy. The official statement served to clear up some remaining ambiguities about the American attitude towards the PCI, particularly the notion that the Carter Administration was in some way "softer" towards Italian Communism than its predecessor (a thesis carefully fostered by the Italian left despite corrective statements by Gardner). This would have had a healthy effect on the Christian Democrat leadership. However, the British Ambassador thought that the Americans overestimated the PCI threat, and the State Department statement served to promote the polarisation of opinion at a delicate political moment. The Communist Party rank and file were probably encouraged to hold out more strongly for something which the leadership knew they could not get (Communist entry into the Government), while the DC was strengthened in its opposition to a lesser step which Andreotti knew that he could hardly avoid conceding (Communist entry into the majority). In this way, the American statement increased rather than reduced Andreotti's difficulties in the short term. Moreover, the Prime Minister had already made clear publicly, in his

---

12 TNA, FCO 33/3566, Rome Tel. No. 18 by Campbell A., WRJ 014/2, 12 January 1978.

13 TNA, FCO 33/3566, Washington Tel. No. 141 by Jay P., WRJ 014/2, 12 January 1978.

end of year press conference in December 1977, that there could be no question of PCI entry into government without anticipated elections.[14]

The Foreign Office was equally surprised by the sense of alarm in the US about the recent political events in Italy, which clashed with the previous attitude. The Carter Administration, in its first months in office, adopted a more balanced and low-key approach to the question of communist participation in Western European governments than that adopted by Kissinger in the past. This "unobtrusive and balanced line", without threatening dire consequences, had been the American approach in 1977; still in October, Brzezinski had confirmed it in an interview in *The Times*. However, by the beginning of 1978, this policy changed: the United States had not only chosen an interventionist line, but also wanted the collaboration of the European partners to present a united front. The Foreign Office blamed the American embassy in Rome for this new course, with its alarming despatch – an unnecessary apprehension, according to Campbell. Moreover, it was Brzezinski and his National Security Council staff that managed the issue of the "reasonably casual statement", and not the State Department.[15] The US statement looked, therefore, like a combination of bureaucratic politics (Gardner's desire to make some impact in the White House) and domestic politics (in particular, the wish by part of the Congress to ensure that the Italian-American vote remained Democratic).[16]

As months went by, the alarm in Washington subsided after the formation of the fourth Andreotti government, although some of the press seemed to think that the upshot of the crisis was to be regarded as a defeat for the Americans. The embassy in Rome showed a cautious optimism: Communism was not inevitable as many Liberals in America thought and the key to the political future probably lay with the economic developments in the world and especially in Europe. Given the right economic climate, there was no reason why Italy should not emerge from its present political and economic difficulties.[17] In the meantime, Gardner's pivotal role in the January events emerged more

---

14 TNA, FCO 33/3568, "The Italian political crisis (January to March 1978)", Campbell A. to Owen D., WRJ 014/2, 23 March 1978.

15 TNA, FCO 33/3567, "US attitude to Italian political situation", Palliser M. to Jay P., WRJ 014/2, 18 January 1978.

16 TNA, FCO 33/3572, "United States view on Italy", by Hughes E., WRJ 021/1, 4 August 1978.

17 TNA, FCO 33/3567, "Italian political situation", by Campbell A., WRJ 014/2, 28 March 1978.

clearly: the American diplomat had a strong bias toward Italy and was prone to see "Reds under every bed".[18]

An attack at heart of the State: Moro's kidnapping and murder

The crisis and the inauguration of the new government were soon tragically overshadowed by the kidnapping of Aldo Moro, captured while he was going to the Parliament for the vote of confidence to the new government on 16 March. British diplomacy and press followed the case in detail, until its dramatic epilogue. The Labour government was struck by the solidarity showed by public opinion and the political class alike against the Red Brigades.[19]

The first despatches from the embassy in Rome stressed how, despite the initial shock, the Italian government reacted "in a measured fashion" to the tense situation, resisting initial demands from the Republican leader La Malfa and other for emergency measures such as a curfew and the introduction of the death penalty. On the positive side, the new anti-terrorism measures introduced on 21 March, designed to strengthen the powers of the police and the courts, had been accepted without reservation by all parties supporting the government, including the Communists.[20]

Despite the tragic situation, the Moro affair was also a fruitful occasion for fostering Anglo-Italian relations. The very day of the kidnapping, Renato Squillante, the Chief of Cabinet of the Minister of Interior Francesco Cossiga, asked for reassurances that the British government, from its experience in Northern Ireland, could give some technical assistance. At that stage, any request for paramilitary help had been ruled out.[21] The British responded swiftly by sending two instructors to the Special Air Service (SAS).[22] The SAS gave a crash training course to their Italian counterparts, providing a capable reaction force for dealing with terrorist hostage-taking incidents. The Home Office saw no need

18 TNA, FCO 33/3572, "United States view on Italy", by Goodison A., WR 021/1, 25 July 1978. Campbell added a note that partly justified his American counterpart: "US Ambassadors have to put up with a great deal and it is not surprising that they sometimes show the strain".

19 See Gentiloni Silveri U., *L'Italia sospesa*, quoted, pp. 206-221.

20 TNA, FCO 33/3577, Tel. No. 170 by Campbell A., WRJ 031/1, 23 March 1978.

21 TNA, FCO 33/3577, Tel. No. 161 by Campbell A., WRJ 031/1, 17 March 1978.

22 TNA, FCO 33/3577, Tel. No. 166 by Campbell A., WRJ 031/1, 20 March 1978.

for further training on this aspect, although the command and control arrangements of the Italian forces "le[ft] much to be desired".[23]

During the days of the kidnapping, Campbell wondered about its effects on PCI's policy. The Communists hoped that the Christian Democrats under Moro's leadership would have allowed them gradually to make more political progress but now these hopes suffered a setback. All would depend on the outcome of the kidnapping; if Moro became a victim of this affair, he would be a martyr – and it would be politically useful for the DC to have one.[24] A first turning point was a holograph letter from Moro on 29 March, which implied the possibility of an exchange of prisoners with the Red Brigades. According to the British Ambassador, while all political parties publicly agreed that the government should not accede to any such proposal, with the passage of time the image of Moro as a "martyred saint of the Christian Democrats", which was of obvious advantage to his party, was becoming eroded. Although extorted, Moro's letter "somewhat discredited him".[25]

As the weeks passed, two central themes emerged from the British documents. Firstly, there was a striking degree of political solidarity among parties; Campbell interpreted it as an Italian peculiarity:

> In Italy all politicians, whatever their party, are members of the same club, and I think they are all shocked and stunned by Moro's sufferings. No party is making a great profit out of the situation, and they are all seeking to help the Christian Democrats to maintain their determination to stand firm.

On the other hand, there was an atmosphere of defeatism, and it was hard to be optimistic about the political outcome of the kidnapping. Even if Moro were released, he would be regarded as "finished politically": Campbell was quoting the example of the Minister of Transport Emilio Colombo, who spoke of him throughout in the past tense. The loss of Moro was in itself a major setback for the DC: the State and the established institutions would survive, but the Christian Democrats were paying a high price for their failure over the years to tackle the underlying social causes for this challenge.[26]

---

23 TNA, CAB 133/486, "Anglo-Italian cooperation on internal security matters", brief by the Home Office for the visit of Signor Andreotti, JMV (78)9, 16 November 1978.

24 TNA, FCO 33/3567, "Italian political situation", by Campbell A., WRJ 014/2, 28 March 1978.

25 TNA, FCO 33/3577, Tel. No. 190 by Campbell A., "Italian political situation: the kidnapping of Aldo Moro", WRJ 031/1, 31 March 1978.

26 TNA, FCO 33/3577, Tel. No. 217 by Campbell A., "Italian political situation: the kidnapping of Aldo Moro", WRJ 031/1, 14 April 1978.

Another element which drew British attention was the attitude of the PSI, in particular the call by its secretary Bettino Craxi for a "humanitarian gesture" to save Moro's life, including the release of three prisoners not on the terrorists' list. According to Campbell, the reason for this choice lay in the Socialists' will to be seen taking a different line from the Communists. Craxi emerged as a "weak link" in the united front of the Italian political parties, which would not change their resolute stance to resist the terrorists' blackmail.[27] When, at the beginning of May, a DC statement authorised the government to examine the Socialist initiative and referred to the possibility of finding "forms of clemency consistent with the constitution", this was widely interpreted as a crumbling of the Christian Democrat attitude. In fact, Andreotti's diplomatic adviser Umberto La Rocca revealed to the British Ambassador that it was a calculated move by the DC to avoid leaving Craxi isolated, and to try to maintain cohesion between the parties of the majority. Andreotti had, however, no intention of modifying his publicly declared policy of refusing to deal with the terrorists – an attitude reaffirmed in a government note to the press on 3 May. The PCI, in the meantime, remained the strongest supporter of Andreotti's firm stand; the Communists were also trying to exploit for electoral purposes (partial administrative elections were scheduled for 14 May) their lead in the hard-line front and were criticising Craxi for seeking to undermine the unity of the parliamentary majority.[28]

The end of the kidnapping, though not unexpected, could hardly have been more dramatic. On 9 May, Moro's dead body was found in the back of a stolen car in the historic centre of Rome, only a few yards from both the Communists' and the Christian Democrat Party Headquarters. The stupefying impudence of the terrorists in driving Moro's remains in broad daylight through central Rome and leaving them parked in a busy street shocked the entire nation. Though most of the Christian Democrat Party leadership had steeled themselves some time beforehand to accept Moro's death, they had not expected to have to walk out of their offices and view the body.

During a sitting of the House of Commons, Callaghan paid tribute to Moro; he hoped that any British government would face such a situation

27 TNA, FCO 33/3577, Tel. No. 234 by Campbell A., "Italian political situation: the kidnapping of Aldo Moro", WRJ 031/1, 28 April 1978.

28 TNA, FCO 33/3577, Tel. No. 244 by Campbell A., "Italian political situation: the kidnapping of Aldo Moro", WRJ 031/1, 9 May 1978. On the PCI's attitude see Barbagallo F., "Il PCI dal sequestro di Moro alla morte di Berlinguer", in De Rosa G., Monina G. (eds.), quoted, pp. 79-85.

with the same courage as the Italian government did. Thatcher joined the Prime Minister in condemning the "callous and brutal murder" and expressing the Conservatives' understanding of the very difficult decisions that faced the colleagues of the DC President during such a great ordeal.[29]

According to British diplomacy, the Moro affair seemed to have had two main consequences. Firstly, the removal of such an important figure from the political scene altered the balance of influences and personalities in Italy, and especially inside the Christian Democrat Party. The politician who seemed subsequently to have emerged most strongly during the year, partly owing to Moro's disappearance and partly because his government was relatively effective, was Andreotti. The other main consequence of the Moro murder was that, to respond to such a shock to the public, the political parties were reconciled to the adoption of at least some of the measures necessary to combat terrorism (e.g. wider police powers of temporary arrest and interrogation) of a sort which the Communists and Socialists could well have found difficult in other circumstances. But this type of solidarity, which was essentially in the tradition of Moro's strategy of compromise, could in the end prove to be superficial, except on the need to stand firm against terrorism. The loss of Moro was seen from London as the likely beginning of a new phase of more confrontational politics: the DC president was perhaps the only long-term strategist capable of holding the Christian Democrat Party together on a course of collaboration with the Communists. Fanfani, the traditional leader of the right wing of the party, could seek to re-establish his authority over the party, at the expense of Zaccagnini, the Party Secretary, who was widely regarded as Moro's closest political heir. Moreover, the outcome of the recent local administrative elections could increase inter-party tensions. As with the PCI, the Communists for their part derived little benefit and some disadvantage. Moro was still the Communists' preferred interlocutor, and his disappearance was a setback to their ambitions. Furthermore, the PCI's image was damaged in the eyes of the public by the Red Brigades repeatedly asserting that they were Communists, though the PCI counteracted this by their staunch support for the government's firm stand against the terrorists.[30]

The Red Brigades phenomenon was extensively analysed by the British Ambassador. If up until 1977 the Red Brigades appeared to be just another

[29] *Hansard*, House of Commons Debates, 11 May 1978, Vol. 949, cols. 1398-1401.

[30] TNA, FCO 33/4046, "Annual review on Italy", by Campbell A., 10 January 1979; TNA, FCO 33/3578, Rome despatch 051/4, "The Moro kidnapping and murder", Campbell A. to Owen D., WRJ 051/1, 26 May 1978.

manifestation of that fringe political violence which was "endemic in Italy", they had since then focused their attention on people of increasing prominence, but no senior political figure. Nonetheless, with the Moro kidnapping, the Red Brigades demonstrated for the first time their ability to strike at the very heart of the establishment. It seemed that their aim was not so much to secure the release of ex-Red Brigade prisoners as to further their own peculiar "brand of revolution" by splitting the Christian Democrat Party and destroying the unity of the Parliamentary majority. If these were their objectives, they failed with the Moro kidnapping, since inter-party solidarity grew stronger. However, their organisation remained intact and almost untouched by the security forces, which were demoralised after their reorganisation and suffered from a lack of cooperation with the public, due to the "natural Italian reluctance to have anything to do with the police – or indeed with any form of authority". Therefore, British diplomacy considered it reasonable to suppose that the Red Brigades would before long seek to mount further attacks on other political leaders, possibly including Communists as well as Christian Democrats: the hypothesis of more potential "Moro affairs" was far from being rash.[31]

Notwithstanding, it is important to note that Britain did not compare Italy's situation with that in Latin America, and excluded any Argentinian-type deviation. A right-wing reaction was impossible because, despite the alarming increase in political violence, it was not yet on anything like the scale of the worst Latin American models. Moreover, after the experience of Fascism, "the antibodies against an extreme right-wing reaction remain[ed] remarkably strong" in Italy. Disappointment with the performance of the Italian political establishment was profound, but equally profound was the sense of attachment to a democratic state which the Red Brigades were seeking to destroy. For Campbell, all the so-called constitutional parties, including the PCI, were publicly committed to the democratic cause. Moreover, the mood of the Italian people seemed remarkably steady.[32]

"Things are not as bad in Italy as many people think"

During the dark days after Moro's kidnapping, the Joint Intelligence Committee asked the collaboration of the Foreign Office for a study of the Italian situation and its probable evolution in the following two or three

31 TNA, FCO 33/3578, Rome despatch 051/4, "The Moro kidnapping and murder", Campbell A. to Owen D., WRJ 051/1, 26 May 1978.

32 *Ibidem.*

years. The exchange of notes between the Western European Department and the British Embassy in Rome allows a precise reconstruction of the ten themes considered fundamental for the future of Italy by the UK government:

- the attitudes within the Christian Democracy and the PCI towards a historic compromise;
- the will of Christian Democrats and Communists to collaborate in countering extremist groups from both Right and Left;
- the extent to which Italian policies were influenced by Communist support for the government;
- the popularity of the PCI and whether it had reached its peak;
- the prospects for a revival of the PSI;
- the probable alternatives to a historic compromise, should it prove to be impracticable;
- the possibility for existing Italian institutions to succeed in facing the challenge of terrorism;
- the extent to which the extreme Left could gain support in the event of a DC-PCI rapprochement, and the threat which this could pose to the stability of the state;
- the probable developments in the Italian economy and their effect on the political situation, particularly on the position of the Communists;
- and the success or otherwise of the PCI in penetrating the media.[33]

By the end of the year, the answer to many of these questions seemed already clear. The most important fact was that the PCI did not gain strength from the turbulent events of 1978. The Italian Communists still represented a significant bloc in the Parliament, and their attitude was also of crucial importance in regional government and the field of labour relations. But the latest indications were of a certain decline in their electoral popularity: in the local elections in May, the Communist share of the vote fell by over 9 per cent as compared with the June 1976 general election. Andreotti assured that there was no question of the PCI entering government before a further general election, and the next election could conceivably leave it in an even more unfavourable position.

---

33 TNA, FCO 33/3567, "Italian political situation", Rhodes P. to Campbell A., WRJ 014/2, 20 April 1978. The last three points were added by Ambassador Campbell in his reply in TNA, FCO 33/3567, Campbell A. to Rhodes P., WRJ 014/2, 28 April 1978.

As for the relations between the Labour Party and the PCI, the possible visit of Berlinguer to the UK in the summer of 1978 became a source of tension and embarrassment for the British government. The CPGB invited the Secretary of the Italian Communist Party to a festival in Britain and asked Michael Foot, then Labour's Deputy Leader, to organise a meeting with a member of the government. Foot asked for Owen's advice on how to react to the proposal, which took the Foreign Office by surprise. Some officials were in favour of a meeting between British ministers and Berlinguer: avoiding him would be counter-productive and strengthen his position in Italy ("Imagine the reaction here if the Leader of the leading Opposition Party was snubbed by all Ministers on a visit abroad").[34] On the other hand, there were many "cons": no member of a major Western government had yet received Berlinguer (the Communist Secretary met only Mintoff and Soares in 1977, although a PCI delegation was received by the Foreign Ministers in Norway, Sweden and Denmark). Britain would, therefore, be "breaking fresh ground" in doing so, and this could undoubtedly be claimed by the Italian Communists as a major advance in Berlinguer's international political respectability, while Andreotti and the DC would almost certainly resent it. Even the American, West German, and French governments would view it with reserve, due to their opposition to conferring respectability on the PCI.[35] Moreover, according to the *Financial Times*, Ambassador Campbell – together with his American colleague Gardner – had no diplomatic contact with Berlinguer, although some other important embassies did, including for example the West German envoy.[36] Such an unexpected change of policy by the British government would seem quite anomalous; moreover, the CPGB would take advantage in being seen to "play host to the most prominent Eurocommunist".[37] At the end of these consultations, the hard-line prevailed, and Owen did not consent to a meeting with Berlinguer, commenting: "We are not in business to promote the Italian Communist Party". If the PCI leader had been an observer at a Party conference or his visit was at Labour Party initiative, things would have been different.[38]

34 TNA, FCO 33/3563, "Possible visit to the UK by Signor Berlinguer", Judd F. to Owen D., WRJ 011/1, 11 April 1978.

35 TNA, FCO 33/3563, "Possible visit to the UK by Signor Berlinguer", by Goodall D., WRJ 011/1, 12 April 1978.

36 "Supping with the Communists", *Financial Times*, 7 March 1978.

37 TNA, FCO 33/3563, "Possible visit to the UK by Signor Berlinguer", by Palliser M., WRJ 011/1, 19 April 1978.

38 TNA, FCO 33/3563, "Possible visit to the UK by Signor Berlinguer", WRJ 011/1, 27 April 1978.

Anyway, it was much ado about nothing: Berlinguer did not visit the United Kingdom in 1978.

Conversely, in British view, the Socialists appeared stronger than the previous year. Whereas in 1976 the PSI was primarily concerned to distance itself from the DC to restore and sharpen up an individual public image blurred by a series of centre-Left governments, Craxi was now preoccupied with the need to distance it from a PCI which was projecting for itself an image easily confused with the PSI. In the process, he was enraging his own Left, but the PSI success in the partial administrative elections gave him greater power in his party and greater confidence in his dealings with other parties.[39] As for the ruling party, the British embassy assessed that the Christian Democrats still had to deal with the loss of Moro; in the longer run, it could strengthen the position of those inside the DC who favoured a more direct opposition to the Communists.[40]

On these premises, Campbell was optimistic about the political scene in Italy: such questions as whether an Italian government which included Communist Ministers could be regarded as a reliable ally or Community partner had become "academic for the time being". Of course, the more fundamental question of the prospects for the Italian Left, including the question whether the PCI could one day become a democratic socialist party, remained of the highest importance; but these were problems of the longer term.

As viewed from London, law and order was a much more immediate question. A few more kidnappings like that of Moro would have put the whole basis of Italian democracy under almost unbearable strain. But the terrorists did not follow up their successful attack on the DC President, and they seemed to have reverted to more modestly placed victims. The State was still vulnerable, but the government showed its willingness to master the situation and Parliament and public opinion had demonstrated unmistakable support. Meanwhile, the degree to which terrorist activities affected the public order in Italy should not be exaggerated: "business [went] on as usual" and it was far from being a "South American situation".[41]

---

39 TNA, FCO 33/3568, "The Italian political situation", by Goodison A., WRJ 014/2, 18 September 1978.

40 TNA, FCO 33/3568, "The Italian internal political and economic situation", WRJ 014/2, 6 November 1978.

41 TNA, FCO 33/3568, "The Italian scene in 1978" – HM's Ambassador at Rome to the Secretary of State for FCO (Campbell A. to Owen D.), WRJ 014/2, 20 July 1978.

Political stability seemed granted, at all events until the end of 1978, thanks to the beginning of the "white semester" – the six-month period when the President of the Republic, close to the end of his mandate, is constitutionally unable to dissolve Parliament. Actually, a new scandal was going to hit the Italian political scene: on 15 June, President Giovanni Leone resigned for his alleged involvement in the Lockheed affair.[42] A strong PCI campaign eventually forced his sudden resignation, leaving the political parties unprepared for the delicate business of electing a successor. Moro's murder had removed the favourite from the race, while the lack of a "white semester" posed new risks and the threat of early elections to the Andreotti government.[43] Although the DC Secretary Zaccagnini would probably have obtained Communist support, the Christian Democrat leadership was prepared to accept a suitable lay candidate enjoying widespread support. The Socialists took the initiative in insisting on a candidate from their party, Sandro Pertini, an 81-year-old with a strong anti-fascist record and a founding father of the Republic. After an initial disagreement, the Christian Democrats accepted the PSI candidate; Pertini won with the largest majority in his favour of any previous President of the Republic, and his election gave relative satisfaction to all but the extreme right-wing parties.

British diplomacy was taken by surprise by Leone's resignation and thought that it occurred mainly because of political manoeuvring between the parties and not because of any sudden realisation that the President was too corrupt to be allowed to continue in office.[44] Conversely, the press in the United Kingdom took the opportunity to stress how the Leone affair was suggesting a country where corruption "on both the petty and the grand scale [was] endemic to the system" and where all parties, with the exception of the Communists, had their "black sheep".[45]

Compared with Moro's murder, the premature resignation of Leone as President of the Republic was a "paltry affair" for Campbell. Nonetheless, in British view it had several political implications. Firstly, his departure did not precipitate a crisis, but on the contrary, tended to strengthen the political framework in which Andreotti's government functioned.

42 See Chapter 1. In the end, the allegations about Leone's involvement proved to be false.

43 TNA, FCO 33/3564, "The 1978 Italian presidential election", by Campbell A., Rome despatch 014/1, 2 August 1978.

44 TNA, FCO 33/3568, "Resignation of President Leone", Adams W. to Goodall D., WRJ 014/2, 22 June 1978.

45 "Leone is only a symptom", *The Guardian*, 17 June 1978.

Secondly, his successor was a Socialist: this was clear confirmation of the improvement of the PSI position under Craxi's leadership. Moreover, Pertini's integrity and moral authority would indeed be an asset for the Socialists, even if, as an octogenarian, he could not be regarded as likely to last the full 7-year course (which in fact he did, completing his mandate in 1985). Thirdly, although the PCI could rightly claim to have forced Leone to resign, the substitution in the Presidency of a "discredited Christian Democrat by a respected Socialist" had to be judged a bad deal from the Communist point of view.[46]

Pertini's election was welcomed favourably in London: he could restore to the Presidency some of the integrity which it lost under Leone. Pertini was very popular, particularly among the young, and his initial actions – for example, cutting protocol and visiting a memorial to the victims of fascist atrocities – showed a "sureness of touch that was often lacking in his predecessor". Above all, his election with the full consensus of all the constitutional parties preserved the unity of the majority which the election had earlier threatened to destroy: this would be a helpful factor for stability in the coming months.[47] In an article in *The Times*, Peter Nichols described Pertini as a "bad politician" (in the most positive sense of the phrase), someone who had never managed to fit into the factious life of the Socialist party, despite a brief period immediately after the war as its secretary. He won a reputation for fairness, and no one could challenge his integrity and honesty. But he would no longer be able to meet his enemies recklessly, like during his youth:

> [...] the enemies of democracy in Italy today are less easily identifiable than they were when Pertini was young. He has to give a lead to a country worried by violence but violence much less attributable than in the past: by disillusion after swift development; by a loss of old values and a failure to find new ones; by an overcomplicated political scene which is no longer black and white.[48]

However, considering the Italian situation as a whole, the outlook was not so bad for British diplomacy and the Foreign Office: it was even "mildly encouraging" in some respects. "Things [were] not so bad in Italy as many [thought]". Of course, not everything "in the Italian garden [was] lovely"; probably there would be some further terrorist success, nor would the economy be rectified at once – although the economic scene already

---

46 TNA, FCO 33/4046, "Annual review on Italy", by Campbell A., 10 January 1979.

47 TNA, FCO 33/3564, "The 1978 Italian presidential election", Campbell A. to Owen D., WRJ 011/2, 2 August 1978.

48 Nichols P., "The 'veteran' who could revitalize Italy", *The Times*, 10 July 1978.

showed many improvements. But Campbell did not doubt Italy's recovery: the Italians had "a great capacity for survival".[49]

Attempting cooperation: the European Monetary System

A peculiar example of the potential Anglo-Italian alliance in the process of European integration was the series of negotiations which led to the creation of the European Monetary System (EMS) in 1978. The timing of the initiative was extremely unfortunate for both countries and the dilemma of joining the EMS or not had profound economic and political implications for Britain and Italy. Despite differing views and positions in the international scenario, close collaboration between the countries could have helped in attempting to correct the presumed inequities in the Community Budget and the Common Agricultural Policy.

The project for the EMS and its reception in Britain and Italy

In October 1977, the President of the European Commission Roy Jenkins revitalised the EC's efforts at establishing a monetary union. This initiative led to the birth of the EMS, which became operational in March 1979.[50]

In his speech at the European University Institute in Fiesole, near Florence, Jenkins summarised the main goals he was expecting to fulfil for the future of the European institutions: the creation of a monetary union would take Europe "over a political threshold" and Europe at the moment

---

49 TNA, FCO 33/3568, "The Italian scene in 1978" – HM's Ambassador at Rome to the Secretary of State for FCO (Campbell A. to Owen D.), WRJ 014/2, 20 July 1978.

50 The literature on the EMS is voluminous. The most accurate narration is probably still the essential volume by Ludlow P., *The Making of the European Monetary System*, Butterworth, London 1982. We quote here: Mourlon-Druol E., *A Europe made of money. The emergence of the European Monetary System*, Cornell University Press, Ithaca 2012; James H., *Making the European Monetary Union*, Belknap Press, Cambridge 2012; Statler J., "The European Monetary System: From Conception to Birth", *International Affairs*, No. 2, 1979, pp. 206-225; Story J., "The launching of the EMS: An Analysis of Change in Foreign Economic Policy", *Political Studies*, No. 3, 1988, pp. 397-412; Coffey P., *European Monetary System: Past, Present, and Future*, Martinus Nijhoff, Dordrecht 1984. See also the reconstruction of one of the British political protagonists: Dell E., "Britain and the Origins of the European Monetary System", *Contemporary European History*, No. 1, 1994, pp. 1-60.

was not prepared to pursue that objective solely for ideological reasons. He developed seven economic arguments in favour of the monetary union, and concluded by quoting one of Europe's founding fathers: "Politics is not only the art of the possible, but as Jean Monnet said, it is also the art of making possible tomorrow what may seem impossible today".[51]

Actually, the task Jenkins was indicating to his European partners seemed impossible. His proposal attracted little attention (according to Edmund Dell, "little but derision") and it was basically set aside and labelled as the product of a "dreamer".[52] Even his Vice-President and predecessor, François-Xavier Ortoli, did not share this enthusiasm, commenting that he did not believe it would be useful to raise a "politically absurd" idea in order to start a debate with a probably negative outcome.[53] However, West German Chancellor Helmut Schmidt had started discussions with the French President Valéry Giscard d'Estaing to create a new European monetary institution: the outcome of this highly personal and secret initiative (the German ministries and the Bundesbank were deliberately not informed of two bilateral meetings) was the proposal at the European Council at Copenhagen in April 1978 to establish a "zone of monetary stability" in Western Europe. According to the British Foreign Office, it was Giscard who had initiated the discussion with Schmidt, since the Chancellor had "never been a European idealist".[54] The Committee of Finance Ministers (ECOFIN), the Monetary Committee, and the Committee of Central Bank Governors were involved in the technical details, although Schmidt relied mostly on a secret committee formed of German, French, and British representatives for the creation of the new European Monetary System. The German Chancellor had eventually involved Britain in this inner circle: an agreement among these three countries would be a guarantee for the other Members States to follow.

The timing of this project was extremely unfortunate for both Britain and Italy: the two countries had been struggling with internal problems for years, and the dilemma whether to join the EMS had profound economic and political implications for the British and Italian governments.

In 1978, the United Kingdom was still recovering from the profound crisis of 1976, although the economy was showing the first signs of recovery. In this scenario, and considering the abortive six-week effort in 1973 to

51 Jenkins R., *Europe's Present Challenge and Future Opportunity* (first Jean Monnet Lecture), European University Institute, Florence, 27 October 1977.

52 Dell E., quoted, p. 2; "A distant goal", *The Times*, 28 October 1977.

53 *Financial Times*, 20 October 1977.

54 James H., quoted, p. 152.

participate in the Snake, Britain was not willing to discuss her participation in exchange-rate arrangements in early 1978. The major argument against EMS membership was that it imposed an asymmetrical burden on weak currency countries, severely reducing growth and government spending. The new monetary system was also likely to become an electoral issue since it was widely expected that Callaghan would schedule a general election for the autumn of 1978. Some Treasury speculations were quite apocalyptic, assuming that membership of the EMS would keep sterling at an artificially and unacceptably high level, resulting in restrictive fiscal measures, a GDP deficit, rising unemployment, and social conflicts, not to mention the suggestion that the whole of Schmidt's proposal was part of a "Machiavellian German plot to boost their exports", to Britain's detriment.[55] However, the main fear in Whitehall was marginalisation. The EMS could be a move towards a "two-tier community", and the political implications, if Britain was not in the top tier, had to be taken into consideration: it was appropriate to ensure either that this was a scheme which the UK could live with, or that it foundered.[56]

Therefore, when Callaghan met Schmidt and Giscard at a private breakfast on the morning of 8 April at the occasion of the Copenhagen European Council, he put aside his reservations and agreed to restrict discussion to a group of three specially chosen confidants. This troika of experts had the task of working out the details of the projects of what would become the Bremen Annex, attached to the conclusions of the European Council in Bremen. The Group of Three – or Gang of Three, as Peter Ludlow labelled it – was formed by Bernard Clappier, the governor of the Banque de France; Horst Schulmann, Schmidt's senior economic adviser; and Ken Couzens, who was nominated weeks later than the others and was second permanent Secretary of the Treasury. The choice of the experts revealed a great deal about the countries' different strategies: Giscard chose one of the civil servants most in favour of Europe, while Schulmann was one of the most trusted advisers of the German Chancellor and had worked in the European Commission. Couzens, instead, had only recently come to deal with international financial matters and "acted throughout as a senior Treasury official", with a professional scepticism that Callaghan failed to counteract.[57] This would also explain the substantial failure of the UK inside the Group of Three: the British representative did not take

---

55 Ludlow P., quoted, pp. 111-112.

56 TNA, PREM 16/1615, "Chancellor Schmidt, the Snake and Pooling Reserves", Note by Hunt J., 6 April 1978.

57 Ludlow P., quoted, pp. 108-109.

part in all the secret meetings during the spring of 1978, and the final document of the group was basically a Franco-German position paper on which Clappier and Schulmann had already been working before the arrival of their colleague from London. In any case, with Ken Couzens' appointment, the British Prime Minister had deliberately avoided people with a pro-European and integrationist stance, like Michael Butler: it was a clear indication of "where he did not want to go".[58]

As for Italy, although its trade balance, and especially its balance of payments, had greatly improved since the agreement with the IMF in April 1977, the crucial economic factor, i.e. Italy's public spending deficit, remained dangerously high, and was certain well to exceed even the revised forecast commitment given to the IMF in the autumn. Agreement on a package was reached only with great difficulty within the government in mid-December but had still to be agreed by the other political parties and by the trade unions. The latter were thought to be hostile even to its less than draconian provisions.[59]

Considering the peculiar internal situation, during the spring of 1978 the Italian government, not surprisingly, paid little attention to the EMS project. Italy had shared with Britain the unfortunate experience of the Snake in 1972-73 and its aftermath; the lira stayed in the system for a period longer than the pound, but also more "nasty and brutish" and, despite encouraging signs of recovery, the Italian economy was still fragile and could be numbered among the "less prosperous" countries.[60]

The government formed a group of experts to discuss the feasibility of joining the Franco-German project: it included Filippo Maria Pandolfi, Minister of the Treasury; Paolo Baffi and Carlo Azeglio Ciampi, respectively Governor and Director-general of the Banca d'Italia; Rainer Masera, a young member of the study department of the bank; and Renato Ruggiero, who had returned to the Ministry of Foreign Affairs following his experience in the Commission, defined by *The Economist* as "Italy's secret weapon".[61] The group – also called "The Club" in Italian documents – had expressed its favour towards an "unconditional adhesion in principle" to the proposal, although timings and ways of proceeding had to be cautiously pondered. Rome's commitment should be accompanied by a strong assurance by the Community, and Germany in particular, to a

58 Mourlon-Druol E., quoted, pp. 171-173.

59 TNA, FCO 33/3566, "US Ambassador's call on the PUS: Italy", by Goodall D., 11 January 1978.

60 Ludlow P., quoted, p. 146.

61 "Italy's secret weapon", *The Economist*, 16 December 1978, p. 38.

substantial transfer of resources to Italy, as a contribution towards solving the structural problems of the Italian economy. Even the Banca d'Italia indicated how a more positive economic scenario and growing financial solidarity inside the EEC would be necessary to the favourable outcome of the proposal.[62]

Beyond economic considerations, there was a basic political constraint which affected Italy's attitude towards the EMS. This was the consensus in Italian politics on the European choice as an important way to maintain the country's link with the Western world. In the words of Ruggiero: "If we did not participate in the EMS, this would show that we are unwilling to accept the challenge […] of being a fully European country".[63]

A special European relationship?

Anglo-Italian relations inside the Community were apparently facing several strains in that period. In April 1978, the UK Permanent Representative to the EEC Donald Maitland drew the attention of the Foreign Secretary David Owen to some difficulties in Britain's relations with Italy over EEC affairs. According to Maitland, Italian suspicions of the UK were causing the Italians to be "obstructive", and British interests were suffering accordingly. However, this state of affairs could be improved if those Italian Ministers who seemed particularly difficult in this respect could be invited to London on goodwill visits by their opposite numbers, in order to avoid misunderstandings.[64]

The relations between London and Rome showed no particular sign of "specialness" in the first months after the launch of the EMS project. After the disclosure of the existence of the Schulmann-Clappier-Couzens group, Italian resentment at being excluded from the inner circle in the secret preparations of the monetary plan was clear, although it was not directed towards the British.[65] However, it must be noted that until *The Economist* revealed the existence of the small group on 26 May, it is almost certain that nobody knew that these parallel discussions were taking place at all.[66]

---

62 Varsori A., *La Cenerentola*, quoted, pp. 318-319.

63 Quoted in Spaventa L., "Italy Joins the EMS: A Political History", *Johns Hopkins University Bologna Center Occasional Paper*, No. 32, 1980, p. 69.

64 TNA, FCO 33/3575, "Relations with Italy", WRJ 026/2, 23 March 1978.

65 See *Il Corriere della Sera*, 7 June 1978 and Ludlow P., quoted, p. 114.

66 Ludlow P., quoted, p. 95.

The prospect of an early general election deeply influenced Britain's attitude in the first phase of the negotiations; the British did not in fact even try to start a proper discussion over the negotiations or to reach at least some results which would suit them. There was a UK "counter-draft" to the Franco-German proposal, although it was never put forward. As for Italy, in a conversation with Campbell at the end of June, Andreotti seemed not to expect that the forthcoming meeting at Bremen would result in remarkable agreements, despite the importance he attached to it. He was not particularly impressed by Schmidt's reassurances, remarking that Germany and Italy had different ideas of what a dangerous rate of inflation was.[67]

At the European Council meeting in Bremen of 6-7 July, Britain found herself quite isolated. Only Andreotti shared the British point of view about the Franco-German scheme, stressing that the paper "read as though everyone agreed". These common criticisms, however, were based on different attitudes: Callaghan did not politically support the scheme, while Andreotti had doubts about Italy's capacity to join, without calling Rome's endorsement into question.[68]

On 25 July, Pandolfi and Baffi met the Chancellor of the Exchequer, accompanied by Ken Couzens. Although Healey gave his Italian counterpart an account of the methods used to control public expenditure in the United Kingdom, the conversation focused mainly on the prospects for a new European Monetary System. By that date, Pandolfi, Baffi, and their colleagues had already worked out the main features of Italy's economic strategy, which consisted of four principal elements: reinforcement of the domestic stabilisation programme; achievement of a monetary agreement which could provide wider bands of oscillation for the weaker countries; a significant revision of the Community budget and, more particularly, of the CAP; and coordination of strategy and tactics with the British, with whom it was believed there was a strong community of interests. The document, which subsequently became known as the Pandolfi Plan, was eventually published on 31 August. The "appointment with Europe" was used as an occasion to place the government's economic strategy within a broader perspective and by doing so to reinforce its authority, stating that "a new direction for our economy and therefore for our society can also be seen as a vote for Europe".[69]

---

67 TNA, FCO 33/3572, "Call on Signor Andreotti", by Campbell A., WRJ 021/1, 30 June 1978.

68 Mourlon-Druol E., quoted, pp. 188-190.

69 Ludlow P., quoted, pp. 148-149.

In the discussion in London, the two governments were similar in their attitude towards the Franco-German initiative, as regards both the necessary conditions for participation in the scheme of monetary co-operation and the importance of resource allocation. The Italians had clearly been surprised at the unqualified political support of the French for a new monetary scheme and the apparent about-turn by Chancellor Schmidt in his attitude towards economic convergence as a pre-condition for monetary co-operation. Baffi also aligned his country with the UK's wish to see changes in the CAP: since Italy had become a major importer of certain goods, especially butter and meat, from the rest of the Community, the Italian government seemed "distinctly unhappy" with the disproportionate resources going to support Northern European agriculture. However, Pandolfi, while sharing the Chancellor's objectives, expressed doubts about finding the practical means to achieve them. The main concern expressed by the Italian delegation was to bring the inflation rate down before committing Italy to enter a monetary scheme. The ambitious counter-inflationary policy of the Pandolfi Plan was not realistically expected to show significant results until mid-1979; domestic policies were therefore "out of phase" with the timetable for establishing a currency scheme by 1 January 1979.[70] Baffi referred to Italy's dilemma as the weakest member state: whether to enter a European monetary system with too weak a currency or whether to stay out, with all the consequent problems. According to Couzens, it would be desirable for the system to lean in an anti-inflationary direction, but Britain wanted to avoid a situation in which countries were forced to deflate or undertake large-scale borrowing to maintain an indefensible rate. Pandolfi agreed: massive credit was not as important as the possibility of a change in rate.[71]

The Italian press and media gave full coverage to the visit, with enthusiastic comments stressing the extent to which Italian and British views converged on European monetary reform and to which Italy could learn from the British government's example in limiting public expenditure, wage increases, and inflation.[72] The meeting, however, had also revealed differences of opinion between Italy and Britain, in particular over fluctuation margins. The Italian negotiators aimed at a looser system for at least a transitional period, while the British preferred a system which

---

70 TNA, FCO 33/3575, "Visit of Signor Pandolfi and Signor Baffi", 28 July 1978.

71 TNA, FCO 33/3575, "Visit of Italian Minister of Treasury and Governor of Bank of Italy", Note from Ingham G., 1 August 1978.

72 TNA, FCO 33/3575, Tel. No. 364 by Campbell A., "Visit of Italian Minister of the Treasury and Governor of the Bank of Italy to London: Italian press reaction", WRJ 026/2, 26 July 1978.

was precisely drafted in order to guarantee the reinforcement that external discipline would give to domestic anti-inflationary policies. Beneath these technical differences, there were two different political visions. On one hand, wider margins would allow Italy to combine her political desire to become a member of the system and at the same time avoid suffering unbearable economic costs. On the other, for the United Kingdom, the most important precaution was a clause allowing members to opt out: "the first was the solution of a government predisposed to join, while the second was the proposal of an administration that was still agnostic". More than a difference in views, the main problem was Britain's hesitancy. By the end of July, the British authorities were still unclear about what they wanted from the EMS and this was also one of the difficulties about forming an Anglo-Italian front: according to the *Financial Times*, the Pandolfi-Baffi visit was "notable for the invention by a very senior British representative of the phrase 'constructive caution', which covered the whole spectrum of UK official responses to monetary union" and was accompanied by the "unspoken assumption" of superiority by British Ministers and officials when dealing with their Italian counterparts.[73]

"Lobbying the Italians on the EMS"

Despite these differences, by mid-September the importance of Italy for Britain's strategy grew stronger. Following the ECOFIN meeting of 18 September in Aachen, with the ratification of the parity-grip option by Schmidt and Giscard, the UK found itself as the most active defender of the so-called symmetry. The Franco-German bilateral agreement meant that Britain had lost its most important technical ally.[74] On these premises, it was decided to approach the Italians: they would not be a fitting replacement of the French, but they could indeed help London's cause, as shown by the British archives. In a note entitled "Lobbying the Italians on the EMS", the Undersecretary in charge of the Community, Michael Butler, made an unequivocal statement:

> The Italians will be an important factor in our strategy. The Chancellor has himself considered making personal contact with his Italian opposite number, but the Treasury also consider that we need to keep Andreotti reinforced against the heavy lobbying that he will receive from Giscard and Schmidt.

73 Ludlow P., quoted, pp. 151-152.

74 On the Aachen meeting and its significance see Mourlon-Druol E., quoted, pp. 216-227.

The Italians, together with Britain, were the "foremost advocates of the need for an EMS to be reasonably flexible and to avoid it being deflationary" and were "at present allies in trying to correct the inequities of the present EEC Budget". Considering the key role played by the respective heads of government in determining their national position, it would be extremely useful to organise a talk with Andreotti. Italy's Prime Minister, "with some unusually effective official support from the Foreign Ministry", seemed to be largely responsible for the "realistic line" taken by the Italians about the CAP, the concurrent studies, and the EMS itself.[75] Yet this Anglo-Italian rapprochement could be undermined by the risky strategy adopted by the British government on revealing – or rather, concealing – its real intentions.

Indeed, it seems clear that, by early October 1978, the British government had already taken the decision not to join the EMS. The reasons behind this choice lay primarily in British internal politics. Despite speculations, Callaghan informed the Cabinet in September that a general election would not be held until 1979. The Prime Minister hoped that the positive economic trends begun in late 1977, when the balance of payments improved and inflation slowly dropped, would continue. Callaghan actively promoted these economic policy successes and trusted to exploit them for electoral purposes.[76] Also, the polls showed an uncertain scenario, with a small Conservative lead in marginal constituencies, and Callaghan did not wish to risk an election on these premises, although there was no reason to think that Mrs Thatcher would suddenly become popular.[77]

With hindsight, Callaghan's decision to delay the general election proved to be a fatal miscalculation: it was naive to ignore the warning signs from the unions that could foreshadow the events of the "winter of discontent" (which will be analysed later). In the immediate future, the postponement of the election made Callaghan "a captive of intra-Labour party struggles over the EMS". Strong opposition came from the left wing of the party, which felt that participation would lead to higher interest rates. At the meeting of the Labour Party's National Executive Committee on 1 October 1978 to consider motions for the upcoming party conference, a proposal "denouncing and rejecting the EMS" was

75 TNA, FCO 33/3570, "Lobbying the Italians on the EMS", Note by Butler D., WRJ 020/1, 20 September 1978.

76 Ludlow P., quoted, pp. 80-81.

77 Cronin J., *New Labour's Pasts. The Labour Party and its discontents*, Longman, Harlow 2004, pp. 189-191.

passed by a vote of sixteen to nine. This motion was not voted at the conference, but it revealed enough hostility to persuade the Prime Minister that he could not count on the party's support.[78]

In a meeting of the Ministerial Group on European Monetary Co-operation on 10 October, Callaghan was explicit: "the Group by a large majority felt that it was clearly not in [British] interests to join the proposed European Monetary Scheme in the form in which it seemed likely to emerge". However, for "tactical reasons", it would seem "unwise" to make this known prematurely to other European partners: Britain had to continue to take part constructively in the negotiations until the European Council in December; otherwise, it could prejudice the chances of a successful outcome to the ongoing studies on resource transfers. There was still scope for influencing the details of the scheme before it began and during the transitional period; the real question was, once the scheme was established, whether Britain would be worse off outside it and unduly exposed to speculation. Meanwhile, it was important that there should be "no advance disclosure of the government's position".[79]

Quite surprisingly, at the same time, some Italian officials and politicians appeared to be inclined to believe that the British would join the French and Germans in accepting the EMS for political reasons, even on conditions which were unsatisfactory for Italy. According to Renato Ruggiero, who was reporting in strict confidence, a reflection of this thinking could be found in *Il Sole 24 Ore*, describing a meeting by leading members of the Republican Party close to the Banca d'Italia, during which the possibility of British surrender to the French and German position was aired. The Foreign Office dismissed the matter as "nonsense": the British Ministers "were holding their cards very close to their chests", but there was no doubt that they could not contemplate the possibility of joining unless the terms were right.[80] On that occasion, the divergence between the actual policy of the British government and its perception on the Italian side was quite striking.

Despite Britain's determination not to join the EMS, collaboration between London and Rome continued in those months. Within the FCO,

---

78 Walsh J.I., *European Monetary Integration & Domestic Politics: Britain, France, and Italy*, Lynne Rienner, Boulder 2000, p. 33.

79 TNA, CAB 130/1047, Ministerial Group on European Monetary Co-operation, 5th Meeting minutes, European Monetary Co-operation, GEN 136(78), Limited Circulation, 10 October 1978.

80 TNA, FCO 33/3570, "EMS: Italian and UK attitudes", by Adams W., WRJ 020/1, 16 October 1978.

there was a widespread conviction that the French wanted to split the Italians from the UK, for example, by talking about resource transfers for Italy (and Ireland) but not for Britain. As the moment for making decisions drew near, it would probably see increasing pressures and incentives on the Italians to accept whatever form of EMS Giscard and Schmidt could agree upon. It was therefore very important that the British government should "encourage the Italians to stay with [the UK] in holding out for an acceptable EMS": this could probably only be done with reasonable hope of success at the level of Andreotti himself.[81]

As for Italy, according to Baffi, as early as 2 November Andreotti wanted to enter the EMS "even without England", a decision which did not encounter the governor's favour. Even Pandolfi disagreed with the Prime Minister. Despite the many rumours circulating not only in the press but also in Brussels about Britain's non-participation, every British official was pursuing the consistent strategy of continuing to say that no decision had yet been made by the Callaghan government.[82]

Different paths: Rome goes in, London stays out

The final act of the British strategy took place on 22 November, when Andreotti visited London at Callaghan's invitation, accompanied by Pandolfi and Baffi as part of an intensive round of Italian consultations before the European Council meeting.[83]

Prior to Andreotti's visit, the Foreign Office stressed how the Italians, together with the United Kingdom, were the "foremost advocates" of the need for an EMS to take into account the needs and problems of all the economies, both strong and weak, and, like the British, they were concerned to correct the inequities of the EEC Budget. The Italian objectives were to focus mainly on the Community side, trying to ensure UK support for the position Italy would adopt at the European Council, particularly regarding the width of currency margins in an EMS and on immediate commitments to assist less prosperous economies. Andreotti would also stress Italy's

---

81 TNA, FCO 33/3570, "Lobbying the Italians on the EMS", Note by Butler D., 20 September 1978.

82 Mourlon-Druol E., quoted, pp. 245-246; Ludlow P., quoted, p. 216.

83 Giscard visited Rome on 25-26 October for discussions on the EMS, and Schmidt paid a one-day visit to Italy on 1 November for discussions on Community issues. Andreotti also visited Luxembourg on 11-12 November and discussed the EMS with his Belgian, Dutch, and Luxembourg colleagues, while Pandolfi saw Colley, the Irish Minister for Finance, on 13 November.

interest in parity of treatment for Mediterranean as against Northern agriculture within the EEC, while encouraging the further "thickening" of Anglo-Italian bilateral relations, in particular, further collaboration on defence projects and in the fight against terrorism. Britain's main objective was to ensure that the Italians stayed as close as possible to the UK at the European Council and thereafter, both on the EMS itself and on related measures to help countries facing economic problems. The meeting with Andreotti would also provide a useful opportunity to consolidate Anglo-Italian co-operation on other Community questions, on many of which the two countries had complementary interests. The FCO then stressed the convenience of demonstrating the importance that the British government attached to the UK-Italy relationship, as well as its readiness to consult Italy on problems of common concern on the same basis West Germany and France were consulted.[84]

Andreotti's visit had a wider meaning, going further merely than immediate negotiations over the EMS, according to Ambassador Campbell. The Italians had always been deeply attracted by European integration, in the wish to correct at a European level the limitations of the Italian administrative system: despite the probable delusion which could spring from it, in that unfavourable economic situation they considered the evolving Community to be the main framework in which to solve their economic problems. In addition, all the democratic forces in Italy strongly felt that integration at a European level was a way of linking the country to the West, avoiding any drift towards pro-Soviet neutralism through the PCI, even though Italian Communists were "sufficiently sophisticated to understand the importance of the Community dimension". In the European integration process, Britain played a key role in Italian eyes: although less important economically than Germany (Italy's largest export market and a major source of investment capital and financial assistance in need), the United Kingdom was regarded as a vital counterweight to the long-feared Franco-German hegemony, as well as a major guarantee of European democracies. Apart from general, long-lasting goodwill towards Britain, more recently in some key sectors of the administration, such as the European Integration Department of the MFA, the Treasury, and the Banca d'Italia, a definite feeling had emerged that the two countries were "natural allies" in the struggle to create a more equitable distribution of the burden of EEC costs. Campbell made himself very clear in this regard: "As I understand it, Italy is in fact our only substantial ally in our

---

84 TNA, CAB 133/486, "Visit of Signor Andreotti, 22 November 1978: Steering Brief", Brief by Foreign and Commonwealth Office, 15 November 1978.

attempt to correct the distribution of injustices inherent in the existing Community system".

Italian officials and the Italian press had, at last, acknowledged that their country, the second poorest in the Community, shared with the United Kingdom the status of net contributor to it. It was in British interests to try to retain this sense of solidarity, otherwise the Italians might be tempted to seek remedies for their problems from other Community partners. If Britain could be seen to be fighting in the interests of London and Rome, then the good relationship with the Italians would survive and become the basis for profitable collaboration in the EEC, even if in the end the UK decided not to join the EMS. In this connection, the Ambassador suggested that the Prime Minister should be as open and as sympathetic as possible towards Andreotti during his forthcoming visit.[85]

In the discussion in London, Callaghan had indeed been sympathetic, but not open at all: he stated that the Cabinet had not reached a conclusion on UK participation and would not do so until shortly before the forthcoming meeting of the European Council on 4-5 December. If the government's decision were to be negative, however, the UK would certainly not wish to prevent a Community scheme from being established, and any Community member which wanted to join should do so. Britain had participated, fully and constructively, in discussions of the scheme so far, and any criticisms by the British side would not be made from the standpoint of an antagonist. However, if the UK were to join the scheme and then found that she had to devalue, it would undermine the government's efforts to beat inflation and restore the country's economic position.

Andreotti stressed how the EMS had been presented to Italian public opinion as an essential stage in the development of Europe and that this was a crucial factor in the stability of Italy's domestic politics, providing the only common ground between all the parties, including the Communists. This favourable view of the future development of Europe would be improved by the EMS, particularly if all members of the Community were to take part in the scheme from the beginning. There was a significant difference between the EMS and the Snake: when Italy had left the Snake, this had been regarded as a purely technical development, while entry into or departure from the EMS would inevitably be a major political decision.

85 TNA, FCO 30/3901, "Signor Andreotti's Visit to London", Tel. No. 544 by Campbell A., MWE 026/10, 16 November 1978.

The two Prime Ministers also discussed the American attitude towards the EMS. It needed to be made very clear that the scheme was not aimed against the dollar, and Callaghan added that the EMS should lead to a wider development in the monetary field: "with or without the EMS, the time would come when a world monetary system including the dollar would have to be recreated". Andreotti stressed the Italian desire to see a balance and a truly European system which would not reduce itself to a confrontation between the dollar and the deutschmark: this was the main argument of Italy's hope that Britain would eventually join the EMS.[86]

Ten days later, these Italian hopes were to be broken: the British government finally showed its hand just before the Brussels European Council meeting. On 1 December, Callaghan revealed to Andreotti the decision not to join the EMS. He chose a somewhat contorted and cryptic form for his message: "I shall not go to Brussels with a closed mind, but I would not wish to encourage you to think that it is very likely that the United Kingdom will be able to take part in the Exchange Rate Mechanism".[87]

Ambassador Campbell wrote in his memoirs that Pandolfi informed him of Britain's decision not to join before he had heard it from his government. Callaghan had told the Germans, who "passed it on".[88]

Italy was now left without her most valuable ally. The British were in any case quite sure of Italian participation in the project. A memorandum by Callaghan himself a week after Andreotti's visit stressed Italy's favourable political approach to the EMS: it provided the only common ground among all the political parties, including the Communists, and the scheme was generally regarded as an important step towards the kind of Europe which Italy hoped to see. Despite this, in Rome there had been significant reservations about the EMS, but these were left aside after the concession of an optional 6 per cent margin for exchange rate fluctuation and the restoration of the level of 25 billion ECU available to debtors. The main concern regarded the need for greater progress on concurrent studies, so that the EMS would harmonise with the Pandolfi Plan, and Andreotti was

86 TNA, FCO 30/3901, "Prime Minister's discussion with Signor Andreotti on Wednesday 22 November 1978: EMS", 23 November 1978. On the Callaghan-Andreotti meeting see also "Enter Most Surreptitiously (otherwise known as EMS)", *The Economist*, 28 November 1978, pp. 58-59.

87 TNA, FCO 33/3571, "European Council: EMS", Tel. No. 277 by Owen D., WRJ 101/1, 1 December 1978.

88 Campbell A., *Colleagues and friends*, quoted, p. 125.

keen to team up with Britain and Ireland to secure concessions on this front at the European Council.[89]

At the Brussels summit in December, Andreotti announced with displeasure a week-long "pause for reflection", but on 12 December he declared before the Chamber of Deputies that Italy would join the EMS without securing further concessions. Andreotti's "pause for reflection" was a result of the complex political situation. Back in Rome from Brussels, the Prime Minister found that the Banca d'Italia firmly opposed Italian entry, while some of the parties supporting the government were moving strongly in favour. In particular, the small Republican Party, which *The Economist* defined as "the self-appointed conscience of Italian politics",[90] threatened to pull out of the support pact unless Italy joined the EMS immediately, and the Social Democrats and a large part of the DC backed them. The main issue at stake, however, was the Communist Party's opposition to the EMS, which would very probably involve a governmental crisis. The PCI's public criticisms were widely seen as "a trial of strength" to demonstrate the party's influence both to its supporters and to other parties. For this reason, many members of the DC believed that forcing the government to join the EMS would isolate – and humiliate – the Communists.[91] In the end, Andreotti decided that Italy would immediately join the European Monetary System and won by a comfortable majority, despite Communist opposition and Socialist abstention (the PSI wanted to distance itself from the PCI, but had proposed a delayed entry). Such a decision, which was consistent with Italy's traditional European commitment, was to lead to the end of the "national unity" government.

At the end of December, Andreotti sent a message to Callaghan about Italy's choice to join the EMS. The purpose of this note was to emphasise that, although the Italian government had taken a different decision, the spirit of its approach to the EMS was similar to that of the UK. The Foreign Secretary, David Owen, assured Andreotti that there was no British resentment over the Italian government's decision: the reasons for it were well understood. Although he believed that there was rather

89 TNA, CAB 129/204, "European Monetary System: French, Italian and Irish views, Memorandum by the Prime Minister", CP (78) 124, 29 November 1978.

90 "How little Ugo delivered giant Italy up to the snake's jaw", *The Economist*, 16 December 1978.

91 Spaventa L., quoted, p. 87.

more rhetoric than reality about the EMS at present, Owen hoped that the scheme would be successful.[92]

According to Ambassador Campbell, the negotiations leading up to the establishment of the EMS had important and mainly favourable effects on Anglo-Italian relations. Italian and British objectives, although not identical, were near enough for collaboration to advance very closely in negotiating technical aspects and attempting to correct "the grosser inequities" of the Community budget and the Common Agricultural Policy. However, Italy and Britain differed in the attitudes of their respective political parties to European integration, hence their different final decisions over joining the system from its outset. On these premises and despite certain well-known differences of emphasis (for example, on Mediterranean agriculture), there was no reason why the harmonious cooperation established between Italy and the United Kingdom over EEC questions should not be continued, to the advantage of both.[93]

Apart from these optimistic evaluations, the problem of Anglo-Italian partnership during the negotiations on the EMS was twofold and had affected the relations between London and Rome since the 1950s. Firstly, there was the British tendency to downgrade Italy's role and the actual benefits which could derive from closer cooperation with the Italian government, as had already happened during the negotiations for Britain's entry into the EEC; it had happened with the EMS; it was to happen in the following years, as in the case of the negotiations for the Maastricht treaty or during the 2003 Iraq war. This peculiar attitude also had a side-effect: British politicians and officials were inclined to act with superiority when dealing with their Italian counterpart, in a sort of teacher-pupil relationship. However, this treatment was not reserved only for Italians. In the aftermath of the Second World War, British diplomacy had a similar approach even towards the Americans.

Secondly, there were the difficulties for Italian governments of trying to reconcile open allegiance to the European ideal with a more concrete strategy inside the Community, of which an "alliance" with the British could have been a sound move. The fear of being excluded from the European circle on many occasions had prevailed over tactical considerations.[94]

---

92 TNA, FCO 33/3571, "Call by the Italian Ambassador on the Secretary of State", Lever H. to Goodall D., WRJ 020/21, 21 December 1978.

93 TNA, FCO 33/4046, "Annual review on Italy", by Campbell, 10 January 1979.

94 Andreotti wrote in his memoirs that both Giscard and Schmidt telephoned him in early December 1978 urging Italian participation. Andreotti G., *Diari 1976-1979: Gli anni della solidarietà*, Rizzoli, Milano 1981, pp. 287-288.

Also, the language of federalism often spoken by the Italians was barely understood by the British. Italy in 1978 was not viewed in London as a worthy and equal partner: it was considered to be in a petitioning position which Britain wanted to avoid. However, the Italians placed too much faith in the alliance with the British, even when it had become apparent that the UK would not join the system. The year seemed to close with a renewed sense of solidarity between Britain and Italy, which had yet to face the changes on international and domestic levels.

A winter of discontent

The winter of 1978-1979 was to be remembered in Britain as the "winter of discontent", a combination of strikes and surprisingly adverse weather conditions. With its dramatic images of industrial conflict, it has entered the country's mythology and still resonates in people's imagination. It was a turning point in twentieth-century Britain, marking at the same time the end of Labour's historic relations with the trade union movement and the beginning of the Thatcher era.[95]

The "winter of discontent" (a Shakespearian reference to the opening line of *Richard III*) lasted from November 1978 to March 1979. It was the biggest British labour stoppage since 1926: in 1979, almost 30 million working days were lost; on 22 January, the "National Day of Action", 1.5 million public sector employees went on strike.[96]

The first signs of the "winter of discontent" actually showed during the summer of 1978. In July, the Labour government introduced a new guideline for wage rises of 5 %: it was not a legal requirement, although sanctions would be imposed on government contractors who broke that limit. The TUC, conversely, insisted on a return to free collective bargaining. Ford Motor Company made an offer within the government's guidelines, which the workers rejected: by 25 September, 57,000 workers were on official strike. In November, Ford eventually accepted government sanctions and revised their offer to 17 %, which the workers accepted on 22 November. On 13 December, the Commons voted for a withdrawal of the sanctions against Ford: the Conservatives, the Liberals, the Scottish

---

95 Shepherd J., *Crisis? What crisis? The Callaghan government and the British "winter of discontent"*, Manchester University Press, Manchester 2013, pp. 1-7. See also Martin Lopez T., *The Winter of Discontent: Myth, Memory, History*, Liverpool University Press, Liverpool 2014.

96 Beckett A., *When the lights went out*, Faber&Faber, London 2009, p. 465.

Nationalists, the Ulster Unionists, and Labour left-wingers all voted against or abstained. The government was left nearly powerless against any workers who followed the Ford strikers' example.[97]

Quite surprisingly, in October 1978, following the annual Labour Party Conference and in the midst of the Ford strike, two leading Italian politicians – the Republican Ugo La Malfa and the Socialist Bettino Craxi – had praised the Callaghan government for its fruitful relations with the trade unions from the pages of their parties' newspapers. La Malfa spoke in glowing terms of the understanding which existed between government and trade unions in the UK and held this up as an example for Italy:

> [...] Andreotti and the leaders of the parties forming the majority [...] can take an example from a government such as the British Labour government with regard to the strictness, conscientiousness and coherence which are needed to face up to situations such as those in which England and Italy have found themselves in recent years. [...] Although it is to the left, the British Labour government is not composed of amateurs as far the economy is concerned. [...] A comparison with what is happening in Italy reveals the full extent of the distance which separates the two conceptions of government: one which aims at safeguarding the future of the country and at defending general interests whatever the political cost, and the other which appears more and more resigned to gaining time, often pretending to govern, by agreeing to all possible compromises with more or less powerful sector, political and financial interests.[98]

La Malfa referred to this theme again in an interview on Italian television on the evening of 13 October.[99]

Craxi stressed how the British Prime Minister offered assurances regarding the future development of the UK economy but refused to modify the present lines of the economic policy which called for strict

---

97 *Ibidem*, p. 464. In the same weeks, *The Economist* stressed the similarities between Italy and the United Kingdom in wage restraints: during his visit in July 1978 to talk about the EMS, Pandolfi also tried to find out how Britain's austerity measures were working and the Andreotti government was applying this British lesson to the hospital strike that was affecting Italy in October 1978. This new Anglo-Saxon approach brought the Italian government to refuse to cave in after the usual token stoppages for collective bargaining, thus causing a new, protracted stoppage "which urbane, well-dressed Italian union leaders used to deride their British counterparts for having to resort to". "Andreotti's 5 %", *The Economist*, 4 November 1978.

98 "Un confronto aggiornato", *La voce repubblicana*, 13 October 1978.

99 TNA, FCO 33/3570, "Government and trade unions in Italy and the UK", WRJ 020/1, 20 October 1978.

controls. Like La Malfa, the Socialist secretary made some comparison between the situation in Italy and the United Kingdom, although he dwelt on the differences between the Italian and British Left. Being in government, the Labour Party could exercise all the responsibility of political power, while the Left in Italy could only control and condition the government and the political power. If in Britain the government were led by Mrs Thatcher and Labour were relegated to a position of simple Parliamentary support, even Mr Callaghan would be "talking a different language", more similar to that of the Italian Socialists. Craxi concluded that "If Callaghan were in our place he would probably behave like us, and if we were in his place we would probably behave like him".[100] Just two months later, it is very likely that neither Craxi nor any other Italian politicians would have liked to be in Callaghan's place.

With the beginning of 1979, the weather conditions worsened, and Britain became almost paralysed in the grip of ice and snow. On 3 January, an unofficial strike of the Transport and General Workers Union lorry drivers began. The following day, Callaghan left a freezing London to fly to the sunny beaches of Guadeloupe, where the French President Giscard d'Estaing had organised a quadripartite meeting to discuss political and security developments of common concern: the relations with the Soviet Union and China, strategic arms limitation, and the recent events in Iran.[101] It was an unfortunate timing for Callaghan, but the summit had been arranged months before and not going would have been a negative sign for Britain. Despite the difficulties, the Labour government wanted to show that it was still able to govern the nation.

From a British foreign-policy perspective, the meeting was successful; Callaghan also talked one-to-one to Carter about replacing Polaris with Trident. Yet, for Britain's internal policy, the Guadeloupe summit was a watershed: it marked the beginning of Labour's downfall, with an indelible blow which left the Party in opposition for the following eighteen years. Actually, what harmed the Prime Minister's public image most happened just after the quadripartite meeting, when Callaghan went to Barbados for an official visit, and pictures of him swimming and sunning himself circulated in the press. When he returned to Heathrow, being asked in a press conference about the worrying state of the country, Callaghan stated: "I don't think other people in the world will share the view that there is mounting chaos". The *Daily Mail* and the *Sun* famously turned this into

[100] Craxi B., "Callaghan e noi", *Avanti!*, 18 October 1978.

[101] See Chapter 4.

"Crisis? What Crisis?".[102] Almost 40 years on, the phrase is still regularly used to accuse British politicians of complacency.[103] As John Shepherd wrote, "it seemed to put in nutshell an out-of-touch Prime Minister and a hapless government battling trade union power as the temperature of industrial relations in Britain soared".[104]

From that moment on, the unrest seemed unstoppable. For the most part, the strikes were unofficial, more "shapeless and anarchic" than "carefully choreographed, centrally directed 'days of action'".[105] The lorry drivers went on official strike by mid-January, putting essential supplies in danger. The strikes affected all sectors, from transport to the press, from civil servants to Heathrow pilots, from hospital staff to dustmen, from caretakers to gravediggers.

The Italian government carefully monitored the British economic and social situation. Uncertainty about the level of wage demands, in both the public and private sector, and the effects of salary increases on the UK economy – in particular about the trend in inflation, on investment and employment – were subject to careful assessment and increasing interest in Rome. Italian diplomats wondered what measures the British government would adopt in that political climate and in an election year to continue its policy of fighting inflation without compromising the development rate.

The Chancellor of the Exchequer Denis Healey was not optimistic: with an average increase in wages to the extent of 15 per cent, the inflation rate would likely exceed 10 per cent during the next summer, reaching 13 per cent by the end of 1979. The cost of such an increase in the public sector would be around three billion pounds, and could not be supported within the existing financial resources of the government. The latter would, therefore, have to adopt a stricter fiscal policy and reduce the level of public expenditure with predictable negative impact on public services and employment. Healey's statements also revealed a certain determination to adopt a firm attitude towards future wage demands. Observers raised some doubts not only about the reliability of the predictions made by the Chancellor of the Exchequer but also and more importantly about the real willingness and ability of the government to adopt a rigid position. Before the elections, it would be harder to make use of tax measures and

---

102 *Sun*, 11 January 1979. The transcript of Callaghan's press conference can be found in TNA, PREM 16/2050, "Interview with the Prime Minister at Heathrow Airport", 10 January 1979.

103 Beckett A., quoted, p. 484.

104 Shepherd J., quoted, p. 2.

105 Andrew Beckett described it as "the Peasants' Revolt"; Beckett A., quoted, p. 465.

cut public expenditure rather than using the more politically attractive loosening of monetary policy.[106]

The industrial unrest in the United Kingdom dominated all reporting on British affairs in the Italian press throughout January. In the main, this reporting came from London correspondents and in the first half of the month tended simply to catalogue the various disputes. However, towards the end of the month, some correspondents tried to analyse the underlying reasons for the unrest.

On 23 January, the leading financial daily *Il Sole 24 Ore* carried an article by London correspondent Carlo Bassi entitled "Ruin lying just around the corner". Asking whether the cries of alarm were justified, the article stated: "Taking into account the fact that the country's economy is one of the poorest in Europe, that the standard of living is very low, [...] that to the old evil of union militancy is added a tax system designed to kill any initiative and any desire to be productive [...] the answer seems to be an unequivocal yes". The origins of this new "British disease" lay in the problematic and painful transition from the Empire's glory and wealth to the status of "ordinary workers' nation". The article went on to suggest a need to review the whole economic system and quoted Wynne Godley, director of the Department of Applied Economics at London University, who stated that income from North Sea oil was not used to regenerate the economy, but rather to help financing an expansion of imports to feed the consumer boom. The warning of the Governor of the Bank of England Gordon Richardson was also quoted. The article ended with the hope that someone would listen to these calls for change.[107]

On 26 January, the *Corriere della Sera* carried a report by London correspondent Renzo Cianfanelli stating that "Callaghan like Napoleon has been defeated by General Winter". He was forced to beat a retreat by the frost as well as by the strategic mistakes and the intrinsic weaknesses of his minority government. However, the threat to Callaghan came not from the railwaymen or the lorry drivers, who belonged to privileged categories, but from employees in the public sector, agricultural workers, and bank workers. All these groups, whose earnings were considerably below the national average, had been sacrificed in three years of the social contract. Thanks to the well-known discipline of the British in times of crisis, the social contract succeeded in bringing inflation down from 28 % to 8 %. However, while the contract levelled out pay differentials, the

---

106 ASPR, busta 125/A, "L'andamento dell'economia britannica", Ducci R. to Forlani A., 30 January 1979.

107 Bassi C., "La rovina dietro l'angolo", *Il Sole 24 Ore*, 23 January 1979.

device of productivity deals was disproportionately advantageous to the great industrial fiefdoms such as the electrical workers (69 % above the national average) and the miners (32.5 % above). By the end of the three years, the growth of wildcat strikes indicated the gap between underpaid workers and the trade union hierarchy, forcing union leaders to take action and renounce the social contract.[108] The *Corriere della Sera* carried further articles on 3 and 4 February. A front-page headline on 3 February read "Soon England will exceed Italy in the European inflation index", with a trend towards figures closer to those of Third World countries than to those of leading industrial states.[109] On 4 February, the headline was "perhaps the English too will take up the '*scala mobile*'" (automatic wage indexation), but with a new element: the categories of workers benefitting from this new formula would be obliged to sign a no-strike clause. Moreover, Cianfanelli gave a very detailed description of the situation throughout the United Kingdom. In London, many schools had been closed since Christmas, and the pavements were full of rubbish due to the strike of caretakers and dustmen. In Liverpool, the gravediggers' strike brought about a "macabre stocking of rotting corpses"; the Medical Officer of Health speculated that burial at sea would be considered. In the meantime, half of Britain's hospitals were not working properly, accepting only patients in critical conditions.[110]

The FIAT-owned *La Stampa* on 31 January carried an article by London correspondent Mario Ciriello under the title "England's cruel January". There were many reasons for the industrial unrest, but all stemmed from one fact, namely that the United Kingdom was on the edge of the abyss; it was equally irresponsible to deny the existence of a profound malaise. Britain was at the tail end of the industrial nations, and not even North Sea oil had halted the decline. While the Labour government had obtained notable results in the battle against inflation, individual and collective productivity was still insufficient. One reason for this was that incomes were lower and more highly taxed than in the rest of Europe. People were tired of austerity and of waiting for the elusive light at the end of the tunnel. Even if there were to be a change of government before the end of the year, and even if the government were to have a clear majority, there was little hope that a cure would be found for the "English vice" which was

---

108 Cianfanelli R., "L'Inghilterra è quasi in ginocchio ma Callaghan non prende decisioni", *Corriere della Sera*, 26 January 1979.

109 Cianfanelli R., "Presto l'Inghilterra supererà l'Italia nella classifica europea dell'inflazione", *Corriere della Sera*, 3 February 1979.

110 Cianfanelli R., "Anche gli inglesi forse si convertono alla scala mobile", *Corriere della Sera*, 4 February 1979.

a deep-rooted resistance to change. Until this virus could be eliminated, certain imbalances could only get worse. The lesson here was important because certain aspects of it recalled the Italian scene. For thirty years British moderation had permitted the country to overcome adversity and disillusionment without any great upset, but now there was disquiet and impatience. The British wanted more and did not hesitate to ask for it, even if their protest caused disruption to the sick, the elderly, to invalids, and to millions of others. Britain could change only if the minds of the people changed first.[111]

The only articles striking a slightly different note appeared in the two Left-wing parties' newspapers. Gino Bianco, London correspondent of the Socialist daily *Avanti!* (and member of the Bureau of the Socialist International) wrote an article on 29 January entitled "For Callaghan the real problem is inflation". Apart from the dramatization of some events deliberately exaggerated and exploited by the Conservative press, the government's central issue was to impose a limit on inflation through wage constraints. Bianco quoted Roy Hattersley, Secretary of State for Prices and Consumer Protection, in setting out the strategy that the Labour government was going to adopt in the following months: there was no reason to assume that inflation would rise again and trying to anticipate such a rise with massive wage increases would only make reality the most dreaded nightmares.[112]

As for the Communist daily *L'Unità*, it published an article on 31 January by London correspondent Antonio Bronda, who dealt with the line followed by the majority of the British newspapers, which were forecasting disaster by the end of January. Bronda wrote of "deceptive hoaxes" by the commercial and "popular" press, which was not only a matter of style, focussing on the visual impact of slogans and titles, detached from reality. It was a "calculated use of violence" addressed to the workers, the trade unions, and class struggle. The Italian correspondent pointed out that the disaster had not yet happened and went on to claim that many newspapers were unable to avoid the temptation to indulge in sensationalism and to provide news which was an advantage to the Conservative Party whose policy could be described as "the worse it is for them, the better it is for us".[113]

Beyond different political tendencies, the picture of Britain which emerged from Italian press during the "winter of discontent" was that of

111 Ciriello M., "Il crudele gennaio dell'Inghilterra", *La Stampa*, 31 January 1979.
112 Bianco G., "Per Callaghan il vero problema è l'inflazione", *Avanti!*, 29 January 1979.
113 Bronda A., "La stampa inglese e la campagna anti-sciopero", *L'Unità*, 31 January 1979.

a weak country. The "British disease" seemed far from being cured; not even North Sea oil proved to be an effective remedy. There were many references to the Heath government, brought down by the coal miners' strike in February 1974, and to Callaghan's willingness to avoid the same political end. It is not the case that the expression "winter of discontent" was first used during the three-day week, when in the midst of the oil crisis after the Yom Kippur war, electricity for commercial users was limited to three specified consecutive days each week to prolong the life of available fuel stocks. The Italian press was struck by the fact that Heath declared a "state of emergency", while Callaghan refused to do so. Most importantly, the articles of Italian newspapers in those months stressed – with a slightly undisguised pride – that Britain was a poor country, with an inflation rate which was very similar to Italy and likely to overtake it in the months to come.

Concluding, 1978 showed the importance of internal politics both for Italy and the United Kingdom, although with different results. In Rome, the most difficult year in the history of the Republic proved to be the stimulus for more daring initiatives. The immediate entry into the EMS had to be a signal for Italy's partners that allegiance to the European ideal had never been under discussion, despite the difficult economic situation and law and order issues. It was also an early test of the so-called European "external bond": by appealing to international constraints decided in Brussels, the Italian government could pursue harsh economic measures without incurring the opposition of public opinion. The European choice was therefore to become not only a powerful political tool but also a vital element of internal economic policy – and hopefully of Italian recovery.

As for Britain, the impression at home and abroad was of a country in terminal economic decline and on the edge of ungovernability. The "winter of discontent" in 1979 was a pivotal event: the rash of strikes in crucial public services against the Labour government's income policies seemed to show that the country was ungovernable, and destroyed the government's reputation for prudent economic management and its ability to gain the cooperation of the unions. The events of winter 1979 brought the question of British decline back into the limelight, despite Callaghan's attempts to minimise the situation. It was the end of the post-war consensus and paved the way for the Thatcherism of the next eighteen years.

a weak country. The 'British disease' seemed far from being cured, not even North Sea oil proved to be an effective remedy. There were many references to the Heath government, brought down by the coal miners' strike in February 1974, and to Callaghan's willingness to avoid the same political end. It is no coincidence that the expression 'winter of discontent' was first used during the three-day week, when in the midst of the oil crisis after the Yom Kippur war, electricity for commercial users was limited to three specified consecutive days each week to prolong the life of available fuel stocks. The Italian press was struck by the fact that Heath declared a state of emergency, while Callaghan refused to do so. Most importantly, the articles of Italian newspapers in those months stressed – with a slightly undisguised pride – that Britain was a poor country, with an inflation rate which was very similar to Italy and likely to overtake it in the months to come.

Concluding, 1978 showed the importance of internal politics both for Italy and the United Kingdom, although with different results. In Rome, the most difficult year in the history of the Republic proved to be the stimulus for more daring initiatives. The immediate entry into the EMS had to be a signal for Italy's partners of an allegiance to the European ideal had never been under discussion, despite the difficult economic situation and law and order issues. It was also an early use of the so-called 'European external bond': by appealing to international constraints decided in Brussels, the Italian government could pursue harsh economic reforms without incurring the opposition of public opinion. The European option was therefore to become not only a powerful political tool but also a vital element of internal economic policy – and hopefully of Italian recovery.

As for Britain, the impression at home and abroad was of a country in terminal economic decline and on the edge of ungovernability. The winter of discontent in 1979 was a pivotal event: the wave of strikes in crucial public services against the Labour government's income policies seemed to show that the country was ungovernable, and destroyed the government's reputation for prudent economic management and its ability to gain the cooperation of the unions. The wreck of winter 1979 brought the question of British decline back into the limelight, despite Callaghan's attempts to minimise the situation. It was the end of the postwar consensus and paved the way for the Thatcherism of the next eighteen years.

Chapter 4

Goodbye Seventies, welcome Eighties

The "long Seventies" ended with many political similarities between Britain and Italy: in 1979, both countries experienced a government crisis followed by general elections. In the United Kingdom, the Conservative Party came back to power under the leadership of Margaret Thatcher: the future "iron lady" was to stay at 10 Downing Street for eleven years. British voters hoped that her political and economic programme could help the country to leave decline behind. In Italy, the elections of 1979 marked the end of the "national solidarity" and a redefinition of the political scene which would culminate with the creation of the *pentapartito* coalition.

For both countries, there was an evolution of internal politics that also reflected a fast and radical change in the international scenario. The Soviet invasion of Afghanistan in December 1979 swept away any illusion of détente, opening a period of almost unparalleled rivalry and tension between the superpowers.[1] The European continent once again became the focus of the East-West conflict, and both Britain and Italy tried to exploit the new situation for gaining more international prestige. Thatcher would become one of the most reliable allies of the new US president Ronald Reagan, who came to power in January 1981, and the two leaders shared a neo-liberal view.[2] As for Italy, the country confirmed in a few months both its loyalty to the Atlantic alliance (accepting the deployment of "euromissiles") and to the European Community, so joining the Western bloc with renovated credentials. It was also the moment when a clear Western perception of the drift and

---

1 Njølstad O. (ed.), *The Last Decade of the Cold War. From Conflict Escalation to Conflict Transformation*, Frank Cass, London 2004; Leffler M.P., Westad O.A. (eds.), *The Cambridge History of the Cold War, Vol. III Endings*, Cambridge University Press, Cambridge 2010; Garthoff R.L., *Détente and confrontation. American-Soviet Relations from Nixon to Reagan*, The Brookings Institutions, Washington 1985.

2 Greenwood S., "Helping to Open the Door? Britain in the Last Decade of the Cold War", in Njølstad O. (ed.), quoted; Treharne S.-A., *Reagan and Thatcher's Special Relationship*, Edinburgh University Press, Edinburgh 2015; Aldous R., *Reagan and Thatcher: The Difficult Relationship*, Arrow, London 2013.

crisis of Communism emerged, with obvious implications for the policy of the largest Communist Party in Europe – the PCI.[3]

Mrs Thatcher in power

Cyclone Maggie

In Britain, the 1970s entered, and left, to "the sound of Labour governments falling".[4] After the "winter of discontent", on 28 March 1979, the Callaghan government faced a crucial vote of no confidence in Parliament. Surprisingly, the administration was defeated by only one vote (311 to 310) by a disparate coalition of Conservatives, Liberals, Unionists, and Scottish Nationalists. As Tony Benn noted, it was "the end of a memorable day in British politics, the first time that any government has been defeated on a vote of confidence" since 1924, when Ramsay MacDonald was dismissed in similar circumstances.[5]

The reason for this defeat lay in devolution, a problem which had affected the Labour governments throughout the second half of the 1970s. On 1 March 1979, two referenda on devolution were held in Scotland and Wales. While the Welsh voted massively against devolution, in Scotland the "yes" camp won, but a threshold requiring 40 % of the electorate to be in favour was not reached due to low turnout. As a result, the Scottish National Party put down a motion of no confidence; after consulting the Liberal Party, even Thatcher put down an Opposition motion, which took precedence. Callaghan initially miscalculated Labour's advantage in Parliament, even stopping his whips from negotiating for votes until persuaded forcefully by his advisors.[6]

The election was fixed for 3 May, with an unusually long campaign (five weeks) which Callaghan had deliberately arranged in the hope that the memories of the "winter of discontent" could fade. He was proven wrong: with hindsight, another miscalculation after postponing the vote in the summer of 1978. From the start of the campaign, the Conservatives led

---

3 Pons S., "Il socialismo europeo, la sinistra italiana e la crisi del comunismo", in Colarizi S., Craveri P., Pons S., Quagliariello G. (eds.), *Gli anni Ottanta come storia*, Rubbettino, Soveria Mannelli 2004, p. 215.

4 Coates K., "What went wrong?", in *Id.* (ed.), *What went wrong: explaining the fall of the Labour government*, Spokesman Books, Nottingham 2008, p. 7.

5 Benn T., *Conflicts of Interest: Diaries 1977-80*, Arrow, London 1991, p. 478.

6 Shepherd J., "The Fall of the Callaghan Government, 1979", in Heppell T., Theakston K. (eds.), *How Labour Governments Fall*, Palgrave Macmillan, London 2013.

the polls, with an advantage of almost 12 per cent, ultimately reduced to seven points. The Tories won by a majority that allowed no argument: they were 43 seats ahead of all other parties put together, enough to guarantee a full-length parliament. The electoral uncertainty that had characterised British political life since late 1973 had come to an end.[7] There was also another and more fundamental element of Britain's politics to come to an end: the post-war "consensus" was to be replaced by a mixed formula of emphasising free markets with restrained government spending and tax cuts – the essence of Thatcherism.[8]

Thatcher's political rise had attracted Italy's attention since her election as leader of the Conservative Party in February 1975, when she defeated the former Prime Minister Edward Heath. Although the electoral defeat of 1974 was the lowest point for the Tories, since then they showed a slow yet systematic recovery. This favourable course clashed with the depth of the crisis of the Labour government, burdened by the austerity measures they had to approve to face the general economic situation. In 1977 the prospects for the Conservatives to come back to government seemed "considerable" from Rome. Their political strategy was already clear: the Tories were in favour of fair and necessary – although unpopular – measures, as long as they would not be the starting point of a greater intrusion of the State into the life of citizens. The Conservative Party was therefore against indiscriminate nationalisation and thought that public subsidies (only when absolutely necessary and not obtainable through the banking system) were the only acceptable government measure. As for the EC, Thatcher's European vision was "slightly softer" than that of her predecessor Heath and the rest of her party. It was an idea in part close to the French "*Europe des Patries*". Thatcher, however, was personally in favour of direct elections to the European Parliament, even if she feared that the breaking up of centre and right-wing forces could pave the way for the creation of a dominant socialist-communist bloc inside the Community. For this reason, the Tories would try to increase

7 Butler D., Kavanagh D., *The British general election of 1979*, Macmillan, Basingstoke 1980, p. 338.

8 Lawson N., *The View from No. 11: Memoirs of a Tory Radical*, Bantam, London 1992, p. 64. On Thatcher's years see the extensive two-volume biography by Moore C., *Margaret Thatcher: The Authorized Biography – Vol. 1 and 2* (Penguin, London 2014 and 2016); the two volumes by Campbell J., *Margaret Thatcher – Vol. 1 and 2* (Jonathan Cape, London 2000 and 2007); Vinen R., *Thatcher's Britain. The Politics and Social Upheaval of the 1980s*, Simon & Schuster, London 2009.

relations with the DC in Italy, as they had already done with the German Christian Democrats.[9]

The first direct contact with the future Prime Minister happened in June 1977, when Thatcher visited Italy as Leader of the Opposition.[10] The visit was part of the strategy to avoid fragmentation of the centre-right forces and to secure strong participation in the project for the European Democratic Union (EDU).[11] The most valuable meeting was with Aldo Moro, "the person at the centre of the policy-making of the [DC] – even more than Prime Minister Andreotti". Moro accepted the broad purposes of EDU Mrs Thatcher outlined to him, and only saw difficulties within the compass of the extremely complex Italian political scene.[12] According to Thatcher, one of the main obstacles to overcome was the choice of the name: "We have grown used to [being called the Conservatives], but I am fully aware that when translated into other languages, the word Conservative acquires completely different overtones. In Italian, for example, it is a term of criticism". That could certainly be a hindrance to cooperation between parties, but it was necessary to concentrate attention on the common ground which existed between the British Conservative Party, and the Christian Democrats and other centre-right parties in Europe.[13]

By March 1979, two weeks before Callaghan's defeat in the House of Commons, the Italian embassy in London was speculating on the chances

9 ASPR, busta 697/B3, "Colloquio di V.E. con la signora Thatcher, leader del Partito conservatore britannico", 22 June 1977.

10 On Thatcher's Tory leadership before 1979 see Caines E., *Heath and Thatcher in Opposition*, Palgrave Macmillan, London 2017.

11 The project for a European anti-socialist alliance (a "European Democrat Party") was formulated by the Tory Shadow Cabinet in 1975. Thatcher met with Helmut Kohl in 1975 and again in 1976 to address the CDU Congress, where she called for "an effective working alliance" of centre and centre-right parties: Thatcher Archive, CCOPR 544/76; Conservative Party Archive (CPA), CCO/508/8/21, "Conservative in Europe", 1979. The European Democratic Union officially came into being in Salzburg in April 1978. See Johansson K.M., "The alliance of European Christian democracy and conservatism: convergence through networking", in Kaiser W., Starie P., *Transnational European Union: Towards a Common Political Space*, Routledge, London 2005.

12 CPA, IDU 34-1, 27 June 1977; "Il leader dei conservatori inglesi cerca alleanza nella DC italiana", *Il Corriere della Sera*, 25 June 1977. In the end, the Italian Christian Democrats did not join the EDU.

13 TNA, FCO 33/3215, "Europe as I see it", The RT. Hon. Margaret Thatcher, M.P. Leader of the Opposition, Speaking at the Centro Italiano di Studi per la Conciliazione Internazionale, Rome, Conservative Central Office News Service, 664/77, 24 June 1977.

for the Tories to win a substantial majority in the upcoming elections. The future of the Labour government was doomed by the end of the social contract with the trade unions, and Britain's political and economic climate was likely to be radically changed. Thatcher's personality was now defining her party's look, despite some dissent about how to reconcile ideals with the economic and social heritage of the Labour government.

After the traumatic leadership challenge in 1975, the main opposition party looked quite hesitant, disunited and virtually powerless. The growing difficulties that Callaghan had to face brought Thatcher into the limelight and made her gain prestige and greater tactical skills without having to modify her programme. Ambassador Ducci stressed how her "petty bourgeoisie environment" gave a new shape to the Conservative Party. Thatcher was reproached with her excessive care for the way she dressed and for her overly-refined eloquence: both indicated "an apparent self-righteousness" which clashed with her violent and dogmatic political ideas. Her apparent intent was restoring the nation's trust in the traditional pillars of British democracy, which were shaken by the downsizing of Britain's financial skills and international responsibilities in the aftermath of the Second World War. Thatcher was offering to the public opinion the rediscovery of Christian moral values in family, school and foreign policy, the reaffirmation of free initiative in the economy and the celebration of state authority and patriotism; she even re-evaluated the Victorian era. In this way, Thatcher renounced Heath's progressive dirigisme to please many voters; yet, this new ideological format had given the party a doctrinaire and populist stance, with some crusade-like tones that were unrelated to its tradition. On the other hand, Labour's government experience required a viable, pragmatic approach.

As for Thatcher's political programme, her guidelines seemed already well-defined to the Italian ambassador. In the economy, the Tories intended to restore a "society of incentives" based on private initiative and market forces, according to Hayek and Friedman. This would imply, after many years of rigid incomes policy, the return to free collective bargaining in the private sector, a vigorous monetary policy, the reduction of government intervention in the economy to a minimum and the progressive de-nationalisation of many firms, together with the downsizing of state economic authorities. Other priorities would be the reinforcement of law and order and closer controls on immigration. As for the international scenario, the Tories intended to re-establish the military credibility of the country, while pursuing a more active diplomacy and coordination among the activities of the EC, NATO, and the Commonwealth. A strong reaffirmation of the European vocation of the party would mean a constructive, albeit critical, participation in the integrationist project.

There were still doubts whether the productive structures, the country's social situation and the international environment could adequately respond to the stimuli of the new Tory policy. However, the Italian embassy stressed how the uncertainties about such radical projects had decreased, partly because of the growing public approval and partly because of Thatcher's reassurance that this new course would be gradual. The Tory leader had to face the uneasy task of trying to reconcile the party's soul, inflexible on principles and represented by politicians like Keith Joseph, with its mind, prone to compromise and embodied by William Whitelaw and Francis Pym, the One Nation centre still close to Heath's vision. As for the former Prime Minister, a rapprochement seemed very unlikely, in consideration of his self-marginalisation.

The greatest concern for Italy was the radicalisation of Britain's political life: two years of unusually harsh political campaigning and a profound economic and social crisis had amplified the dichotomy between the Labour left and the Conservative right, while the country needed "to find the middle way that best suited British character again".[14]

The Italian press covered the British elections with attention and curiosity. Two days before the vote, *Il Corriere della Sera* analysed "cyclone Maggie", a phenomenon which could either bewitch or frighten with its raging against the British system. Mrs Thatcher was against dependency culture and income levelling, against the trade unions, against "Labour moral indulgence" as a cause of Britain's decay. In contrast, Callaghan and his party were blaming "lazy Tory morality" for the decline of the country. The United Kingdom had not seen such an underlying dispute since 1945 when the debate about British economic decay began:

> In the beginning, it seemed a temporary malaise, due to the end of the Empire and privileged markets. But thirty years have passed, and other nations had prospered without the protection of colonial markets. Then it was time to blame the heavy burden of the pound, a reserve currency with no means to remain so. But now the Deutsche Mark and the yen have taken the pound's place. Then it was time to blame the limit of an insular market, outside the Common Market and far from the Commonwealth. But Britain entered the Common Market a long time ago. Finally, it was time to blame the scarcity of raw materials, after the decline of coal. But now Britain has North Sea oil.

With her look of a "common Chelsea lady", Thatcher was now simply blaming taxes, "old news" with which even the Labour government seemed

14 ASPR, busta 125A, "La signora Thatcher e la sua filosofia politica", Ducci R. to Forlani A., 13 March 1979.

to agree. Therefore, 3 May would be remembered as the "tax cutters' elections". The outcome could be troublesome since the voters could be tempted by a break with tradition.[15]

The Italian press placed great emphasis on the fact that the British democratic system proved its efficiency: "The British government crisis opened after that in Rome but the UK has had a new Prime Minister for the past two days while the Italian electoral campaign is only just beginning and the type of government which will emerge from it is only a hypothesis of futurologists".[16]

As regards the election result, most Italian newspapers considered the Conservative victory in Britain as symptomatic of a general swing to the right in Europe. There was also a feeling that a Conservative government meant the end of British hesitations over the EC. Indeed, *Il Sole 24 Ore* reported optimism in Brussels that Britain's entry into EMS was now imminent; the strengthening of the pound in the latest months could make abandoning monetary isolation easier.[17] The fact that for the first time in a European democracy a woman had become head of government also attracted interest. Thatcher – the "grocer's daughter who took the place of Churchill" – was now welcomed as the "second Queen of England".[18]

Comments by Italian politicians, on the whole, dealt with the European dimension. In an editorial, the Christian Democrat daily *Il Popolo* commented "the United Kingdom, which always remains a point of reference of the first order in the evolution of an advanced industrial society, seems to have decided to meet the inevitable problems of the next five years with a government which is committed to restoring order – economic, social and political – correcting some tendencies which on the whole are considered negative and dangerous". According to Andreotti, Labour's reservations on Europe, which prevented Callaghan from "moving quickly into the Community and joining the EMS", were the first cause of their defeat.[19] Luigi Granelli, director of the Foreign Affairs Department of the DC, commented that Thatcher's victory was a turning point in the British political scene and would bring new elements to

---

15 Cianfanelli R., "Il ciclone Maggie", *Corriere della Sera*, 1 May 1979.

16 Rizzo A., "Tra Roma e Londra", *La Stampa*, 6 May 1979.

17 Piccione U., "L'Inghilterra dei Tories forse entra nello SME", *Il Sole 24 Ore*, 5 May 1979.

18 Cianfanelli R., "La figlia del droghiere ha preso il posto di Churchill", *Corriere della Sera*, 5 May 1979.

19 "Andreotti: i laburisti pagano anche lo scarso europeismo", *Corriere della Sera*, 6 May 1979.

the foreign policy of the country. The dynamic Tory leader would need to learn from the mistakes of her predecessor and choose a flexible and prudent strategy to face Britain's unresolved problems: the economic crisis, trade unions' inflexibility, the terrorist threat, and the weakness of welfare. As for the EC dimension, it was well known that the Tories were more pro-European than Labour, but relations inside the European Parliament could still be complicated.[20]

Not surprisingly, a different tone could be found in the PCI daily *L'Unità*. Thatcher's election was indeed a turning point in British politics, and she represented the "hope for a new climate of entrepreneurial confidence"; yet, the Communist paper focused on the many uncertainties about her programme. Thatcher was not a "cyclone": she had been repeating for two years her willingness to "reduce the State", but it was "the same chimera that Heath embraced". Foreign policy would be her real testing ground, to show the gap "between the extremist statements of Tory propaganda and the diplomatic line" of the new government.[21]

The PSI daily *Avanti!* was, if possible, even more critical towards the new British Prime Minister. On the eve of the election, the newspaper stressed the uncertainty of the results, with a slight Labour lead. With Thatcher's victory, "Britain could break two records: being the first European country with a woman as Prime Minister, and giving birth to the most reactionary government of the century". Thatcher was "almost unbearably unscrupulous" and epitomised bourgeois and Victorian England, which considered Labourism as the devil's product. The United Kingdom "went back while trying to change" and even Anglo-American relations would be strained by the new Conservative government.[22]

No longer the top of the class?

There was genuine curiosity in Italy about the realisation of Thatcher's programme, not least because, just one month after the elections, the question of British decline was brought back to the limelight once again

---

20 "Elementi di novità in politica estera", *Il Popolo*, 5 May 1979.

21 Bronda A., "Ma la Thatcher può realizzare il suo programma?", *L'Unità*, 6 May 1979; *Id.*, "Signora Thatcher e adesso che ha vinto?", *L'Unità*, 10 May 1979; *Id.*, "La politica estera primo scoglio per la Thatcher", *L'Unità*, 9 May 1979.

22 Bianco G., "Con la Thatcher Londra rischia il rischio del buio", *Avanti!*, 3 May 1979; *Id.*, "Londra va indietro cercando di cambiare", *Avanti!*, 5 May 1979; *Id.*, "Diffidenza e timore verso la Thatcher: alla prova i rapporti speciali Londra-Washington", *Avanti!*, 8 May 1979.

with the case of the "Henderson despatch". Sir Nicholas Henderson, British Ambassador to Paris, in his valedictory despatch leaving the French post, gave quite a discouraging portrait of the United Kingdom in the world scenario. Britain still ranked among the great powers immediately after the War, and in the mid 1950s it was still the strongest European power militarily and economically. It was British decline in comparison to the other European partners since then that had been so marked, so that Britain was not only no longer a world power, but was not in the first rank even as a European power. Besides economic issues, the weakness of British foreign policy was blatant: the United Kingdom was no longer able to influence events because it did not have the power or will to do so. The special relationship with the United States had declined in comparison with relations between Washington and Bonn or Paris. As regards Europe, for the first time for centuries British policy could not be based upon preventing other powers from dominating the continent because, out of weakness, the UK would be unable to do this. Britain had continued too long to try to play a world role and "failed to cut [its] coat according to [its] cloth".[23] The document, however harsh in its assessments, would have been nothing more than a paper circulating in Whitehall and among British Embassies; the scandal happened when the despatch leaked to the British press a few weeks later during the General Election campaign, to the great displeasure of the Labour Party. It certainly did not praise the departing Callaghan government. Moreover, after the election, the document was published in near entirety in *The Economist* of 2 June 1979.[24]

The Italian newspapers broadly commented on the document, stressing how the United Kingdom could be overtaken in GDP per head by Italy and Spain in less than 20 years. The crisis was so blatant that the despatch could be leaked by one or more Foreign Office diplomats, anxious to make the public aware of the "British disease" and urge the new administration to "farsighted efforts". In any case, Britain was no longer "the top of the class".[25] Most of the press, moreover, was struck by how Henderson had been rewarded. The diplomat wrote the despatch because

---

23 TNA, FCO 33/3941, WRF 020/1, "Britain's decline; its causes and consequences", 31 March 1979.

24 *The Economist* wrote: "The despatch does not, needless to say, reach us from him and was presumably written for very limited circulation. But it is so unusually forthright and timely, particularly in its middle and concluding passages on British policy in Europe, under governments of every stripe, as to merit publication virtually in full". *The Economist*, 2 June 1979.

25 Ciriello M., "L'Inghilterra non è più la prima della classe", *La Stampa*, 3 June 1979.

he thought he was going to retire; instead, Thatcher invited him to return to service as Ambassador to Washington, where he remained until 1982 (a position first offered to Heath, but he refused). The *Corriere della Sera* noted that, apparently, Carrington agreed on that "unpleasant opinion" of Britain's place in the world; however, it was "still a mystery how the Tory government [could] make British society more dynamic and vital".[26]

Despite this unpromising scenario, the first assessment by the Italian embassy in London stressed that Thatcher's foreign policy was unambiguous, and the contrast with Callaghan seemed striking. The judgement on the former Labour government was quite unforgiving:

> [It] waver[ed] between an American and a European choice, between Europeanism and anti-Europeanism, between an ideological favour for détente and an ideological enhancement of human rights, between the need for Africa to remain loyal to the principles of decolonisation and liberation and the need of sound temperaments to realise a flexible procedure.

For the Italian Ambassador, this fluctuation resulted in a perceived inability to find effective solutions: the special relationship with the United States contributed, thanks to Callaghan's mediation, to smoothing the friction between Carter and some European leaders, but Britain did not gain much from this intermediary role, while the confrontation with Brussels grew stronger. In the meantime, the relations with Eastern Europe were unproductive on both the diplomatic and the economic side; notwithstanding, the United Kingdom showed no willingness to strengthen NATO military deployment.

In Ducci's view, in comparison with a "confused Labour strategy", permeated by ideological contradictions, Thatcher's politics looked like a clear formula: "détente but from a strong position". This method had several implications. Firstly, in their relations with the United States, the Conservatives did not want to play the role of the "brilliant second" often pursued by Owen and even Callaghan with Carter. Without falling back into Heath's anti-Americanism, the Tories were trying to create a complementary relationship with Washington: in the Middle East, this would mean acting autonomously either alone or in the context of the

---

26 Cianfanelli R., "Tra 20 anni Italia e Spagna supereranno la Gran Bretagna", *Corriere della Sera*, 3 June 1979. Lord Carrington asked Henderson to take over in Washington from Peter Jay, Callaghan's son-in-law. Henderson's period in Washington, from 1979 to 1982, proved to be the most important and by far the most demanding of his career, especially during the Falkland war, when he was successful in putting the British side of the Falklands War in 1982. See his obituary in *The Telegraph*, 16 March 2009.

European Political Cooperation to develop further agreement between Israel and Egypt. As for the SALT, Britain's approval was not blind; it came after a thorough examination. This, however, did not mean weaker relations between London and Washington: Thatcher knew exceptionally well that the American privilege increased Britain's weight in Europe. Secondly, the more precise definition of Tory politics did not turn into curt and harried methods but was instead shown in professional, rational, and calculated schemes.

According to the Italian embassy, this combination of doctrine and practice reflected the mix of personal approaches of the two main characters of British foreign policy. The relationship between Thatcher and Carrington was very different from the way of working of their predecessors; Callaghan and Owen used to apply a clear division of roles, with the former supervising general issues and the latter focusing every time on a particular problem. As for their styles, despite some ethical and sociological similarities between Mrs Thatcher and Callaghan, nothing could diverge more than Owen's optimism and Carrington's "patrician disenchantment". Ducci did not review positively the behaviour of the Labour Foreign Secretary: too ambitious, vigorous and Kennedy-like, Owen saw the Foreign Office serving as a springboard for the party leadership. In contrast, Carrington was quite detached and not careerist at all, not ostentatious and "almost colourless", deliberately ironic and admired for his professional commitment, with no ideological prejudices (nor hobbies, as stressed by the Italian ambassador). Lord Carrington belonged to a proper Britain heritage and had already been able to soften some of Thatcher's hardness; he looked "like a man who would be included in the best tradition of Foreign Secretaries".[27] For *L'Espresso*, Carrington was the opposite of "iron" Thatcher: a flexible man resolved not to distance himself from reality but to take into consideration also the needs of his interlocutors and adversaries. For this reason, the weekly indicated him as the most likely Prime Minister of the coalition government which could be born from the alliance of Conservatives and Lib-Dem after the next elections.[28]

In the autumn of 1980, two visits – by the Queen in October (her first since 1961) and Thatcher in November – gave the opportunity for Italian diplomacy to make an appraisal of the Conservative government after a year and a half in power. From the Italian documents emerges a

---

27 ASPR, busta 125A, "La politica estera del governo Thatcher: modalità e protagonisti", Ducci R. to Forlani A., 19 July 1979.

28 Gambino A., "L'Europa? D'accordo, ma senza illusioni", *L'Espresso*, 11 October 1981.

sharp contrast between Britain's successes in foreign policy and her poor economic results.

According to the new Ambassador in London, Andrea Cagiati, Mrs Thatcher gained a freedom of action objectively even greater than the one secured by a comfortable majority in Parliament. This was due to three factors: firstly, the paralysis of the Labour opposition, which was prey to a form of ideological self-destruction and unable to elaborate a coherent strategy. The party seemed to split into two different fronts: an "apocalyptic maximalism", unjustified even to the most progressive voters; and a social democratic centrism not appealing to militants. In such a situation, the future leader – either Callaghan, Healey or a third compromise candidate – would need some time to reshape a feasible opposition to Thatcher without falling into an idealistic furore. Secondly, the trade unions looked quite bewildered after the successes of the 1970s and were now afraid that their members would not follow in a new battle against a government that was neutralising their political strength. Cagiati described the trade unions as a "timid and unstable giant who doesn't know any more if his enormous weight is still made of muscles"; even without muscles, that giant could still crush a government with his weight, but the Labour Party was not the political point of reference for the TUC. Lastly, the Conservative Party lacked credible alternative leaders.[29]

In this internal scenario, the Italian Ministry of Foreign Affairs reported that recession was still haunting British economy. The gross national product was still decreasing (it fell 1.5 per cent in the second quarter of the year). Even industrial production declined in all sectors, losing 4 per cent compared to 1979 (the textile industry alone fell 11 per cent). The CBI expected for 1980 a reduction of industrial production between 6.5 and 7 per cent, thus equalling the negative record of the 1975 recession.[30] The Conservatives' economic policy had only partially fulfilled the electoral program of the spring of 1979. In Cagiati's view, the United Kingdom was far from that "economic revolution" championed by Thatcher. The government's strategy considered heavy social costs inevitable, in a temporary reorganisation of the economy, but there had been many problems in reaching the fundamental goal of the containment of public spending. Despite the hard cuts in the Education and Health sectors, there was no satisfactory result overall. Local authorities seemed reluctant

29 ASPR, busta 887/B8, "Viaggio Regina Elisabetta in Italia – politica interna britannica", Tel. No. 1134, firmato Cagiati A., Riservato, 9 October 1980.

30 ASPR, busta 713/B3, "Rapporti economici bilaterali anglo-britannici", November 1980.

in following the government line for reducing costs and personnel. In the short term, therefore, there was going to be no "reason for comfort".[31]

Conversely, as for British foreign policy, the Italian Ambassador stressed how the Conservative government was more successful, being able to solve two issues inherited from its predecessor: the Rhodesian problem and the budget question in the EC. On both occasions, Carrington showed the traditional qualities of British diplomacy: a stubborn determination to pursue his goals, the ability to switch between hardness and openness, and a remarkable intuition about finding the best external support. In the aftermath of this triumphant first phase, Carrington had now to face a harder task, that is improving Britain's global role, bringing her back to East of Suez while integrating into the most important fora in the Western world. Cagiati reported that, in this strategy, from a Tory point of view, East-West and North-South relations had no particular importance; for this reason, ties with Moscow and the Third World were moved to the background ("London prefer[red] armed peace to détente"). What mattered most were trade links and the relations with Brussels and Washington; the United Kingdom aspired to be part of both the Western directorate and of the European directorate. That had also been a Labour goal, although Callaghan followed a different path: the former Foreign Secretary used to move from the United States to reach Europe. As seen from Italy, Callaghan was Carter's "right-hand man" in the Third World; drawing upon this close collaboration, he liked to present himself to Giscard and Schmidt as the European voice of the American president and as a politician able to soften Carter's ideological biases in East-West relations. In contrast, the Tories' coldness towards the Third World and their preference for traditional diplomatic tools (more efficient and yet less Carter-like) cooled the Anglo-American understanding down. For the Italians, the relationship between London and Washington did not seem special any longer.

Moreover, Cagiati thought that Britain's intransigent position on détente widened the gap with France and West Germany: Giscard and Schmidt looked quite suspiciously at any policy which could encourage the United States to extremism. There seemed to be no easy solution for the Thatcher government, and Carrington could only try to avoid any drastic choice between the American alliance and the Franco-German axis. Opting for one of the shores of the Atlantic over the other would just

31 ASPR, busta 887/B8, "Viaggio Regina Elisabetta in Italia – politica economica e rapporti economici italo-britannici", Tel. No. 1123, firmato Cagiati A., 7 October 1980.

be to the detriment of the United Kingdom, which would distance itself from Washington while getting stuck in an unsatisfying European policy.

According to the Italian Embassy in London, therefore, in this second phase, Thatcher's foreign policy showed some indecision about which methods to adopt, and the Labour opposition was too weak to put any pressure on the government. The European allies could be more helpful, but both France and Germany did not want to play any special role for Britain. In this scenario, there could be some place for Italy: the government in Rome could decide "if, and to what extent, it would be useful to play the British card, especially in Community matters". There was the basis for a successful outcome: Italy's positive results in Brussels were a heritage to exploit in the weeks to come, provided that the government could give the British the impression of a clear and constant policy.[32] As we will see, the European dimension would be a pivotal element for Italy not only in improving relations with London but also in creating a new dynamic phase in foreign policy.

First hints of recovery

The end of the national solidarity

After two and a half years of relative, if precarious, stability under Andreotti's Prime Ministership, Italy seemed to have returned once more to the political unease and uncertainty which characterised much of the previous decade. The political truce had started to waver in the early autumn of 1978 when the PCI accused Andreotti of a change in political direction since the death of Moro. By December, the Communists had broken ranks with the majority and voted against the government on two occasions, firstly because of the immediate entry of Italy into the EMS and secondly because of the nomination of new chairmen of major public bodies. The Communist withdrawal from the majority provoked the longest period of government crisis in post-war Italian history, which was finally resolved with the formation of the Cossiga government in August 1979. A more detailed analysis is therefore required, to have an account of the complexities of the Italian political scene and its insightful interpretation by British diplomacy and the Foreign Office.

---

32 ASPR, busta 887 B8, "Visita Regina Elisabetta in Italia – politica estera britannica: tendenze generali", Tel. No. 1121, firmato Cagiati A., Riservatissimo, 7 October 1980.

By the beginning of 1979, the Parliamentary majority on which Andreotti's minority government depended for support began to look increasingly fragile. Although a government crisis did not yet appear to be imminent, the PCI had started an offensive which could lead to the break-up of the majority. Campbell thought that the Communists were divided on how to proceed: according to the polls, their popularity was suffering from an alliance with the government, and there was an impulse to dissociate themselves from the Cabinet; but too much dissociation could lead to an early election, the results of which they feared.[33]

Over time, however, the PCI decided that early elections were a "lesser evil" than continued association with the government majority.[34] On 26 January, the Communist Party announced its withdrawal from the parliamentary majority. Five days later, Andreotti handed his resignation to the President of the Republic, thus formally opening a period of political "crisis". As viewed from London, the Communists' move originated from their being "trapped in association with government policy but without any real increase in power"; they had, therefore, felt obliged to provoke a change in advance of their party congress in March, when Berlinguer and other moderates in the leadership would otherwise have come under heavy attack.[35] One new factor was the attitude of the Socialists. Their recent local election results did not confirm the upward trend that was apparent in the middle of 1978. Conversely, they expected to do well in the European elections to be held in June and were concentrating all their efforts on this objective. As confirmed by Andreotti's diplomatic adviser La Rocca, in these circumstances Craxi could be willing to move some way away from the Communists in the Parliament to avoid having a national election before the European one. If so, this could point the way to the reconstitution of an Andreotti government with socialist abstention and communist opposition, or even with socialist support and communist abstention. Anyway, the crisis would take a long time to be resolved, but without causing "disquiet to Italy's allies and partners".[36]

In the following weeks, the crisis did indeed worsen: Andreotti failed in his first round of consultations and, in an attempt to overcome this impasse, Pertini gave a mandate to the President of the Republican Party

33 TNA, FCO 33/4047, Tel. No. 56 by Campbell A., WRJ 014/2, 22 January 1979.
34 TNA, FCO 33/4047, Tel. No. 70 by Campbell A., WRJ 014/2, 26 January 1979.
35 "Italian Communists risk losing workers' support", *Daily Telegraph*, 10 February 1979.
36 TNA, FCO 33/4047, Tel. No. 80 by Campbell A., WRJ 014/2, 1 February 1979.

Ugo La Malfa.[37] It was the first time that a "lay" (i.e. non-Christian Democrats) candidate had been asked to attempt to form a government in Italy since the war, apart from a brief exploratory mandate which was given to Pertini himself, as President of the Chamber of Deputies, in 1968. The choice of 75-year-old La Malfa was favourably received by the political parties, though DC reactions were mixed.[38] Eventually, even La Malfa gave up the attempt to form a government, although the PCI had moderated its demands, by offering to settle for the inclusion of representatives of the independent left who had been elected on the Communist list.

Pertini's next move was the joint appointment of Andreotti, La Malfa and the veteran Social Democrat and former President of the Republic, Giuseppe Saragat, for a final attempt at forming a government. The PCI insisted on several unacceptable conditions, such as the Communist right of veto over the choice of all ministers and the participation of the Communists in certain regional councils. It was too high a price to pay, and Andreotti was left with no alternative but to cobble together a three-party government, his fifth, presented on 20 March, which he knew would risk defeat on a vote of confidence because it had no prearranged majority. The Communists were sure to oppose it, and the only acceptable chance of survival (since Andreotti had announced that he would not accept the support of the extreme right) lay in the possibility of abstention by the Socialists. The sudden death of La Malfa on 29 March left no possible excuse for the PSI to support the government. In the event, the Socialists were unwilling to disassociate themselves in this way from the PCI, and the government was defeated in the Senate on 31 March, by one vote (just like Callaghan). This precipitated the dissolution of Parliament and left Andreotti in charge of a stillborn administration whose primary task would be to manage elections, both national and European.[39]

It was not easy to understand such "political suicide" or "hara-kiri".[40] *The Economist* caustically commented that "it [was] pure Pirandello. [...] As in Britain three days before, the government's defeat was by a margin of one vote. But, unlike Britain's, nothing would have dismayed Italy's

37 "Non-Christian Democrat may be Italy Premier", *Financial Times*, 22 February 1979; "Outsider tipped to lead Italy", *The Guardian*, 22 February 1979.

38 TNA, FCO 33/4047, Tel. No. 117 by Campbell A., WRJ 014/2, 22 February 1979.

39 TNA, FCO 33/4048, "The fourth and the fifth Andreotti Governments, March 1978 to March 1979", Campbell A. to Owen D., 30 April 1979.

40 See TNA, FCO 33/4048, Tel WTGR0727 from the Canadian embassy in Rome, 2 April 1979.

government more than winning; Mr Andreotti's relief at being thrown out of office was plain to all".[41]

Apart from the Andreotti government, the crisis made another victim: the historic compromise. The PCI's policy since 1973 proved to be a failure. On paper, the historic compromise remained the strategy of the party, but it no longer necessarily meant that the Communists had to enter a coalition government. As Berlinguer remarked during the fifteenth PCI Congress in March-April 1979, there was a clear distinction between the historic compromise (which was reminiscent of Togliatti's strategy) and the policy of national solidarity: the latter had been broken by the Christian Democrats, who wanted to defend by any means their "system of power".[42]

According to Luciano Barca, Berlinguer's secretary, the historic compromise meant the acceptance of the Communist Party as a party of constitutional dignity; thus, it embraced the idea of the Communists both coming to power with the Christian Democrats and the Socialists, or alternating in power with the Christian Democrats. After the election, the PCI would ask to join in a government of national emergency with the Christian Democrats; if excluded, they would go into opposition. There was going to be no middle way. Barca insisted that opposition would be of a "constructive" kind and that the party had learned from its two and a half years close to the government. The prospect of a moderate Communist opposition recouping its lost votes was intended to worry the DC, and the Communists even seemed well-disposed towards the Socialist for a new left-wing alliance – although the PSI had "rarely been so anti-Communist" as at the time.[43]

British diplomacy interpreted this change of policy and the return of the PCI to a role of "responsible" opposition as an able orchestration by Berlinguer. In British view, it seemed clear that he had decided at the outset to have a showdown with the other parties of the majority. Communist manoeuvring in the initial stages of the crisis was merely an attempt to put the blame for provoking elections on to others. According to Campbell, Berlinguer no doubt hoped that the forthcoming government would run into political and economic difficulties; in that situation, the PCI could expect to recover any ground lost in the elections and events could lend force to the argument that Italy was ungovernable without Communist

41 "The government that didn't want to live", *The Economist*, 7 April 1979.

42 See Barca L., *Cronache dall'interno del vertice del PCI Vol. 3: La crisi del PCI e l'effetto domino*, Rubbettino, Soveria Mannelli 2005, pp. 769-782.

43 "*Ciao, ciao*, compromesso", *The Economist*, 7 April 1979.

help. The Communists could also hope that their demand to introduce their ministers in the government ("which remain[ed] the main objective of their historic compromise policy) would prove "irresistible".[44]

After one of the longest electoral campaign, the results of June 1979 partly confirmed the expectations and fears of the parties: the Christian Democrats performed well even though they did not increase their share of the vote, while the Socialists gained several seats but did not improve their percentage. British attention focused on the two most noteworthy features of the results: on the one hand, the Communists lost four per cent, and it was the first time they had lost ground in a general election since the war. Although "the myth of their inexorable advance ha[d] thus been broken", they remained above the psychologically important threshold of 30 per cent. In contrast, the smaller parties registered the most significant gains. The Italian electorate did not give the politicians any great shocks, but it gave no-one a vote of confidence.[45]

In the meantime, Alan Campbell left Rome – and the diplomatic service – in June 1979; with him, Italy unquestionably lost a valuable and uncommon interpreter of its politics and society, able to understand the complexities of a country so difficult to comprehend from outside. After all, as Campbell wrote in his valedictory despatch, "it is hard to take a very sanguine view of the health of Italian democracy if one judges it by the standards of the rest of Western Europe. Perhaps it is better to think of the Italian political scene more in terms of 18th century England when political patronage was such an important factor".[46] His successor, Ronald Arculus, was less well-disposed towards Italy.

As correctly predicted by Campbell, the new government was not likely to be formed until shortly before the start of the Italian summer break.[47] The good showing of the smaller centre parties could make it marginally easier to create a stable coalition in the centre leaving the Communists in opposition, but such a government would lack a majority without the support of the PSI. After several attempts by Andreotti, Craxi (the first Socialist ever to

---

44 TNA, FCO 33/4048, "The fourth and the fifth Andreotti Governments, March 1978 to March 1979", Campbell A. to Owen D., 30 April 1979.

45 TNA, FCO 33/4049, "Italian general election: 3/4 June", Tel No. 190 by Campbell A., WRJ 014/2, 5 June 1979.

46 TNA, FCO 33/4051, "Some impressions on leaving Italy", by Campbell A., Foreign and Commonwealth Office Diplomatic Report No. 158/79, WRJ 014/4, 28 June 1979.

47 TNA, FCO 30/4048, "Italian political situation", Saving Tel. No. 11 by Campbell A., 28 June 1979.

be given a mandate) and the Treasury Minister Pandolfi, public opinion seemed "bemused and not a little disgusted with the continuing failure of Italian politicians to put national interests before party advantage".[48] Then, by early August, another Christian Democrat, Francesco Cossiga, emerged as something of a surprise choice. His government was a coalition of DC, PSDI, PLI and two independent "technicians", and the Socialists considered it sufficiently different from its predecessor to allow them to abstain – and therefore to guarantee its political survival.

From its formation, the Cossiga government was regarded as little more than a "stop-gap". Once the parties could clarify their political relationships, it was thought that a more permanent government would be formed to reflect the new scenario.[49] According to British diplomacy, it was a government "weak even by Italian standards", and yet, its main weakness – the fragility of its political base in Parliament – was paradoxically also its strength.[50] Cossiga's strongest card remained the lack of a credible alternative to the present parliamentary formula: as no new element to break the stalemate was likely to emerge before the beginning of 1980, there was no objective justification for provoking a new crisis.[51]

However, for the United Kingdom, Cossiga was "probably the most helpful Italian Prime Minister possible at present".[52] The two Cossiga governments of 1979-80 marked one of the highest moments in Anglo-Italian relations, in particular due to the "special" personal connection established between the Italian Prime Minister and Margaret Thatcher. The British Premier had profound respect for Cossiga, as witnessed in her memoirs:

> Italian politics and Italian politicians do not evoke much understanding or sympathy from the British, or indeed from the Italians, and I confess to sharing some of that disenchantment. But Francesco Cossiga was himself a sceptic about the usual Italian practices. He was the nearest thing to an independent in Italian politics; in negotiations he always played a straight hand; he could be relied upon to keep his word [...]; and he was an undoubted Anglophile and a strong admirer of the Glorious Revolution of 1688 as the birth of true liberal politics.[53]

---

48 TNA, FCO 30/4048, Tel. No. 309 by Goodison A., 2 August 1979.

49 TNA, FCO 33/4049, "The political scene in Italy", by Foreign and Commonwealth Office, 18 December 1979.

50 TNA, FCO 33/4049, "Italian political situation", Tel. No. 547 by Arculus R., WRJ 014/2, 26 November 1979.

51 TNA, FCO 33/4049, Saving Tel. No. 19 by Arculus R., 17 December 1979.

52 TNA, FCO 33/4533, "Italy: Annual Review for 1979", 21 January 1980.

53 Thatcher M., *The Downing Street years*, HarperCollins, London 1993, pp. 82-83.

This genuine appreciation clashed with her dislike – allegedly reciprocal – for Andreotti.[54] As for Cossiga, he said that Thatcher "combined all her innate qualities of charm and femininity with those of an exceptional negotiator"; someone even complained that she "bewitched" the Italian Prime Minister.[55]

Apart from personal relations, Italy and Britain were able to develop a fruitful collaboration since 1979, particularly in the field of European integration. The reasons for this new rapprochement lay not only in a convergence of interests between London and Rome inside the Community – although it proved to be fundamental for Anglo-Italian relations in the early 1980s – but also in the first signs of recovery showed by Italy.

In search of a new prestige

Recovery for Italy went through the two fundamental elements of its foreign policy: the Atlantic and the European dimensions. In both cases, the cooperation with Britain proved to be fundamental.

With regards to the Atlantic policy, the turning point was the Guadeloupe quadripartite summit of January 1979. In the sunny French territory in the Caribbean Sea, the United States, France, West Germany and Britain agreed on what became known as the "dual-track" approach, linking the deployment of US Pershing II and Cruise missile in Europe with progress in arms control negotiations on intermediate-range weapons with the USSR. The modernisation of nuclear weapons in Europe, or Theatre Nuclear Forces (TNF), was seen as a solution to the Soviet deployment of the new medium-range ballistic missile SS-20.[56]

The Guadeloupe summit can be considered a watershed for both Britain and Italy, although for different reasons. In the United Kingdom, it marked the real beginning of the "winter of discontent" and gave an indelible blow to the Labour government. For Italy, Guadeloupe epitomised

---

54 In her memoirs, Thatcher was not very forgiving in describing Andreotti: "This apparently indispensable participant in Italian governments represented an approach to politics which I could not share. He seemed to have a positive aversion to principle, even a conviction that a man of principle was doomed to be a figure of fun". *Ibidem*, p. 59.

55 TNA, FCO 33/4329, "Signor Cossiga and the Prime Minister", Adams W. to Gladstone D., 7 February 1980.

56 See Nuti L., Bozo F., Rey M.-P., Rother B. (eds.), *The Euromissile Crisis and the End of the Cold War*, Stanford University Press, Stanford 2015.

the country's weakness and loss of prestige resulting from the long crisis. But this episode also worked as a stimulus for the next government to try and find a new, more decisive role for the country in the international scenario. It was not an easy gain: Italy had been excluded from a series of multilateral initiatives during 1978, such as the tripartite and quadripartite consultation on military technology. Nonetheless, when the "Big Four" met in Guadeloupe in January 1979 to discuss East-West relations and the new SALT II agreement, Italy was the only non-permanent member of the Nuclear Planning Group (NGP) not to be invited.

This exclusion from the group of the big Western powers deeply irritated the Andreotti government. Ducci stressed how Italy's main concern was the weakening of political co-operation among the Nine and of political consultation in NATO caused by privileged discussions by three member states with the US, and the Italian government viewed this development "with grave disquiet".[57] The meeting set up, at least in fact, a "directorate for the management of the main problems of the Western world", thus risking depriving the existing consultations, within both NATO and the EC, of part of their relevance. The Atlantic and the European spirit "would thereby suffer through a resumption of [...] Gaullist practices".[58] According to the Foreign Office, if and when another Guadeloupe occurred, the British government should show some "special consideration" to the Italians, although there was no question in bringing them into the quadripartite scenario. In case of future slips, it was always possible "to take refuge in the Berlin cover-story": officials were talking about Berlin and happened to mention some other subject in passing ("no-one believes this story, but it inhibits non-quadripartite partners from making a fuss").[59] However, Italy resented the Americans and the French more than the British, since they had not played a leading role in organising the meeting. The French should make special arrangements over the briefing; as for the Americans, they "time and again [broke] the

57 TNA, FCO 33/4056, Tel. No. 18, "Guadeloupe summit: Italian reactions", WRD 021/2, 24 January 1979.

58 TNA, FCO 33/4055, Tel. No. 19, "Guadeloupe summit: Italian reactions", WRD 021/1, 24 January 1979.

59 TNA, FCO 33/4056, "Italian exclusion from quadripartite and other small groups", Palliser M. to Campbell A., WRD 021/2, 31 January 1979. The Permanent Under-Secretary Michael Palliser used a Melvillian metaphor to resume the best attitude for the "Big Four": "Britain, France, Germany and the US will have to go on organizing quadripartite work among themselves and we shall simply have to put up with the fact that every so often the quadripartite whale will break surface and blow, for all to see. When the Italians and others get their harpoons out, the only remedy for the whale will be to dive and disappear again for a while".

rules of confidentiality" and the Germans were "nearly as bad", as shown on the occasion of the Puerto Rico summit. At least the British could preserve a reputation for discretion.[60]

According to Campbell, this concern derived from Italy's uneasy position as the least powerful of the major Western nations and had been endemic since Italian unification. However, it should not be ignored, "if only because Italians who feel strongly about this tend to be those most devoted to the Western alliance". The matter needed careful watching in the Anglo-Italian as well as the general Western framework.[61]

This "Guadeloupe complex"[62] – a mix of willingness to avoid both marginalisation from the big powers and the creation of a "directorate" – would provide a new impetus to Italian foreign policy. The Andreotti government was profoundly irritated and interpreted Italy's exclusion as the failure of the other allies to acknowledge the positive economic results and the readiness in joining the European Monetary System. Being left outside the Guadeloupe meeting reinforced the perception that Italy had lost its middle-power status: NATO's dual-track decision provided the occasion to confirm Italian loyalty to the Atlantic alliance and to show to the other partners that the country was still a valuable and strategic ally.[63]

Britain played a key role in the renovated Atlantic policy of Italy.[64] By the beginning of February, Ducci started to emphasise to Michael Palliser, the Permanent Under-Secretary of State and Head of the Diplomatic Service, that Italy felt just as exposed to Soviet nuclear attack as Germany or Britain; that Italy had existing theatre nuclear weapons deployed on its soil, and that this was at present broadly acceptable to Italian opinion – not least because very little was said about it. The Italian government

60 TNA, FCO 33/4056, "Italian exclusion from quadripartite and other small groups", WRJ 021/2, 30 January 1979. As mentioned in the document, in summer 1976, American "clumsiness" [*sic*] made sure that the Italians knew that a quadripartite meeting was taking place to which they were not invited, and Chancellor Schmidt then disclosed that the Italian internal situation had been under discussion.

61 TNA, FCO 33/4046, "Annual review on Italy", by Campbell A., 10 January 1979.

62 Bagnato B., "L'Italia vista da Palazzo Farnese: la missione di Gilles Martinet (1981-1984)", in Di Nolfo E. (a cura di), *La politica estera italiana negli anni Ottanta*, Marsilio, Venezia 2007, p. 220.

63 Evangelista M., "Atomic ambivalence: Italy's evolving attitude towards nuclear weapons", in Verbeek B., Giacomello G. (eds.), *Italy's foreign policy in the twenty-first century: the new assertiveness of an aspiring middle power*, Lexington Books, Lanham 2011, p. 127.

64 For British attitude towards the "dual-track" decision see Stoddart K., "Creating the 'Seamless Robe of Deterrence': Great Britain's Role in NATO's INF Debate", in Nuti L., Bozo F., Rey M.-P., Rother B. (eds.), quoted, pp. 176-195.

was just as sensitive to the deployment of new or modernised weapon systems as any of the other European countries. For Palliser, the Italians were "erecting unreal bogey men": no firm conclusions had been reached at Guadeloupe, and there would have to be further detailed consultation in the Alliance.[65] On 22 February, the British accepted a bilateral meeting with an Italian delegation, with a broad exchange of views and some useful agreement. Most of all, the talks in London showed to the other allies – and in particular to the United States – that Italy was genuinely interested in a positive conclusion of the TNF modernisation.[66] This would be fundamental in the following months when the Italians were able to confirm on several occasions to Carter's special envoy to Europe, David Aaron, a strong commitment to giving a decisive contribution to the programme.[67]

By October, both Cossiga and Pertini became fully convinced of the need to go ahead with the deployment.[68] But Cossiga needed the external support of non-majority parties (i.e. the PSI) to guarantee that Parliament authorised the modernisation of TNF: against this background, Craxi had a pivotal role in granting unconditional support to the government, and in proving to the Americans his Atlantic credentials. In the end, the Parliamentary debate on TNF on 4-6 December 1979 saw Christian Democrats, Liberals, Social Democrats, Republicans, and Socialists voting in favour of "Euromissiles", while the PCI voted against. A few days later, on 12 December, Italy together with the other allies approved the modernisation of NATO Theatre Nuclear Force. In a meeting with Thatcher, Cossiga said that he would try to make the PCI accept that the vote on TNF was an opportunity to prove that they were independent of the Soviet Union.[69] Instead, the Communist "no" formalised the end of the process of distancing from the "majority" initiated twelve months earlier with the vote on EMS. The Italian political scene emerged deeply divided from this debate. The Catholic world, usually pacifist and antinuclear, dissociated itself from the DC from the very first time. The rift between

65 TNA, FCO 33/4054, "Grey areas and modernization of Theatre Nuclear Force (TNF)", by Palliser M., WRJ 202/4, 2 February 1979.

66 Ciarrapico A., "Rapporti Est-Ovest 1977-79. La vicenda degli euromissili", *Rivista di Studi Politici Internazionali*, Vol. 69, No. 3, 2002, pp. 374-375.

67 Nuti L., "The Nuclear Debate in Italian Politics in the Late 1970s and the Early 1980s", in Nuti L., Bozo F., Rey M.-P., Rother B. (eds.), quoted, pp. 234-238.

68 TNA, FCO 33/4058, "Record of a discussion in plenary session between the Prime Minister and signor Cossiga at the Palazzo Chigi", 5 October 1979.

69 TNA, FCO 33/4058, "Brief record of main points discussed at the tete-a-tete meeting between the Prime Minister and signor Cossiga at Palazzo Chigi", 4 October 1979.

the centre-left and the PCI was even wider, and the Communists, trying to play the card of "loyal opposition", found themselves isolated on the main decision of internal and foreign policy.[70] The Euromissile debate not only showed a new dynamism in Italian foreign policy but was also a useful tool for causing problems to the PCI, thus continuing the *conventio ad excludendum* policy (or agreement to exclude – the informal pact among governing parties to exclude the Communist Party from office) to avoid further rapprochement with the government majority. This trend was confirmed two months later, at the Fourteenth Christian Democracy Party Congress in February 1980, when the right-wing *correnti* joined under the banner of an anti-communist "preamble". This coalition won the majority of votes, advocating that, "given the continued contrast of views" between the DC and PCI, it was no longer possible for the Christian Democrats to share government responsibility with the Communists.[71]

Britain acknowledged the Italian commitment to the TNF cause and praised the "skilful and robust" campaign conducted by Cossiga. In this way, "Italy became a key country in the battle of the missiles (TNF). She was the largest and the most reliable of the lesser NATO countries, one at least of which the Americans needed to be sure of as a safe recipient of missiles".[72] On the other hand, the level of Italian defence expenditure was such as to undermine the effectiveness of Italy's contribution. Of thirteen NATO countries, only Canada spent less as a per centage of GDP than Italy; this low absolute level of expenditure inevitably meant equipment deficiencies, and low levels of training and professional competence.[73]

Besides the Atlantic dimension, the most valuable collaboration between London and Rome happened during 1979 in Community policy, although it proved to be a mixed blessing for Italy. According to British documents, both countries had a major EEC interest in common: despite having the seventh and eighth lowest per capita gross domestic product in the Community, both were net contributors to the Community Budget. They had accordingly together promoted the argument that Community policies should contribute to a convergence of economic performance and not, as it was at the time, the reverse. The two governments also

70 Nuti L., "The Nuclear Debate", quoted, pp. 238-242; *Id.*, *La sfida nucleare*, Il Mulino, Bologna 2007, pp. 372-374.

71 Leonardi R., Wertman D., *Italian Christian Democracy: the politics of dominance*, Springer, New York 1989, p. 85.

72 TNA, FCO 33/4533, "Italy: Annual Review for 1979", 21 January 1980.

73 TNA, FCO 33/4924, "The Italian defence scene", Arculus A. to Carrington P., Departmental Series, Western European Department, WRJ 060/3, 8 May 1981.

shared a wish to see a radical reform of the CAP that would prevent such a considerable proportion of the EEC Budget from being consumed by the storage and disposal of surplus agricultural produce.[74]

The problem of the British contribution was not new nor unexpected; it had already been raised during the 1975 referendum campaign and it was entirely predictable in advance that the United Kingdom was going to be a net contributor to the EEC budget. Nevertheless, Britain began to claim for a reduction in its net contribution before the transitional measures for its contribution expired in 1979. During Thatcher's first term her relations with the European partners had been poisoned by the interminable dispute over Britain's contribution to the Community budget, the "British Budgetary Question" (BBQ) or, as Roy Jenkins started to call it, the "bloody British question".[75]

An informal Anglo-Italian alliance in trying to correct the inequities of the budget had already emerged during the negotiations with the Callaghan government for joining the EMS. Since the inauguration of the Conservative government, it appeared clear not only that the Italians shared Britain's aims on the Community Budget and the CAP, but also that Italy would be a key partner in avoiding isolation inside the Community and trying to present a "united front" to the remaining Seven. For practical purposes, the Foreign Office considered it essential to cement that tactical alliance before Thatcher's Community debut at the European Council in Strasbourg in June 1979, both to give more strength to British demands and to prevent the Commission having a qualified majority – and thus avoid having to invoke the Luxembourg compromise.[76]

Thatcher's visit to Rome in October 1979 had the primary task of strengthening the alliance with the Italians without imperilling the British timetable before the European Council in Dublin. Italy's requests were imprecise and likely to be almost as unwelcome to the other Community partners as Britain's demands for a budget refund. The tactic of the Conservative government was clear: the "Italian nuisance value" could be great, but making too precise promises to Cossiga would be expensive for the United Kingdom, as well as for the rest of the Community. In the

74 TNA, FCO 33/4052, "Italy internal situation and UK/Italian relations", Western European Department, 15 May 1979.

75 Wall S., *A stranger in Europe. Britain and the EU from Thatcher to Blair*, Oxford University Press, Oxford 2008, pp. 6-40; Young H., *This blessed plot*, The Overlook Press, New York 1998, pp. 313-325.

76 TNA, FCO 33/4057, "Community budget", Butler M. to Owen D., WRJ 026/9, 11 May 1979.

words of the Cabinet Secretary John Hunt: "We want cash in Dublin: the Italians will probably have to be content with words".[77] During their meeting, Cossiga offered to develop "a line of common action" whose basis would be that the EEC could not count on a full contribution from Italy and Britain if they were not getting satisfaction from the partnership.[78]

In the end, this proved to be a miscalculation for the Italian government. The Dublin summit in December showed that Britain's and Italy's interests were in direct conflict. The Italians were anxious to secure British support for their proposals for restructuring the Community Budget, which involved target shares of spending on structural and investment policies well above the current levels. While restructuring could in principle be a common aim, there were serious differences of interest between the United Kingdom and Italy regarding the form it should take. The Italians wanted to increase expenditure to improve agricultural structures, and to promote Italian production of Mediterranean crops.[79] Moreover, in Dublin Thatcher adopted a strongly confrontational style towards her European partners,[80] while Italy was not allowed enough space nor attention for mediating and discussing its own request.[81]

On 1 January 1980, therefore, the six-month Italian Presidency did not seem to begin under favourable auspices, in a moment when political solidarity among the Nine had reached one of the lowest points in years. The Soviet invasion of Afghanistan in December 1979 opened a wide cleavage between the British, in favour of the American sanctions against the USSR, and the Franco-German position of non-alignment with Washington. Moreover, internal disputes further weakened the Italian government, which also lost a valuable Minister of Foreign Affairs (Franco Maria Malfatti, former President of the European Commission, resigned in January for health reasons), while a new government crisis was initiated in March, with the creation of a new executive still led by Cossiga. This provided the Nine a pretext for postponing the European Council in

77 TNA, FCO 33/4058, "Visit in Rome", by Hunt J., Ref. A0350, 2 October 1979.

78 TNA, FCO 33/4058, "Record of a discussion in plenary session between the Prime Minister and signor Cossiga at the Palazzo Chigi", 5 October 1979.

79 TNA, FCO 30/4329, "Visit of Prime Minister of Italy, 29-30 January 1980 – Budget/ Convergence", Brief by the Treasury, 22 January 1980.

80 Roy Jenkins described the dinner on the first day, when Thatcher spoke for four hours "without pause, but not without repetition" about the British budget problem. Schmidt pretended to sleep; Giscard looked on in unfeigned horror; Cossiga "wrung his hands". Jenkins R., *A Life at the Centre*, Macmillan, London 1994, pp. 498-499.

81 Istituto Affari Internazionali, *L'Italia nella politica Internazionale (1979-1980)*, Edizioni di Comunità, Roma 1981, p. 226.

Luxembourg until April. Nonetheless, Italy's role in mediating for a positive outcome of the British budget question was widely acknowledged in London: Cossiga made a tour of European capitals, while an ad hoc group led by Renato Ruggiero worked on different ways to reduce British contribution to the budget.[82] At the Luxembourg Council there appeared to be a real possibility of an agreement, although Thatcher initially refused the offer, only to then accept it one month later after minor adjustments.[83]

Despite the positive mediating role, Italy was once more left outside of a trilateral meeting. After the Council, Schmidt, Giscard and Thatcher met in the French embassy with the apparent aim of talking about Berlin. Actually, they spoke about Schmidt's visit to Moscow to find a solution to the Afghanistan crisis through a more flexible European line. The exclusion of Cossiga from the meeting proved Italy's minor role in the elaboration of Community policies, a gap that even the EC Presidency could not fill. Even the failure of the British negotiations was first announced to the French and only as a second step to the Italian Presidency.[84]

The same alternation of progress and regression also characterized the Italian economy. In the first half of 1979, British reports showed good economic performance in Italy on the external front, and figures on industrial production were encouraging. But there was still considerable unease about the rate of inflation, which reached nearly 14 %. The Italian government was also particularly worried about the economic impact of recent international oil prices increases, while the visit of an IMF team for routine consultations in early April was the occasion for some severe warnings about inflationary prospects. The Foreign Office gave an interesting insight of the extensive use of the "external constraint", which was not only European: there were rumours that Italy was to seek a one-billion-dollar IMF credit so that the government could blame the conditions which would be attached to such a loan for the implementation of restrictive policies which it knew were necessary but which it would itself be unable to introduce.[85]

In terms of economic performance, the gap between Italy and the United Kingdom had considerably narrowed over the years 1955-1979. In

82 *Ibidem*, p. 230.

83 Gowland D., *Britain and the European Union*, Taylor & Francis, Abingdon 2016, p. 226.

84 Istituto Affari Internazionali, *L'Italia nella politica internazionale (1979-1980)*, quoted, p. 232.

85 TNA, FCO 33/4052, "Italy internal situation and UK/Italian relations", Western European Department, 15 May 1979.

1955 GDP per head in Italy was less than half that of the UK. In 1978, it was within 15 per cent of the British figure. Between 1955 and 1978 the Italian share of world exports doubled, from 2.2 per cent to 4.4 per cent, while Britain's declined from 10.3 per cent to 5.3 per cent. Productivity in Italy grew by an average 5.2 per cent between 1950 and 1977, while the figure for the UK was 2.6 per cent, exactly half. According to Campbell, Italy would probably overtake Britain economically within the next few years – unless the United Kingdom began to do much better.[86]

For Italy, therefore, the 1980s were starting with conflicting results. Despite its honourable victory on the TNF issue, the Cossiga government was beset by difficulties. The country had to face the EC Presidency with a precarious internal political situation, although the economic performance showed a positive trend. The road to recovery was a long and arduous one.

The new five-party experiment

The creation of a "lay bloc"

In October 1980, Cossiga resigned as Prime Minister after the rejection of the budget (*finanziaria*) by the Italian Parliament. The loss of Cossiga was a "big blow" for Britain; Arculus described him as "one of the best Prime Ministers Italy has produced in recent years".[87] The start of Cossiga's decline could be seen in the Donat Cattin affair when he was accused of aiding and abetting in a "trial by Parliament". The eventual acquittal did not mitigate the effects of what British diplomacy described as an "ordeal". The economic decree, judged necessary to defend the lira and restrain domestic demand, twice failed to get through Parliament – the second time being the occasion of the government's fall. The view from London was very disapproving, and not only because Cossiga would "be missed": "Once again the Italians permitted themselves a government crisis when the international scene is troubled and a domestic crisis particularly untimely".[88]

86 TNA, FCO 33/4051, "Some impressions on leaving Italy", by Campbell A., Foreign and Commonwealth Office Diplomatic Report No. 158/79, WRJ 014/4, 28 June 1979.

87 TNA, FCO 30/4046, "The Forlani Government: October 1980 to May 1981", by Arculus R., 22 June 1981; TNA, FCO 30/5241, "Italy's Communists", by Arculus R., 3 November 1982.

88 TNA, FCO 33/4436, "Italian Government changes", Arculus R. to Fergusson E., 9 October 1980.

After Cossiga, the mandate was given to another Christian Democrat, Arnaldo Forlani, former Minister of Foreign Affairs and Defence and DC Party Chairman. The press in the United Kingdom showed some concern about the umpteenth Italian government, the fortieth since the war.[89] However, in only three weeks (a positive record for Italian political history), Forlani secured a good working majority in Parliament, thanks to the support of the PSI. Craxi agreed on a "unity of action" pact with the Social-Democrats led by Longo, which enabled him to demand and get parity for the lay parties in the new coalition. In London, the new quadripartite coalition (DC, PSI, PSDI, PRI) was seen as "another step on the road to Craxi's Prime Ministership".[90]

British opinion of the Forlani government was not positive, although it was acknowledged that he had "a very unfortunate run of bad luck". A grave earthquake in the South (Irpinia), which left almost 3,000 people dead and 280,000 homeless, showed the deficiencies of the country in organising relief; terrorism grew stronger with the kidnapping of a senior magistrate. There was also a major scandal over the evasion of duty payable on oil products, leading to the resignation of the Minister of Industry, Antonio Bisaglia. The economy showed a negative trend as well, with worsening recession, high inflation, large trade deficits and declining reserves; the Bank of Italy had to take a series of increasingly tight monetary measures and to adjust the lira within the EMS in March. However, this was not exceptional in comparison with other Italian governments, and Forlani coped well with a series of domestic crises "that might have destroyed a Prime Minister less capable of dispassionate manoeuvring". He also had some successes, in NATO and the struggle against terrorism; by retaining Colombo at the Ministry of Foreign Affairs and Lagorio at Defence, he ensured continuity and competence in Italy's policies in NATO and the European Community; and he had a reasonably strong economic team.

Despite internal difficulties, Italian foreign policy showed a new impetus, assuming for the first time military commitments in the Middle East and the Mediterranean. In 1979 Italy took part in the United Nations Interim Force in Lebanon (UNIFIL) to restore international peace and security in that area, and in September 1980 an agreement on the neutrality of Malta was signed – Malta agreed not to enter into

89 "Another fragile political child is born", *Financial Times*, 31 October 1980. Actually, the Forlani government was the 38th Government since the foundation of the Republic of Italy – but the 40th since the end of the war in 1945.

90 TNA, FCO 33/4436, "The new Italian government", Arculus R. to Carrington P., 28 October 1980.

any alliance while Italy would guarantee Malta's neutrality.[91] Also, the European dimension was further strengthened at the beginning of 1981 when Foreign Minister Colombo joined his German colleague Dietrich Genscher in urging further initiatives towards political union. Colombo and Genscher presented their draft European Act to the European Council meeting in London in November 1981: it was a declaration of intent by the Ten who made a solemn commitment to move towards a European Union. The final document would be adopted by the Stuttgart European Council in the form of the Solemn Declaration on European Union on 17-19 June 1983: however, it was a somewhat edulcorated result, since it was not legally binding.[92]

According to British diplomacy, the weakest element in the Forlani government was Forlani himself. The new Prime Minister was coolly detached (so different from Cossiga's warmth), "by nature and habit a short-term tactician, skilled in party in-fighting and content to leave the wider issues to others". But Italy's economic, political and social problems required "a skipper with a more seaworthy craft equipped with a rudder and engine, and with a clearer idea of his intended destination".[93]

Forlani's weakness fully emerged on the occasion of the "P2 scandal", which caused his government to fall after seven months. The scandal – which Arculus defined as "pervasive, complex and disturbing, even by Italian standards"[94] – involved the implication of politicians, journalists, officials and members of the armed and secret services, in a secret masonic lodge Propaganda Due (P2). Originally a traditional Masonic lodge based in Arezzo, Tuscany since the end of the 19th century, P2 started to develop a new character in the 1950s; under the lead of Licio Gelli, who became Grand Master in 1971, it was transformed it into a "secret power centre". Public attention was first drawn to the lodge in 1976 when, in the course of anti-terrorist investigations, it was the subject of a report to the Ministry of the Interior. The report described P2 as the most powerful masonic organisation in Italy.

---

91 "Italy-Malta: Agreement on the neutrality of Malta", *International Legal Materials*, Vol. 21, No. 2, 1982, pp. 396-398; Chipman J., *NATO's Southern Allies: Internal and External Challenges*, Routledge, London 2004.

92 The Stuttgart Declaration defined four fields of activity for the European Union: the European Communities, foreign policy, cultural cooperation and approximation of national laws. "Solemn Declaration on European Union (Stuttgart, 19 June 1983)", *Bulletin of the European Communities*, No. 6, June 1983, pp. 24-29.

93 TNA, FCO 33/4898, "The Forlani Government: October 1980 to May 1981", by Arculus R., 22 June 1981.

94 *Ibidem*.

In March 1981, detailed lists of 953 alleged members of the lodge were seized by the *Guardia di Finanza* during a raid on Gelli's home. Press speculation about the Lodge built up throughout spring, while Forlani tried to play for time. Details of the list were eventually released on 21 May. The publication of the lists caused much public alarm and suspicion that membership of the P2 lodge constituted a state within a state which determined the country's real political and financial affairs. The names of those appearing on the lists linked to the major Italian scandals in the last decade. There was particular concern over the involvement of the secret services and the Carabinieri; among politicians, the most prominent names were the Minister of Justice Adolfo Sarti (DC), the Minister for Foreign Trade Enrico Manca (PSI), and PSDI Secretary General Pietro Longo.[95]

When the scandal broke, the Forlani government first tried to carry on with business as usual. But pressure from the Communists – the most important political party whose members did not figure in the list of alleged P2 members – and the Socialists quickly built up. Forlani immediately set up a commission of "three wise men" to determine whether or not, unlike normal masonic lodges, P2 was an illegal secret organisation in violation of Article 18 of the Constitution. This plus the offer of a cabinet reshuffle was not enough to satisfy Socialist demands for more drastic changes to the coalition and the government subsequently resigned on 26 May.[96]

After Forlani fell, the Foreign Office predicted that Italian politics were going to be "even more unpredictable than usual" in the months ahead.[97] Indeed, Pertini wanted to avoid either a long power vacuum or anticipated elections and asked Forlani to form a new government, but he renounced. Pertini turned instead to Giovanni Spadolini, the leader of the Republican Party. On 18 June, Spadolini accepted and became the

---

95 Among the other "excellent names": Admiral Giovanni Torrisi (Commander in Chief of the Armed Forces); General Orazio Giannini (Commander of Guardia di Finanza); General Giuseppe Santovito (Head of Military Intelligence – SISMI); General Giulio Grassini (Head of Civilian Intelligence – SISDE); Angelo Rizzoli Jr. (publisher and part owner of *Corriere della Sera*); Franco di Bella (editor of *Corriere della Sera*); Franco Colombo (Director RAI TG1); Giovanni Palaia and Renato Croce (Secretaries of High Council of the Judiciary – CSM); Guido Barbaro (President of Turin Assize Court).

96 TNA, FCO 33/4899, "Masonic Lodge Propaganda Two", Tomkins W. to Osborne R., WRF 014/2, 9 July 1981.

97 TNA, FCO 33/4898, "The Forlani Government", Gladstone D. to Fergusson E., WRJ 014/2, 30 June 1981.

first non-Christian Democrat Prime Minister in Italy in 36 years, after Ferruccio Parri in 1945.[98]

British government and diplomats alike welcomed the advent of the first "lay" premiership with relief: Spadolini was a definite improvement in comparison with his predecessor, who had not succeeded in gaining London's sympathy. Instead of the "dull" Christian Democrat, Thatcher could now count on a partner defined as "a hardworking intellectual, genial and popular".[99] He was a college professor at the Faculty of Political Sciences "Cesare Alfieri" of the University of Florence, and former editor of the *Resto del Carlino* and *Corriere della Sera*. Spadolini's choice, moreover, reflected the importance of the P2 scandal and the degree to which it was recognised that fundamental political change in Italy was necessary.[100]

Despite the good personal records, the Foreign Office considered the Spadolini government doomed and not likely to survive the summer. Whereas Forlani began his period in office with some fairly good cards in his hand, Spadolini appeared to have none. He would have to prove "either a wizard of the finesse or an outright card-shaper" if he was to survive even as long as Forlani. There were also speculations about the reasons for Spadolini's fall (probably one among "another scandal, a PSI bid for the premiership, a change of PCI tactics, and DC impatience to regain control", or a combination of all four).[101]

This prediction proved to be too pessimistic: the Spadolini government not only survived until the summer, but it stayed in power until November 1982 (although in August 1982 Spadolini resigned and formed a new cabinet identical to what it had been previously). Spadolini's appointment was the first result of the new political formula which became known as the *pentapartito* (meaning "five parties"), formed by Christian Democrats, Socialists, Republicans, Socialist-Democrats, and Liberals. Most of all, it was the acme of the "lay bloc" strategy in which the PSI was the leading force – as well as a constant threat of early elections for the DC.[102]

---

98 On the "lay premiership" see, among others, Curini L., Martelli P., *I partiti nella Prima Repubblica. Maggioranze e governi dalla Costituente a Tangentopoli*, Carocci, Roma 2009, p. 139.

99 TNA, FCO 33/5746, "Italy: annual review for 1981", by Arculus R., 25 January 1982.

100 TNA, FCO 30/4046, "The Forlani Government: October 1980 to May 1981", by Arculus R., 22 June 1981.

101 TNA, FCO 33/4898, "The Forlani Government", Gladstone D. to Arculus R., WRJ 014/2, 29 June 1981.

102 See Galli G., *I partiti politici italiani (1943-2004)*, Rizzoli, Milano 2004, pp. 210-211.

Spadolini's programme was founded on four emergencies: economic, moral (with references to the "aberrant parallel organisation" P2), terroristic, and international.[103] The programme was judged positively by the British government, although it still seemed too ambitious for a cabinet which depended on DC and PSI to stay in power.[104] If the economic emergency was still urgent, with high rates of inflation and unemployment (although in 1982 the petrol price decreased for the first time since 1960), the Republican secretary was reaping his first successes in managing the P2 scandal with a resolute stance that contrasted sharply with the weak attitude of his predecessor. According to the Foreign Office, many Italians had already sensed "a wind of change" brought by Spadolini, to the great displeasure of the Christian Democrats.[105]

The other new element in Italy's political scene was the PCI's weakness. With the creation of the *pentapartito* and the strengthening of the lay bloc, the chance to open a government majority to the Communists was waning for good. At the same time, the PCI diverged from Moscow, openly condemning the Soviet invasion of Afghanistan.[106] In November 1980, with a second "Salerno turn"[107] (after the first one in 1944 when Togliatti agreed to set up a government of national unity, supporting democracy and abandoning the armed struggle), Berlinguer announced the end of the historical compromise and launched the new strategy of "democratic alternative". This turn, however, did not create the proposal for an alternative government nor had real political interlocutors.[108] Even the PCI's influence over government foreign policy appeared minimal: according to London, "as long as the party remain[ed] outside government, it [was] likely to continue in its foreign policy to take account of Western attitudes wherever possible, and thus to pose problems for the Soviet Union".[109]

---

103 De Rosa G., "Il Governo Spadolini di fronte alle "quattro emergenze", *Civiltà Cattolica*, quaderno 3146, 1981, pp. 191-199.

104 TNA, FCO 33/4899, "Spadolini's programme", Culshaw R. to Osborne R., WRJ 014/2, 23 July 1981.

105 TNA, FCO 33/4899, "Spadolini's August", Osborne R. to Culshaw R., WRJ 014/2, 30 September 1981.

106 Pons S., *Berlinguer e la fine del comunismo*, quoted, pp. 489-519.

107 See Macaluso E., *50 anni nel PCI*, Rubbettino, Soveria Mannelli 2003, p. 173.

108 Pons S., *Berlinguer e la fine del comunismo*, Einaudi, Torino 2006, pp. 551-554.

109 TNA, FCO 51/475, "The foreign policy of the Italian Communist Party", Research Department Memorandum, West and Southern European Section, RRW 334/1, October 1980.

Internal struggles viewed from the outside: terrorism in Italy in the early 1980s

Of the four emergencies outlined by Spadolini, British attention turned in particular to the terrorist problem. Britain's concern for the phenomenon of terrorism in Italy did not reach its peak with the Moro kidnapping: actually, it was just the beginning. From 1978 to 1981, terrorist actions continued uninterrupted: almost half of all victims of terrorism fell in those four years.[110]

The 1970s ended with another challenging year due to terrorism: during 1979, the killing or wounding of magistrates, police officers, and business executives (mainly from FIAT) filled the front pages of the newspapers. The government tightened up anti-terrorist measures, and the police had some successes, despite the problems of the judiciary system; the British ambassador reported that magistrates had difficulty in confirming charges against several ultra-left-wing university professors accused of master-minding the campaigns.[111]

Italian terrorism had also hit the United Kingdom directly: in August 1979 Rolf Schild, a German-born, British-based businessman, was kidnapped while on holiday in Sardinia with his family. Schild was released after two weeks, while his wife and daughter were set free in January and March 1980 respectively after the payment of a ransom.[112]

On 2 August 1980, a bomb exploded at the Central Railway Station of Bologna, killing 85 people and wounding more than 200. The choice of the day (the first Saturday of August, when summer holidays start for most Italians) and the location (one of the main connection stations in the

110 Of the total 429 victims of terrorism in Italy, 210 died between 1978 and 1981; 1980 was the record year, with 125 victims – 85 in the attack on Bologna train station on 2 August. Zavoli S., *La notte della Repubblica*, Nuova Eri-Mondadori, Roma, 1992, p. 476.

111 TNA, FCO 33/4533, "Italy: Annual Review for 1979", 21 January 1980. It was a reference to the "7 April trial": on 7 April 1979, Padua's Public Prosecutor Pietro Calogero arrested the main leaders of the *Autonomia Operaia* movement, who were also university professors (among them Toni Negri), with the charge of being involved in the political wing of the Red Brigades and the Moro kidnapping and murder and being the moving intellectual and political force behind Italian terrorism. See Ginsborg P., *A History of Contemporary Italy*, quoted, pp. 386-387.

112 Cossiga himself took up the cause for a prompt and positive solution of the case. See, for example, TNA, FCO 33/4353, "Record of a conversation between the Prime Minister and the President of the Council of Ministers of the Italian Republic, Signor Cossiga, at 10 Downing Street", 29 January 1980.

country) showed that the bombing aimed at causing as many victims as possible. It remains the most devastating terrorist attack in Italian history.

The Bologna attack was described as entirely unexpected both in methods and ideology: the bombing was attributed to right-wing extremists. British diplomacy stressed how there had been no significant act of random killing of that kind in the previous six years, and before 2 August, the primary threat seemed to be the continued series of single crimes against selected targets in the systematic campaign of the extreme and violent left.[113]

Despite the large death roll, the Bologna attack seemed to have less significance than the running series of left-wing attacks on the establishment. These culminated, a few months later, in the seizure of judge Giovanni D'Urso in December – "a serious blow to Forlani and unpleasantly similar to the Moro case" – and the killing of Carabinieri General Enrico Galvaligi on New Year's Eve: December showed that the battle against terrorism was far from being won.[114]

After the events in Bologna, the new Ambassador in Rome, Ronald Arculus, tried to sketch a sociological outline of the phenomenon of terrorism in Italy, of which he acknowledged four "social causes". Firstly, the universities had to be blamed: due to their long inadequacy, they became fertile grounds for the terrorist movement of the Seventies. The introduction of free access to higher education in 1969[115] brought overcrowding and chaos, making it more difficult for graduates to find a job; many of them felt "cheated by a society which cannot create worthwhile opportunities". Secondly, massive migration from Southern Italy to the North of the country in search of employment broke the traditional links with the church, the family and the supportive structure of the moral community and replaced them with an uncaring and disorderly industrialised society. The giant factories increased this feeling of alienation and were often fertile recruiting grounds for terrorism, while young people sought refuge in

113 TNA, FCO 33/4594, "Terrorism in Italy", despatch (051/4) by Arculus R., WRJ 051/3, 8 August 1980.

114 TNA, FCO 33/4897, "Italy: annual review for 1980", 7 January 1981.

115 Until 1969, only one high school (the "*liceo classico*", corresponding to British grammar school) granted access to every department. After the "hot autumn" (a series of large strikes in factories and industrial centers of northern Italy), access to universities was progressively liberalized and opened even to students of the vocational institutions, attended primarily by the working classes. The reform was expected to reduce class inequality in university attendance. See Shavit Y. and Westerbeek K., "Educational stratification in Italy: reforms, expansion, and equality of opportunity", *European Sociological Review*, Vol. 14, No. 1, 1998, pp. 33-47.

"sub-groups and sub-cultures". The third cause was the low regard for the State and its agencies by Italians, even the law-abiding ones. According to Arculus, it was a widespread and reasonable phenomenon, and both main parties had to be equally blamed for it. With few honourable exceptions, DC leaders sought power "without much principle and secure[d] it by patronage"; as for the PCI, it was regarded by the young left as "hopelessly middle-aged, a bourgeois establishment party" offering no valid alternative to the Christian Democrat establishment. Finally, the judicial process was held in often justified contempt, due to its abnormal slowness, with trials prolonged for years waiting for a general amnesty.

If such social factors helped motivate the terrorists, for Arculus their objectives were rarely consistent or expressed with much coherence. Terrorism was a "destructive but understandable" product of Italian society, like the drug problem, criminal violence, or the corruption of much of public life. The same processes which had brought about Italy's economic miracle, its combination of private wealth and public squalor, enterprise and anarchy, would continue both to breed terrorism and to contrive ways to live with it. Terrorism was therefore likely to remain a fundamental problem for Italy for many years to come unless a new economic boom comparable to that of the 1950s and early 1960s could be used to build a new society. The Ambassador concluded with some considerations on the fight against terrorism. Italian society was "resilient and capable of improvisation" and positive response to problems, as shown by its economic success in the face of failures of government and lack of resources: indeed, it was not near collapse. On the other hand, terrorism could not be broken in the short run; its roots went too deep, and the resupply of recruits was easily assured, through the universities and a whole generation of the unemployed and alienated young. The most likely outcome in the near future, therefore, was a continuing bloody struggle with severe losses on both sides.[116]

Anyway, it is important to note that, in British view, the successes of terrorism were not leading the way for the entry of the Communist Party into government: on the contrary, they were acting as a deterrent. This was primarily because of the terrorists' ideology, described as often "half-baked or confused" and whose importance should not be exaggerated. Even the attraction of violence for its own sake was just as important, coupled with despair about the system. On these premises, many of the groups on the left were "pure Leninists" in their organisation and outlook, and that

---

116 TNA, FCO 33/4594, "Terrorism in Italy", despatch (051/4) by Arculus R., WRJ 051/3, 8 August 1980.

embarrassed the PCI and partly explained the party's stand on law and order: and yet, "for the PCI leadership, examining left-wing terrorism [was] too much like looking through the family album". On the other hand, the ideology of the extreme right was crude anti-Communism with a "dash of nostalgia for Il Duce" and shared with the left a general hatred of the status quo, epitomised by large corporations, Parliament, and the Security Services. Speaking of the latter, the British government was concerned about the state of the services in Italy, particularly their fragmentation: six different services worked in competition on the Moro case. In such a scenario, terrorism was not seen as a catalyst for the entry of the PCI into government, although it put a strain on society and the political system, thus providing opportunities (like Bologna) to the Communists to launch attacks upon the government. However, the PCI did not as a result get any nearer to power, despite Cossiga's fall. The British Ambassador expected that terrorism, despite the vulnerability of some institutions like the magistracy, would continue to reflect the weakness of Italian society rather than bring about radical change.[117]

Even after the bombing in Bologna, British interest in Italian terrorism did not diminish. The Foreign Office created a monthly bulletin for 1981 with a "calendar of terrorism events" to monitor the main law and order issues. As emerged in a talk with Rapisarda, Deputy Head of UCIGOS (Ufficio centrale per le investigazioni generali e per le operazioni speciali – Central Bureau of General Investigations and Special Operations), the Red Brigades were reconsidering their strategy. Their previous attack had been the kidnapping of Judge D'Urso, who represented the magistrates and the prison system; the killing of General Galvaligi, representing the Carabinieri, "perhaps the most dangerous adversary of the Red Brigades"; and the murder of Roberto Peci (brother of Patrizio, a former member of the BR and their first informant) had been an obvious warning to actual or would-be "pentiti". The kidnapping in April of Ciro Cirillo, DC councillor for the Campania region, revealed a new tactic of exploiting the aftermath of the earthquake and general discontent in the area.[118] In contrast, the killing of the Montedison executive Giuseppe Taliercio on 5 July 1981, just as Spadolini's government was about to go before Parliament for the vote of confidence, was to be included in the most consolidated strategy. The Red Brigades showed themselves still to be

---

117 TNA, FCO 33/4594, "Terrorism in Italy", Arculus R. to Gladstone D., WRJ 051/3, 27 October 1980.

118 TNA, FCO 33/4919, "Italian terrorism", by Culshaw R., WRJ 051/1, 2 December 1981.

well enough organised to carry out crimes at a time designed to have the maximum impact. Three years after the Moro case, the BR wished to signal that they would not be satisfied with "minor" changes to the political system, namely the appointment of the first "lay" Prime Minister since the war. More generally, the Red Brigades always wanted to keep themselves on the front pages at a moment of political change.[119]

With the beginning of the 1980s, the possible international links of Italian terrorism became an issue of great importance in Anglo-Italian relations, both for the consequences of a hypothetic manoeuvring from the outside – maybe from the Soviet Union – in one of Britain's European partners and also a member of NATO, and for the experience of Irish terrorism and its likely links with groups in Italy. During a visit to London in January 1980, Cossiga informed Thatcher of two small guided missiles which had fallen into the hands of an Italian terrorist group: he had feared they could be for use in Northern Ireland, but it was later established that the missiles had been intended for use in Italy. The terrorists had been arrested, and it appeared they had connections with the George Habash Palestinian organisation.[120]

The most striking and controversial case originated from a declaration by President Pertini about the alleged international control of Italian terrorism. Already after the Bologna attack, Arculus reported that Pertini alluded to international links and even Cossiga and Foreign Secretary Colombo did not exclude the possibility of outside support. The British embassy in Rome did not believe there could be evidence of these allegations, yet the internal dynamics of these statements were apparent: since the PCI had tried to exploit the Bologna massacre to prove the fundamental weakness of Italian society under the DC, the government could respond with hints to international links, implying that "the Communists' own house need[ed] to be put in order".[121]

In November 1980, the charges became more pressing: during a meeting with the President of the European Commission Roy Jenkins, Pertini said that he had many doubts about the internal origin of the terrorist threat in Italy. In a conversation with the President of Algeria Chadli Bendjedid,

119 TNA, FCO 33/4919, "Terrorism: calendar of events", Culshaw R. to Osborne R., WRJ 051/1, 20 July 1981.

120 TNA, FCO 33/4353, record of a conversation between the Prime Minister and the President of the Council of Ministers of the Italian Republic, Signor Cossiga, at 10 Downing Street, 29 January 1980.

121 TNA, FCO 33/4594, "Terrorism", Tomkins W. to Gladstone D., WRJ 051/3, 11 August 1980.

he learned of a training camp in the Libyan desert for terrorists from Italy, Spain, and Germany. For this reason, Pertini regarded the Red Brigades as part of an "international conspiracy against democracy". He also thought that the Italian constitution was itself under threat, due to the growing pressures for a presidential government which could bring some risk of a coup, despite the loyalty of the Carabinieri. Pertini feared that terrorists were taking advantage of the wave of discontent caused by government scandals and the earthquake in Irpinia.[122]

The apparent allusion to the Soviet Union not only provoked a sharp reaction from the PCI – Forlani was under pressure to state whether the government shared the assessment of the President of the Republic – but also from the Soviets. Vice Foreign Minister and former Ambassador in Rome Nikita Ryzhov summoned the Italian Ambassador in Moscow, Giuseppe Walter Maccotta, to protest against Pertini's accusation, which was offensive and in sharp contrast to the recent friendly character of Italo-Soviet relations.[123] It was the first formal protest from the Moscow government in many years (apart from critical articles in the state-controlled press). The case eventually subsided when Speranza, the DC Under-Secretary at the Ministry of Foreign Affairs, gave an oral reply to the Soviet Ambassador, emphasising that no accusations against the USSR had been intended: no real damage was done to Soviet/Italian relations.[124]

The British embassy stressed that there were links between the Italian terrorists and other countries: for example, many took refuge in Paris or Southern France; they received German terrorists passing through; they went to Czechoslovakia; they got weapons from various sources; there were reports of some having been trained in Libya. However, Arculus concluded that there was no evidence that they were directed from outside. President Pertini was nonetheless right in affirming that the destabilisation of a country in a strategic position like Italy had to be a Soviet interest.[125] Even the Foreign Office agreed with the absence of substantial evidence of international links with terrorism in Italy: the domestic gangs needed

---

122 TNA, FCO 33/4594, Record of conversation between the President of the European Commission and the President of the Italian Republic: Palazzo Quirinale, Rome, 15 November 1980.

123 Zucconi V., "Mosca protesta per l'intervista di Pertini sul terrorismo. Quirinale e governo: ma nessun Paese è stato accusato", *Il Corriere della Sera*, 28 January 1981.

124 TNA, FCO 33/4919, "Italian terrorism: international links", Culshaw R. to Osborne R., WRJ 051/1, 10 March 1981.

125 TNA, FCO 33/4919, "Italian terrorism: international links", Tomkins W. to Gladstone D., WRJ 051/1, 30 January 1981.

little support from abroad. On the other hand, it was surprising that no captured terrorist confirmed nor denied reports of outside involvement.[126]

The battle against terrorism in Italy was far from being won, despite some progress of the authorities, in particular with the liberation of the NATO General James Lee Dozier in January 1982. The Dozier kidnapping had a great symbolic value for public opinion, helping the moral relaunching of the institutions; it is considered the episode which started the decline of the Red Brigades.[127] However, as seen from London, terrorism was not a phenomenon destined to disappear in the short run, because of its ability to recruit new members, especially among young people. Given this new wave of recruiting, it was necessary to avoid any generalisation about the purposes of the Red Brigades and other groups. Their early leaders used to be "equipped with relatively uniform ideologies and tactics", while new members came from a wider social and cultural environment, often of lower quality and with less coherent purposes: groups in one city could have very different objectives from those elsewhere. The phenomenon, therefore, grew more varied, but no easier to eradicate.[128]

Concluding, 1979 would mark a watershed in the history of both countries, albeit with differing results. Italy was set to full realignment with the major Western powers, as shown by the will of the Italian government to comply with NATO's decisions on euromissiles. The Italian government overestimated the impact of participation in the EMS: it did not represent the end of the uncertainties of the 1970s, nor did it give the country a new international stance. On the eve of the revived conflict between the superpowers, it was Italy's support to TNF modernisation that would be interpreted by her partners as the defining moment for the Italian way out of the crisis. Italy, therefore, entered the 1980s with many unresolved problems, but also with a recovering economy, new political characters and the first steps toward a renovated image. This trend was even more apparent for Britain, with the clearly new path of Thatcherism, although the results of the first years of Conservative government seemed disappointing. It took a 74-day war to change the situation for good.

---

126 TNA, FCO 33/4594, "Terrorism in Italy", Gladstone D. to Arculus R., WRJ 051/3, 15 September 1980.

127 See Valiani L., *I governi Spadolini e la lotta al terrorismo*, Edizioni de La Voce Repubblicana, Roma 1983.

128 TNA, FCO 33/4919, "Terrorism: calendar of events", Culshaw R. to Osborne R., WRJ 051/1, 20 July 1981.

Chapter 5

Of faraway wars and Socialists in power

In 1982, after almost three years in government, the Conservative Party appeared divided and weak. Internal dissent spread, and Thatcher's own political survival was at risk. Few believed that she could ever lead the Tories to another election win. The British economy did not show enough signs of recovery, while the government dealt with reducing double-digit inflation and cutting public spending. The polls indicated that Thatcher was the most unpopular Prime Minister ever and the Conservative Party's ratings stood at 23 per cent.[1] The Argentine invasion of the Falkland Islands in April 1982 was to change this apocalyptic scenario: Thatcher emerged from the 74-day war as a new leader, the personification of a modern and imperial warrior queen. But was Britain actually great again?

The Falklands war also caused some tension between the United Kingdom and Italy, in a moment when the political formula of the *pentapartito* began to show its limits for Italian stability. 1983 was an election year for both countries: while in Britain continuity was granted by Thatcher's confirmation, Italy saw a significant change in her political history, with the first Socialist Prime Minister since the foundation of the Republic.

Is Britain great again?

> What has changed since Margaret Thatcher came to power? The Iron Lady says without a moment of uncertainty: "Everything's changed". She's exaggerating. The glorious revolution against the Mandarins of the welfare State has yielded results. But the British imperial lion, after the Falklands war roaring, went back to sleep. The country remains lazy, resigned to rest on Victorian laurels. The cruel whipping of the terrible lady does not have the awaited effect.

---

1 Berrington H., "Change in British Politics: An Introduction", in *Id.* (ed.), *Change in British politics*, Frank Cass, London 1983, p. 5.

These are the opening words of the book *Thatcher the iron doll* by Italian journalist Paolo Filo della Torre, published in 1983.[2] The assessment, albeit harsh, is indicative of the widespread dissent and even disappointment regarding Thatcher's Britain in the early 1980s. In the three years of Conservative government that preceded the Falklands war, the drastic programme of the Prime Minister did not fail to provoke criticisms on issues of economic policy even on the part of Tories' moderate wing. Former premier Edward Heath became the spokesperson of this internal opposition at the Blackpool Party Conference in September 1981, while other leading figures, like the then Chairman of the Conservative Party Peter Thorneycroft and the then leader of the Commons Francis Pym, openly diverged with the Prime Minister. This prompted Thatcher to undertake a Cabinet reshuffle, which was intended to reduce the influence of the critical elements and present the public with a renewed image of the government in view of future electoral campaigns.

Economic measures were just one of the issues at stake: from the very beginning, the Thatcher government experienced unexpected difficulties in fulfilling its manifesto promises. Social and racial unrest were a major problem. Britain suffered serious riots in many major cities, especially on the weekend of the 10-12 April 1981, when hundreds of mostly black youths rioted in Brixton, South London. The worst incidents occurred on the evening of 11 April, when 279 policemen and 45 members of the public were injured. Home Secretary William Whitelaw commissioned a public inquiry into the riot headed by Lord Scarman.[3] The "Scarman report" was published on 25 November 1981, pointing out the problems created by unemployment, poor housing, ethnic conflict, and low educational achievement.[4] In the meantime, the Irish Question came back to the limelight overwhelmingly, with a new wave of hunger strikes in an attempt to break the British policy of criminalising paramilitary prisoners.

---

2 Filo della Torre P., *Thatcher la bambola di ferro*, Rizzoli, Milano 1983. It must be noted that Paolo Filo della Torre was also London correspondent for the left-wing daily *La Repubblica*.

3 TNA, PREM 19/484, "Brixton: inquiry", 13 April 1981.

4 *The Brixton Disorders 10-12 April 1981*, Report of an Inquiry by the Rt. Hon. The Lord Scarman, Cmnd. 8427 (HMSO, 1981). On the riots see Benyon J., *Scarman and After. Essays Reflecting on Lord Scarman's Report, the riots and their aftermath*, Pergamon, Oxford 1984. Scarman advocated special training to make the police sensitive to racial resentments, urging "positive discrimination" to overcome the sense of negative discrimination felt by the black population. Although Thatcher agreed with much of the analysis of the Scarman Report, she insisted that inner-city problems did not justify rioting and crime, especially if carried out under the guise of social protest.

This culminated with the death of the member of Provisional IRA and MP Bobby Sands, which led to worldwide anti-British protests.[5]

In the spring of 1982, the popularity of the Thatcher government drastically decreased, and there were very poor chances for the Prime Minister to be granted a second mandate in the forthcoming elections. Unexpectedly, the way out for Thatcher's doomed political fate came from a group of scattered islands in the South Atlantic Ocean.

The Falklands effect

The Falklands crisis broke out on 19 March 1982, when a group of apparently civilian workers of a fishing company landed in South Georgia, which was part of the Falklands archipelago, and raised the Argentinian flag. Then, on 2 April, around 3,000 Argentine special forces invaded Port Stanley, the islands' capital, which was renamed Puerto Argentino, seizing the airfield, the Royal Navy barracks, the government house and the harbour.[6]

The attack took the British government by surprise, although Argentina and the United Kingdom had disputed sovereignty over the Falkland Islands/Malvinas throughout the previous two centuries.[7] More than 8,000 miles away from mainland Britain and three hundred miles off the southern coast of Argentina, in 1982 the Falklands had approximately 1,800 inhabitants, known as "kelpers", the majority being of British descent.

---

5 Hennessey T., *Hunger Strike: Margaret Thatcher's Battle with the IRA, 1980-1981*, Irish Academic Press, Kildare 2013; Beresford D., *Ten Men Dead: The Story of the 1981 Irish Hunger Strike*, Atlantic Monthly Press, New York 1997.

6 On the Falklands war see Boyce G.D., *The Falklands War*, Palgrave Macmillan, Basingstoke 2005; Freedman L., *The official history of the Falklands campaign*, Vol. 1. *The origins of the Falklands War* and Vol. 2. *War and diplomacy*, Routledge, London 2005; Hastings M., Jenkins S., *The battle for the Falklands*, Pan Books, London 2010; Cawkell M., Hunt R., *The History of the Falkland Islands*, Anthony Nelson, London 2001; Parsons M., *The Falklands War*, Sutton, Stroud (Gloucestershire) 2000; Goebel J., *The Struggle for the Falkland Islands: A Study in Legal and Diplomatic History*, Yale University Press, New Haven 1982; Strange I.J., *The Falkland Islands*, David & Charles, London 1983; Borsani D., *La "special relationship" anglo-americana e la guerra delle Falkland (1982)*, Le Lettere, Firenze 2016.

7 Britain took control of the islands in 1833, when the British Navy occupied the archipelago, which in 1820 had become an Argentinian colony. The islands were a focus of international conflict already in the 18th century: Britain claimed the right of discovery and early settlement of the islands, while Spain lay claims over the archipelago in accordance with the Treaty of Tordesillas of 1494. Since its independence in 1816, Argentina intended to enforce its rights of succession to Spain.

In 1965, Argentina had brought the Falklands case in the UN on the basis of resolution 1514 (on the Granting of Independence to Colonial Countries and Peoples), and negotiations between the two countries had continued without significant progress for 17 years.[8] In March 1982, the talks were interrupted again, and Argentine representatives said ominously that the government in Buenos Aires would implement more drastic measures to defend its cause. These warnings were not taken into account by the United Kingdom since the Falklands were not the primary concern for British ministers in 1982. Defence policy focused mainly on the Soviet Union, the Middle East and Northern Ireland; even the small part of intelligence dealing with Latin America worried more about the threat that Guatemala posed to Belize than the threat that Argentina posed to the Falklands.[9]

Moreover, the warnings from Buenos Aires received poor consideration due to the weak position of Argentina. Following a coup, the country had been under military rule since 1976, and in December 1981 a new junta led by General Leopoldo Galtieri came to power. The new junta hoped to divert public attention, while Argentina was falling into a deep economic crisis, with a great recession and inflation reaching 90 %. Galtieri needed a quick success abroad to secure his government at home and decided to invade the Falkland Islands, embarking on a military adventure imbued with nationalism. In hindsight, he made a severe error of judgment. The Argentine attack was moved by two assumptions, namely the backing of the United States and Britain's lack of interest for the Falkland Islands, and both proved to be wrong. The first hypothesis arose from Galtieri's firm belief in the support of the Reagan Administration after the warm welcome received in a trip to Washington in 1981 and by the Inter-American Treaty of Assistance (Rio Pact) and the support provided to the CIA in Nicaragua. In fact, the United States, after an initial phase of official neutrality and mediation of US Secretary of State Alexander Haig, chose a pro-British position, giving the go-ahead to US military aid to the United Kingdom. As regards the second condition, namely disinterest in London, the Thatcher government had imposed substantial cuts of the Royal Navy as part of a more general downsizing to the armed forces in 1981; the Argentine press emphasised the event for propaganda purposes. Also, the new nationality law adopted by the British government in 1981 played a role in the dispute with Argentina over the Falklands. The "Gibraltar amendment", which gave Gibraltarians exclusive access to British citizenship, was extended to

---

8 González M.A., *The genesis of the Falklands (Malvinas) conflict. Argentina, Britain and the failed negotiations of the 1960s*, Palgrave Macmillan, Basingstoke 2013.

9 Vinen R., quoted, p. 136.

Falkland Islanders only after the war. At the time of the conception of the Bill, it seemed possible that a special gesture towards the Islanders, making it easier for them to leave if they wished, could adversely affect negotiations with Argentina. There was the risk of giving the impression that Britain was trying to strengthen its position in the talks or strengthen its hold on the islands and perhaps discourage Argentina from proposing that the inhabitants could also hold Argentinian citizenship.[10] The gesture, however, turned against the British, since the Buenos Aires government interpreted it as a lack of interest on the part of London.[11]

If the British were surprised by the invasion, the Argentines were surprised by the strength of Britain's response. The action of the Thatcher government took place simultaneously on several fronts: the UN request for intervention, the military mobilisation, the imposition of sanctions on Argentina and the request of Community solidarity.

As for the first point, on 2 April, the British Permanent Representative to the United Nations, Anthony Parsons, asked for and obtained an emergency meeting of the Security Council to vote on a resolution for an immediate ceasefire and the Argentinean retreat. On the following day, 3 April, with ten votes in favour (including the United States), one against (Panama) and four abstentions (including the Soviet Union, which did not use the veto power) the Security Council passed Resolution 502, calling for the withdrawal of all Argentine forces from the Falklands. The governments in London and Buenos Aires were also invited to solve the dispute through diplomatic channels.[12]

Also on 3 April, after a stormy session of the House of Commons – exceptionally convened on a Saturday for the first time since the Suez crisis – the Thatcher government decided to form a task force to retake the Falklands. The Cabinet was accused of inertia and lack of foresight for not recognising the real Argentine intentions: Foreign Secretary Peter Carrington took full responsibility and resigned, to be replaced by Francis Pym.[13]

---

10 TNA, FCO 9/3134, "Memorandum: The Falkland islanders under UK immigration and nationality law", December 1980.

11 For the importance of 1981 Nationality Act on British internal and foreign policy see Bentivoglio G., "Redefining immigration through citizenship? Britain and the case of the 1981 Nationality Act", in Calandri E., Paoli S., Varsori A. (eds.), *Peoples and Borders: Seventy Years of Migration in Europe, from Europe, to Europe (1945-2015)*, Nomos, Brussels 2017.

12 "Council calls for withdrawal of Argentine forces from Falklands", *UN Chronicle*, Vol. 19, No. 5, May 1982, pp. 5-10.

13 Theakston K. (ed.), *British Foreign Secretaries since 1974*, Routledge, London 2004, p. 130.

Meanwhile, the British government broke diplomatic relations with Argentina and imposed heavy economic sanctions on Buenos Aires: these included a freeze on Argentine assets in British banks, an embargo of arms sales to Argentina, suspension of export credit insurance, and a ban on Argentine imports. At the same time, Britain was asking her partners to take economic action against Argentina.[14] The initiative of London focused no longer on the United Nations but on the European Community, with an intense series of negotiations described by British officials as the backbone of the diplomatic strategy aimed at isolating Buenos Aires.[15] The issue of EC sanctions would become a cause for tension between the United Kingdom and Italy, which will be analysed in more detail below.

On 14 June, the last line of Argentine defence in the Falklands fell, and the islands were brought under full British control: after 74 days, it was the end of the conflict. Despite its brevity, the war had a high number of deaths (900 between military and civilian) and profoundly affected world opinion. The military defeat accelerated the fall of the junta of Galtieri and Argentina's return to democracy, while Thatcher's popularity rocketed, guaranteeing her re-election for a second term in 1983: before the war, this was not the expected outcome. The victory avenged the humiliation of Suez in 1956 and gave a new voice to British ambitions, well summarised in the slogan "Britain is great again".[16]

It was a political triumph for Margaret Thatcher: "the woman with no experience of defence or foreign policy was now a warrior queen".[17] But this did not mean that the government's popularity – which reversed the past climate in public opinion – would surely last. Just after the announcement of victory, the *Corriere della Sera* wondered about the convenience for the Tories to exploit the popular mood and call for early elections: the negative experience of Edward Heath in 1974 could show the danger of a vote called on a single theme.[18]

Britain's status, influence and prestige were all enhanced by the Falklands victory, which restored confidence and a strong image in

---

14 Martin L.L., "Institutions and Cooperation: Sanctions during the Falkland Islands Conflict", *International Security*, Vol. 16, No. 4, 1992, pp. 143-178.

15 "UK Bans All Argentine Imports", *Financial Times*, 7 April 1982.

16 Turner M.J., *Britain's International Role, 1970-1991*, Palgrave Macmillan, Basingstoke 2010, pp. 198-220.

17 Vinen R., quoted, p. 151.

18 Vergani L., "Londra esulta ma non dimenticherà gli orrori di questa guerra", *Corriere della Sera*, 16 June 1982.

international affairs. The importance of perception cannot be ignored: "power had as much to do with what allies and enemies thought Britain could do as with what Britain could actually do".[19] On these premises, it is worth noting how the United Kingdom and Margaret Thatcher were perceived in Italy in the aftermath of the Falklands war.

The Italian press of the time split into two factions: on the one hand, mainstream magazines celebrated Britain and the personal success of her Prime Minister. On 25 June 1982, the weekly *Epoca* (one of the point of reference for Italian middle-class in the 1960s-early 1970s, back then adopting more a tabloid style) dedicated its cover to "the fairy tale prince" William, Charles and Diana's first son, and published a long article on Thatcher, with the title "Defeat is a men's thing". Like Winston Churchill during the Second World War, the "blond lady with a governess look" was a firm model for all those who would rather have chosen a softer approach. She was "cold, hard and resolved, adjectives which become qualities when they represent the patriotism and the never dormant imperial nostalgia of the ruling class". Her slogans seduced even the keenest opponents; she overcame unpopularity and was able to give a new impetus to the uncertain fate of the Conservative Party. After 74 days of war, for Maggie there were flowers and applause.[20]

Conversely, a large part of the press did not share this optimistic view. *L'Espresso* dedicated harsher tones to Thatcher, starting from the cover showing an unforgiving close-up of the Prime Minister with the title "What sort of woman is this?". She could well receive the greatest glorification in British history since 1945, but this was not going to cancel the fact that Thatcher was the most unpopular Prime Minister of all time. The article reported a long series of slogans and insults used against Thatcher, from the 1970s "milk-snatcher" to other unreportable ones; this dislike transcended national boundaries, and she was called "Madame Non" in France, "Perfidious Albino" in Italy (a wordplay with Albion), "Maggie Messer" (Maggie the Knife) in Germany, while for Helmut Kohl she was a "rhino". And yet, Thatcher had suddenly become "Britannia with the trident" and swept away her most valuable competitors. She was part of the "hard-handed club" together with Henry II Plantagenet, Elizabeth I, Oliver Cromwell and, of course, Winston Churchill. But Thatcher's conservatism had nothing in common with the aristocratic Toryism of Lord Carrington or William Whitelaw. Her dream was to build "a social environment where a well-born but poor young woman can marry an

---

19 Turner M.J., quoted, p. 199.

20 "La sconfitta è una cosa per uomini", *Epoca*, 25 June 1982.

ironworks owner and where a hardworking person can move from zero to hero". Such a philosophy had instead raised unemployment to 3 million. In the first three years of her mandate, Thatcher failed to meet all the expectations: the economy was still in recession, and even criminality had grown, despite the electoral importance of law and order. The Prime Minister had succeeded only in showing her inflexibility, and maybe that was the only reason why she continued to hypnotise British crowds. Thatcher's destiny was the sad paradox of a triumph totally detached from the task she had been assigned: reviving the economy and the sense of initiative and entrepreneurship of her people.[21]

The PCI daily *L'Unità* was sceptical about the real positive outcome of the Anglo-Argentine conflict: Britain had taken the law into her own hands but, should this unilateral approach continue, it would open an area of chronic tension in the South Atlantic.[22] As for British foreign policy, the Falklands crisis had started a new course: now Thatcher "felt stronger" and the United Kingdom could take a more radical stance in the international arena, also showing more independence towards the United States.[23]

Furthermore, this critical attitude was not limited to left-oriented papers. For example, an article in *La Stampa* of 27 July described how the enthusiasm for the return of the victorious soldiers had been immediately dampened by old and new problems: strikes, economic difficulties, terrorism. The only person to come out well from that situation was the Queen. England was torn between past and present, and unfortunately the former was more glorious than the latter. The past was epitomised by the Falklands war, which by that time seemed only "a romantic Victorian adventure", while the present was "grey and muggy" like that unusual British summer. It was a peculiar moment, rich in "psychological paradoxes", whose strains had been alleviated by the two traditional English medicines: "phlegmatism and humour". It was a return to normality, to "troubles, delusions, concerns".[24] This analysis matched Filo della Torre's assessment quoted at the beginning of this chapter.

Italian diplomacy analysed the impact of the "Falklands effect" on British policy at home and abroad. The Argentine conflict had marked a political relaunch of the Conservative Party as a result of popular mobilisation. However, the Tories' popularity was already recovering at

21 Russo F., "Che razza di donna è questa?", *L'Espresso*, 13 June 1982.

22 Bronda A., "Euforia a Londra, ma la guerra finisce davvero a Port Stanley?", *L'Unità*, 16 June 1982.

23 *Id.*, "Londra protesta con Israele e polemizza con Washington", *L'Unità*, 4 July 1982.

24 Ciriello M., "Londra soffre il dopo-Falkland", *La Stampa*, 27 July 1982.

the beginning of 1982, in conjunction with the partial successes of the government's economic policy. The trend reversal was amplified by the Argentine conflict, so much so that Gallup polls in May-June 1982 showed 51 % of preferences for the Conservatives against Labour's 25 %. As the effect of the nationalist wave started to fade away, the overall economic trend continued to be uncertain. Industry showed no turnaround, even in the medium to long term, to pull the British economy out of recession. Unemployment had reached 3.2 million, and according to the CBI it was likely to rise again. Notwithstanding, according to the Italian Embassy in London, Thatcher did not seem willing to give up the monetarist and anti-interventionist line announced in the Conservative manifesto of 1979. The inflexibility of the Prime Minister had won widespread support among public opinion and proved to be successful in the fight against inflation (which was then below 10 %). Thatcher's resistance to compromise on economic rigour was nevertheless raising doubts in the same Tory milieu, although after the party conference held in Brighton in October, the Conservative Party had shown a return to a more deferential line to the leadership – the ultimate move to present a united front at the forthcoming elections.

The end of the Falklands War had also coincided with widespread trade union unrest involving the transport and health sectors, which the government tackled with extreme decision. Thatcher emerged from these events significantly strengthened. The Italian ambassador wondered if a winter of relative union peace could let Britain out from the tunnel of recession.[25] Therefore, as seen from Italy, the ultimate Falklands effect did not lie as much in a renewed imperialism, but rather in the strengthening of Thatcher's internal position. Having settled the differences inside the Conservative Party and won an overwhelming popular consensus, the British Prime Minister could focus her second mandate on the real emergency for the United Kingdom, which was not in faraway islands in the South Pacific, but in the very real economic difficulties of the country.

As predicted, Thatcher easily won the general election on 9 June 1983: the Tories had their most decisive election victory since that of the Labour Party in 1945. Although Thatcher was confirmed for her second mandate, gaining 58 more seats in Parliament, the electoral significance of the Falklands was all in all limited: few voters admitted that the victory over Argentina had exercised any influence over them and less than a third of

---

25 ASPR, busta 757/B3, "Appunto per l'Ufficio del Consigliere Diplomatico del signor Presidente della Repubblica. Oggetto: Gran Bretagna: situazione politica interna", 29 January 1983.

Conservative candidates referred directly to the Falklands during their campaigns.[26] Nonetheless, such an electoral success would have been inconceivable 14 months earlier.

Italian reactions to Thatcher's re-election were mixed. As we will see, a general election in Italy had been scheduled for 26 June, only a fortnight after the British vote. The UK results were therefore also interpreted for their likely implications on the Italian political scene. All political leaders agreed in stressing the diversity of the situations in Britain and Italy. DC Secretary De Mita stated that "there [was] a huge difference between the British Conservatives and the Italian Christian Democrats. [...] The competition in Italy [was] between popular forces". There were speculations about a possible "Thatcher effect" in Italy (a mix of stability and economic austerity which could favour moderate parties). In any case, few exulted with the winners, and nobody wanted to identify with the losers. Republicans and Socialists distanced themselves from the Labour Party. According to Spadolini, the British election confirmed the profound crisis of the class rules of European Left; Labour utopia had proved to be inconceivable both in internal and foreign policy.[27] For Craxi, Thatcher's victory was predictable: Labour had been weakened by splits and divisions, while "maximalist trends", extremism and international policies took potential Labour voters away.[28]

The left-oriented press in Italy was of course critical of the electoral results in the United Kingdom, although with some differences. While the Socialist daily *Avanti!* stressed how Thatcher had actually lost votes, but gained seats due to the British electoral system,[29] *L'Espresso* talked of a Conservative triumph and hailed "Queen Margaret", although the tones used were quite harsh. Thatcher was not loved but was undeniably popular. According to the magazine, she "embodied the dream of a national resurgence": despite the lowest rate of industrial production in British history, the Tory Prime Minister was suited to a "cult of personality" based on the country's "will of faith in a miraculous healing". As for the defeat of the Left in Britain, it had been a sort of political suicide: Thatcher's fortune in the Falklands campaign simply made Labour "flip out", and now Britons had to face five or even ten more years of Thatcherism.[30]

---

26 Vinen R., quoted, pp. 151-152.

27 Cianfanelli R., "I leader politici italiani respingono le analogie con la situazione inglese", *Corriere della Sera*, 11 June 1983.

28 *Avanti!*, 11 June 1983.

29 Bianco G., "In maggioranza gli scontenti per la ricetta Thatcher", *Avanti!*, 12 June 1983.

30 Russo F., "La regina Margaret", *L'Espresso*, 19 June 1983.

Only a few months after the electoral triumph, Thatcher was to meet a series of challenges. For the British economy, the figures for 1983 showed considerable uncertainty in its evolution. On the positive side, inflation slowed down, stopping at 4.8 per cent, but industrial production had decreased, the public debt was likely to reach 10 billion pounds, and unemployment did not show signs of stopping and affected 12.5 per cent of the labour force. The outlook for the short to medium term was clouded.[31] On the political side, the papers of the Italian Ministry of Foreign Affairs highlighted the divisions inside the Conservative Party: internal dissidence emerged during the conference in Blackpool in October, and many Tory MPs signed a document against Britain's presence inside the EEC. In any case, Thatcher's position was still sound and she was determined not to abandon her well-known programme for the economic and political renewal of British society.[32]

The Falklands crisis and Anglo-Italian relations

The Falklands conflict marked not only a watershed moment for the two combatants, the United Kingdom and Argentina, but also a test of Western and European solidarity in the new phase of the "second" Cold War.

Within the Western bloc, the position of Italy was somewhat peculiar. As pointed out by more recent historiography on the Italian role in the Falklands crisis, Italy was apparently divided between Community solidarity and the special relationship with Buenos Aires.[33] On the one hand, Europeanism had been a constant theme in Italian foreign policy for almost forty years, one of the founding elements of the very identity of Republican Italy; on the other hand, about half of Argentine citizens were of Italian origin, and the two countries were important trade partners.

31 ASPR, busta 515/B1, Ministero degli Affari Esteri, Segreteria Generale, Visita a Londra del Signor Presidente della Repubblica, "Situazione economica britannica", 18 February 1984.

32 ASPR, busta 515/B1, Visita a Londra del Presidente della Repubblica (22-24 febbraio 1984), "Politica interna", February 1984.

33 Mechi L., "'Fra solidarietà europea e vincoli di sangue'. L'Italia e la crisi delle Falkland/Malvinas", *Annali della Fondazione Ugo La Malfa*, Vol. XVI, 2001, pp. 139-173; Mechi L., Chiampan A., "Des intérêts difficilement conciliables: l'Italie, l'Europe et la crise des Falkland (avril-juin 1982)", *Guerres mondiales et conflits contemporains*, Vol. 245, 2012, pp. 115-132; Savignoni D., "The Internal Dissenter: Italy", in Stavridis S., Hill C. (eds.), *Domestic Sources of Foreign Policy: West European Reactions to the Falklands Conflict*, Berg, Oxford 1996. On the special relationship between Rome and Buenos Aires see Devoto F.J., *Storia degli italiani in Argentina*, Donzelli, Roma 2007.

The Anglo-Argentine conflict of 1982 marked a redefinition of these two features of Italy's policy: blood ties with Buenos Aires were subordinated to the pursuit of a common position within the European Community, while for the very first time the Italian Government distanced itself from the other Member States and began to question its reputation as a "good European". There is also another aspect which has not been considered previously, namely Anglo-Italian relations during the conflict.

For the British government, it soon became clear that its economic pressure on Argentina would not matter if other countries did not also block imports, export credits and arms sales. Since the EC was the recipient of about 20 per cent of Argentine exports, a European embargo would cause many troubles to the junta of Galtieri.[34] On 10 April, the Ten released a statement on the Falklands crisis, outlining the three types of sanctions to be taken against Argentina: an embargo on the shipment of weapons; a blockade of imports from Buenos Aires in the Community area; and Argentina's exclusion from favourable credit arrangements. The European Community showed an unusual promptness (as one EC official said, "We have done in a day what it usually takes a year to do"),[35] which was closely linked to the British budgetary question. In an attempt to defuse the situation, the other member States decided to accept the imposition of economically disadvantageous sanctions in the belief that the United Kingdom would make concessions on the budget issue.

With great surprise for the British, Italy voted in favour of the sanctions. It was not an easy decision for the Spadolini government, which fully supported the United Kingdom over the principle at stake, although public opinion in Italy was very aware of blood ties with Buenos Aires, and for this reason it could not tolerate a complete humiliation of Argentina. Furthermore, such a disgrace would lead to the collapse of the junta, and it was feared that "whatever came afterwards could be worse" than Galtieri. Also, there was increasing pressure from the Socialist Party. The Foreign Office assured that the possible impact of the crisis on the Italian political scene was well known; nevertheless, the government in Rome needed to be patient, since it could be some time before Argentina was brought to negotiate seriously.[36]

Historiography has usually stressed the dependence of Italy's fashion manufacturing sector on Argentine leather as a key factor in its attitude

---

34 Martin L.L., quoted, p. 154.

35 "Waging Economic Warfare", *Time*, 26 April 1982, p. 31.

36 TNA, FCO 33/5754, "Italian reporting on Argentina", Tel. No. 91, WRD 020/6, 29 April 1982; *Ibidem*, "Italy/Argentina", WRD 020/6, 26 April 1982.

towards the Falklands crisis.[37] In fact, the economic relations between Rome and Buenos Aires were much more extensive and complex. The effect of sanctions which most worried the Italians was not so much on trade (which had declined over the last two years, and where the balance of payments was marginally in Rome's favour), but on Italian contracts and investments in Argentina. Italy was the second largest foreign investor in Argentina after the United States, for a total of 340 million dollars, and the Buenos Aires government had already threatened reprisals against companies from countries applying sanctions. The Argentine Embassy told the Italian Foreign Ministry informally that the junta had taken no decisions on concrete retaliation measures, but in the event of a renewal of sanctions after 17 May they had threatened Italy and the rest of the EC Member States with boycotting their firms – excluding them from tenders, blocking payments and sequestering their assets in Argentina.[38]

In addition to the economic pressure on the Italian government against the renewal of sanctions, there was a "confused" political situation, in which Spadolini exercised all his skills of mediation to keep his coalition partners united. In the meantime, Craxi was taking advantage of the weakness of the DC and PCI to strengthen the "lay bloc" and keep himself in centre stage. In that situation, a government crisis would occur at any time even without a "deliberate provocation" by the Socialist Secretary.[39]

Among the Italian parties, it was the PSI which worried the Thatcher government the most; the British Ambassador was unsuccessfully trying to obtain a meeting with Craxi.[40] In a note in the PSI daily *Avanti!*, the Socialist Secretary stated that Italy should actively support any possible form of international mediation to avoid conflict and promote reason. The government was invited to follow the line of prudence and gradualism suggested by the PSI.[41] Craxi claimed to follow the steps of the Labour Party in its opposition (actually, quite marginal) to the British military undertaking: Europe was wrong, while Italy and the PSI were on the right side.[42]

37 See, for instance, Hastings M., Jenkins S., quoted, p. 310; Martin L.L., quoted, p. 155.
38 TNA, FCO 33/5754, "Italy/Argentina: economic relations", WRD 020/6, 11 May 1982.
39 TNA, FCO 33/5754, "Italy internal", Tel. No. 15, WRD 020/6, 13 April 1982.
40 TNA, FCO 33/5754, "Falklands: Italian views", Culshaw R. to FCO Falklands Emergency Unit, WRD 020/6, 26 April 1982.
41 Craxi B., "Il PSI sollecita un impegno italiano", *Avanti!*, 23 April 1982.
42 Fondazione Bettino Craxi, Fondo Bettino Craxi, UA 71, Riunione della Direzione, "Resoconto dell'intervento nel dibattito sul tema della guerra delle Falkland", 15 July 1982.

While military operations continued in the Falklands and were exacerbated as a result of the sinking by the Royal Navy of the Argentine Cruiser *General Belgrano* on 2 May (with the death of 350 sailors), the tension between the United Kingdom and Italy also reached its highest point. The sinking of the "Belgrano" had certainly helped the expansion of the pacifist and neutralist front, now no longer limited to the PSI. On 11 May, in a parliamentary debate about the Anglo-Argentine crisis, the majority of the statements by MPs were sharply against the maintenance of the embargo; only the PSDI and the Republican Party supported the renewal of sanctions, stressing the importance of Atlantic and EC solidarity.[43]

As a last resort to secure Italy's support, on 16 May Thatcher telephoned Colombo just before the Council of Foreign Ministers in Luxembourg, where they were preparing to vote on the renewal of sanctions. The British Prime Minister appealed to different topics to win the Italian resistance, remarking how the decision on the continuation of Community sanctions against Argentina was of great importance not only for the United Kingdom but also for the EC as a whole and for all who believed in upholding the rule of law throughout the world. The United States and the majority of third world countries had supported Britain in her stand against aggression, but Washington alone could not solve the problem. The decision that the Member States were about to take was considered by the government in London as a test of the solidarity of the Community. Schmidt and Mitterrand had already publicly supported the renewal of sanctions; the failure to extend the sanctions would completely split the Community and serve the interests of the government in Buenos Aires and those who believed that the international order could be changed by force. Only the continuation of economic sanctions could ensure the chances of success in the negotiations with Argentina. Thatcher stated that she would "be most upset if Italy, a country from which Britain derived a lot of its law, was supporting aggression". The Italian government had helped the United Kingdom a great deal in the Community and, "given that special relationship", it would be a tragedy if Italy, "which had given its name to the Treaty of Rome", were to cause a fundamental split and crisis in the Community on this matter. The British Prime Minister hoped Colombo's counsels would prevail with the Italian government but, despite his goodwill, the Foreign Minister admitted that he could not guarantee that he would be successful in changing Italy's approach.[44]

---

43 Atti Parlamentari, Camera dei Deputati, VIII legislatura, Discussioni, Seduta antimeridiana, 11 May 1982.

44 TNA, FCO 33/5754, "Italy and sanctions against Argentina", WRJ 020/6, 17 May 1982.

As feared and expected, Italy did not renew the ban on EC imports from Argentina, while maintaining in force until October 1982 the embargo on the supply of weapons. British diplomacy tried to understand the reasons for this shift – and the lessons which should be drawn from it. The Socialists were the first to speak against the import ban, and it had taken a lot of effort by Spadolini and Colombo to persuade their Foreign Trade Minister, Nicola Capria, to sign the April decree. In the meantime, the DC had complained from the outset that it had not been consulted. The British Embassy in Rome believed that Christian Democrat attitudes were equally questionable, given the party's strong links with Latin America. Conversely, the other three coalition parties – PLI, PSDI and PRI – were considered more reliable. After all, the *pentapartito* implied, among other things, a vast "range of people to be lobbied" and often the Ministers themselves were less important than their party secretaries. As regards the domestic political scene, there was an open clash between London and Craxi. The Socialist Secretary had attempted to exploit the Anglo-Argentine crisis opportunistically, although one should recognise that he had found fertile ground for his criticism. A man with only 10 per cent of the vote was making life difficult for Spadolini. The British Embassy in Rome believed that Craxi's primary motive was to show that his coalition partners were obliged, once again, to "jump to his tune" and that the final decision was up to the party secretaries, not the government. Political justifications came later: still, the parties were now beginning to realise the consequences of the non-renewal of sanctions.[45] Arculus then chose to respond to Craxi in the press with an article in the Rome daily *Il Tempo*, intended to refute a long series of claims from the Socialist Secretary.[46]

Arculus stated that the reasons for the failed Italian renewal of the embargo were manifold: first of all, there were ties of blood with the large Italo-Argentine community, which counted 1.3 million Italian passport holders in Argentina and several more millions of Italian descent; a degree of pacifism, especially but not exclusively on the Italian left; the Pope's equivocal attitude, whose statements had a greater impact than those of any politician; a deep-rooted conviction that everything is negotiable ("Italian life is a constant compromise. The problems must be cajoled not addressed directly"); the widespread notion that the future of the Falkland Islands and their inhabitants was not worth fighting for; the constant references to the conflict as British colonialism's last fling, "a

45 TNA, FCO 33/5755, "Italy and the Falklands", Simpsons-Orlebar to Goodison, WRD 020/6, 25 May 1982.

46 "L'ambasciatore inglese risponde all'On. Craxi", *Il Tempo*, 2 June 1982.

nineteenth-century reaction out of time"; and last but not least, many people saw sanctions as contributing to the escalation of the conflict. There were also more specific reasons, like Italian business interests in the entire continent of South America and the prospect of obtaining the votes of Italians living abroad, especially in Latin America, in the event of a change in the voting system. Four arguments, however, were in favour of London: firstly, many people from Spadolini downwards believed that aggression should be resisted and international law upheld; secondly, it was recognised that the United Kingdom had tried to negotiate a fair agreement; thirdly, the Italians disliked military regimes; the fourth and most important reason was Italy's traditional role as a good European: this first serious parting of the ways with other Community partners in thirty years had provoked a sense of shame and guilt. The most striking feature was how the case for supporting the United Kingdom rested largely on European rather than Anglo-Italian ties. In any case, the ties that predominated were Italo-Argentine-Italian, that is, ties of blood.[47]

A few days later, a new event risked jeopardising the relations between Rome and London even more seriously than the sanctions vote. On 23 May, in an article published in *The Sunday Times*, political editor Hugo Young reported the statement of an unnamed member of Thatcher's government. According to the reliable – albeit anonymous – source, the outcome of the war would be determined by the racial characteristics of the enemy: "the Argies are half Spanish and half Italian. If the Spanish side comes out on top, I reckon they'll fight. If it's the Italian side, they'll surrender. It may be as simple as that".[48] The open accusation of cowardice brought the Italian Embassy in London to take the case to the attention of the Foreign Office. The Foreign Secretary Pym was keen to let it be known that he could not believe one of his colleagues in the Cabinet would speak that way, no more than he should himself.[49] Only the intervention of Pertini seemed to settle the disagreement. The President of the Republic raised the question with Arculus during a reception for the diplomatic corps at the Quirinale and gave great publicity to the Ambassador's denial on the press.[50] In any case, the *Sunday Times* article seemed to have hit a

47 TNA, FCO 33/5755, "Italy and the Falklands", 25 May 1982.

48 Young H., "Heroes of an unheroic war", *The Sunday Times*, 23 May 1982.

49 TNA, FCO 33/5755, Tel. No. 123 by Pym F., WRD 020/6, 27 May 1982.

50 "L'ambasciatore britannico smentisce a Pertini una frase sull'Italia attribuita a un ministro inglese", *Corriere della Sera*, 29 May 1982, "Gli Italiani non sono vili", *Paese Sera*, 29 May 1982; "Arculus a Pertini: nessun ministro inglese ha sparlato degli italiani", *Giornale nuovo*, 29 May 1982; "'Italiani codardi', Londra smentisce", *Il Resto del Carlino*, 30 May 1982.

nerve: according to Arculus, the Italians felt embarrassed for their failure to continue the economic sanctions and the relations between London and Rome had been spoiled by that incident.[51] *L'Espresso* dedicated its cover to the Anglo-Italian controversy, with a cartoon of Spadolini dancing the tango with a mysterious Argentine woman and a Hamletic title: "Are we traitors?".[52]

In the analysis of the role of Italy following the conclusion of the conflict, British documents revealed a somewhat divided political scene, with clear differences between the Cabinet and the parties and within the same coalition. The Italian government, notably Spadolini and Colombo, had supported Britain during the whole crisis. Even President Pertini had demonstrated his support to the United Kingdom in talks with Arculus while keeping a lower profile in his public statements. This dualism was more evident – with greater disappointment to the British – in the attitude of the parties. The PSI, the DC, and the PCI continued to express doubts about the policy of the Thatcher government, and in particular about the degree of force used. Socialists and Christian Democrats were under intense pressure from the business world: according to the British Embassy, persistent rumours reported that FIAT had funded at least one of the South American delegations that had come to Italy to plead the cause of Argentina. The non-renewal of EC sanctions had reduced the level of criticism, and many prominent members of the main political groups had declared privately that they personally were entirely behind the British government, despite the line their party was taking in public. Social Democrats, Liberals and Republicans had instead continued to express their support for British policy.

The reaction to the Falklands crisis in the Italian media differed significantly from the political response. The independent press, led by *La Repubblica* with its editor Eugenio Scalfari, expressed substantial support for the British case. Other newspapers, such as the *Corriere della Sera* and *Il Tempo*, had less clear and more impartial editorial lines. Predictably, the loudest criticism came from the party press. *Avanti!*, *Il Popolo* and *L'Unità* agreed on their main argument: while Argentina was in the wrong, the Falklands were not worth spilling blood over, and there had to be some way of finding a negotiated settlement. British attention, however, focused more on radio and television, the most important Italian media

51 TNA, FCO 33/5763, Arculus to Wood, WRD 020/7, 7 June 1982. The British embassy in Rome continued to receive letters from "indignant" Italian citizens all summer long.

52 *L'Espresso*, 30 May 1982.

(relatively few Italians read daily newspapers). The Ministry of Defence had implemented a massive information campaign in the second half of the crisis when still pictures from British sources had begun to fill newspapers and TV screens.[53]

The annual Anglo-Italian summit scheduled in early July would be an excellent opportunity to strengthen the relationship between London and Rome and the question of the Falkland Islands was going to be a central topic of the meeting. The Republican Party prided itself on its European credentials, and Italy's inability to renew economic sanctions against Argentina was the first significant parting of the ways with other European partners. On the other hand, that episode had shown once again how Spadolini and Colombo, "with the best will in the world, [had to] take account of the leaders of the parties in the always fragile coalition".[54] The visit would give British Ministers an opportunity to show that, despite the weakness of the Italian government and the tensions derived from the Falklands crisis, the United Kingdom continued to seek close relations with Italy in a wide range of activities.[55] One of the main objectives of the Thatcher government was to explain to Italian Ministers and also in public, through press conferences and TV interviews, the British attitude towards the Falklands dispute, the future of the Community, and other issues where Italian public opinion had not understood or had failed to give full support to the United Kingdom. The ultimate goal of the bilateral meeting was, in any case, consolidating good working and personal relations between Thatcher and Spadolini and seeking to make Anglo-Italian relations as important a factor in Italian thinking as were Italian relations with Paris or Bonn.[56] The only political backlash concerned Craxi and the Socialist Party: in order to avoid any controversy with the PSI, it was decided to exclude the Falkland issue from the plenary discussion, which would be attended by the Finance Minister, the Socialist Rino Formica.[57]

---

53 TNA, FCO 33/5755, "Italy and the Falklands", Richardson T. to Wood A., WRD 020/6, 1 July 1982.

54 TNA, FCO 33/5763, "Anglo-Italian summit", Arculus R. to Gladstone D., WRD 020/7, 18 May 1982; *Ibidem*, "Anglo-Italian summit: 7 July", WRD 020/7, 10 June 1982.

55 TNA, PREM 19/1295, "Anglo-Italian summit: 6th-7th July", Ref. A08773, 21 June 1982.

56 TNA, FCO 33/5763, "Anglo-Italian summit: 7 July", WRD 020/7, 10 June 1982.

57 TNA, FCO 33/5764, "Anglo-Italian summit: Prime Minister's briefing meeting", Wood to Bridges, WRD 020/7, 2 July 1982.

In his annual review, the British Ambassador in Rome defined 1982 as a difficult year for Anglo-Italian relations. The Falklands crisis became entangled with real Italian interests and with party politics. The media tended to give prominence to the Argentine version, and a major campaign was necessary by the British Embassy in Rome to restore the image of the conflict. Britain won many admirers for the brilliant military operation, but the general feeling was that it was an "absurd war" which put the Italians in a very awkward spot.[58]

According to the British papers, the most obvious lesson that emerged from the Falklands crisis was that Italy, and especially an Italian government subject to precarious coalition arithmetic, would always try to find a middle way in a crisis. The horror of bloodshed and the feeling of closeness to many Argentines of Italian descent were powerful emotional factors. The line proposed by Craxi, for his own ends, had found an echo not just among the Italian public, but also in other political parties. This was because "Italy has a natural temptation to mediate and usually believes, or affects to believe, that a compromise achieved through negotiations is the correct solution to any problem".[59]

In conclusion, the Falklands conflict represented a moment of crisis – although rapidly overcome – for Anglo-Italian relations. However, there are some considerations to be made. Firstly, Italy's support to British politics rested mostly on Community ties, rather than on the will to show solidarity with the United Kingdom. The relationship with London was not strong enough to determine the course of Italian foreign policy and the British Government was aware of not having the same influence over the Italians as France and the Federal Republic of Germany, not to mention the United States.

Secondly, the episode of the Italian lack of solidarity in the EC could be put on the back burner compared to the primary objective of maintaining Italy in the Western camp. To this end, it was necessary that the Rome government was thoroughly integrated into the system of NATO, the European Community and the OECD: for its part, the United Kingdom was willing to engage in bilateral relations with Italy, even if it was not always rewarding.[60]

---

58 TNA, FCO 33/6663, "Italy: Annual review for 1982", by Arculus R., WRD 014/2, 20 January 1983.

59 TNA, FCO 33/5755, "Italy and the Falklands", Richardson T. to Wood A., WRD 020/6, 1 July 1982.

60 TNA, FCO 33/5746, "Italy: annual review for 1981", by Arculus R., 25 January 1982.

The first Socialist Government in Italy

A new foreign policy in an unsettled political scene?

Still in 1982, Italy was not a country out of the crisis and yet maintained its value in the Western bloc. Nevertheless, there were many signs of recovery in the economy as well as in the way of life.

The international image of the country was gaining a new status, while "Made in Italy" bloomed with the emergence of a new entrepreneurial class. It was an early example of "nation-branding": the "Made in Italy" campaign revamped the image of Italy abroad, reviving certain fascist mythologies about the country as a centre of art and culture.[61] Italian designers made fashion more accessible and became real celebrities: Armani was on the cover of *Time* magazine in April 1982, which paid tribute to "Giorgio's gorgeous style".[62] Also, the interest in Italian art flourished, particularly in the United Kingdom: many exhibitions in London were dedicated to Italy's Renaissance and the metaphysical painter Giorgio De Chirico, West End theatres hosted plays by Italian writers, and the Edinburgh Festival explored Italy's influence on European culture.[63]

More impetus to the country's revival came – not very orthodoxly – from football. In July 1982, Italy won the FIFA World Cup and football fever played a big part in securing the longevity of the Spadolini government. According to *The Economist*, the World Cup did almost as much for Spadolini as the Falklands campaign did for Mrs Thatcher. The football triumph "put the seal on a spell of remarkably good news from a country more commonly associated with scandals and disasters"; Italy was also enjoying a tourist boom.[64]

As regards more traditional politics, the strengthening of the European dimension with the Colombo-Genscher initiative went hand in hand with the broader policy of emphasising Italy's contribution to the Western strategy. To this end, the Spadolini government tried to give new strength to the founding pillar of Italian foreign policy – the relations with Washington – while trying to play a more active role in the Middle East.

---

[61] Ritter C., "The double life of the Italian suit", in Cinotto S. (ed.), *Making Italian America: Consumer Culture and the Production of Ethnic Identities*, Fordham University Press, New York 2014, p. 196.

[62] *Time*, 5 April 1982.

[63] Russo F., "E poi, va di moda l'Italia", *L'Espresso*, 14 March 1982.

[64] "Saved by the ball", *The Economist*, 17 July 1982.

Solidarity with the American ally was stressed during Colombo's visit to the United States in February 1982. The Minister of Foreign Affairs gave a speech at Georgetown University on transatlantic relations, calling for a formal act to reaffirm the common political aims shared by the US and the EEC:

> It is essential that the political will of America and Europe (that is the European Community in its political and economic forms) must be strongly reaffirmed so that we act together in order to pursue the common ideals of security, freedom and peace. My preference is for a formal instrument. I would propose that this common political will be solemnly reaffirmed in a text, for example, a Euro-American friendship pact strengthening democracy and cooperation which should, naturally, cover the political aspects of East-West relations, actions to be taken in favour of the Third World and the coordination of our economic policies. This pact [...] should provide for periodic meetings between foreign ministers to coordinate their respective views, particularly in times of crisis.[65]

Colombo reiterated his proposal some months later, in front of the European Parliament.[66] The British government showed great interest in the Italian project, but it soon emerged that Colombo was "floating a trial balloon" and that the Farnesina was still working to produce precise proposals: the Minister of Foreign Affairs had no clear answer to the problem and the US State Department did not favour any new institutions within the Atlantic Alliance. According to the British embassy in Washington, the US hoped and believed that the Colombo proposal "would disappear of its own accord": they proved to be right.[67]

As for the Middle East, Italy participated in the Multinational Force and Observers (MFO), an international peacekeeping force created in 1981 to operate in the Sinai Peninsula with the aim of overseeing the terms of the peace treaty between Egypt and Israel. Moreover, from 1982 to 1984 Italy joined the United States, France, and Britain in the peacekeeping operations of the Multinational Force in Lebanon (MNF). Italy contributed the largest number of troops to the MNF, with

65 TNA, FCO 33/5272, Washington Tel No. 772 by Henderson N., "Colombo's proposals on US/European relations", WRJ 020/3, 5 March 1982.

66 Gazzetta ufficiale delle Comunità europee. Discussioni del Parlamento europeo. No. 1-289, 14 October 1982.

67 TNA, FCO 33/5752, FCO Tel No. 48 by Carrington P., WRJ 020/3, 11 March 1982; *Ibidem*, "Colombo's visit to Washington: US/European relations", Richardson T. to Lambert S., WRJ 020/3, 11 March 1982; *Ibidem*, "Pertini/Colombo visit to the US", Pakenham M. to Osborne R., WRJ 020/3, 30 March 1982.

nine battalions rotating through Beirut at various times. It was a huge improvement for the Italian armed forces: for the first time, professional soldiers had been deployed together with many conscripts.[68]

To British relief, Spadolini managed to overcome a crisis in the summer of 1982, creating a new government virtually identical to the first one (the so-called "photocopy government"). But the fundamental differences between the DC and the Socialists – primarily over economic policy – remained. Still, because of the forced dependence on the confidence of the major political parties, the alacrity of the PRI Prime Minister was not sufficient to fix the structural defects that plagued the Italian political system. The apparent weakness of the coalition government heavily conditioned bilateral relations and Italian foreign policy. The experiment of the *pentapartito* was viewed with apprehension by the Thatcher government because it could make more politically unstable a country that represented to London the very essence of instability.

In the autumn of 1982, British diplomacy took active steps to overcome the controversy aroused during the Falklands war. Arculus talked with Charles Hargrove of *The Times* about the damage done by the "hen-feathers episode".[69] The resulting article was published inside a five-page special report by Peter Nichols on Italy, to investigate the unity of the country in the centenary year of the death of the Risorgimento hero and "father of the fatherland" Giuseppe Garibaldi. Despite a fresh effort to bring greater flexibility to the political scene with the nomination of Spadolini as Prime Minister, there remained signs of malaise. The gap between public opinion and the politicians was still wide, while the executive remained weak. There was "an aura of unchangeability"; at the same time, urgent treatment was required to continue stability, and a reasonable degree of good government looked "difficult but crucial".[70] As for Hargrove's article on Italian foreign policy, it pointed out two "surprising paradoxes of Italy's paradoxical political situation". Firstly, the country afflicted with chronic governmental instability was managing to play a substantial role in international affairs, and often made its voice heard both in Washington and in the EEC. Secondly, the weakness of the state had not produced any substantial drift towards political

68 Katz S., Russell L.E., *Armies in Lebanon 1982-84*, Bloomsbury, London 2012; Nuti L., *La sfida nucleare*, quoted, p. 359. On the mission to Beirut see Lagorio L., *L'ultima sfida. Gli euromissili*, Loggia de' Lanzi, Firenze 1998, pp. 114-115; Caligaris L., "Western peacekeeping in Lebanon: lessons of MLF", *Survival*, No. 6, 1984, pp. 262-268; Davidson J.W., *America's Allies and War*, Palgrave Macmillan, Basingstoke 2011, pp. 48-51.

69 TNA, FCO 33/5750, "Britain and Italy", by Arculus R., WRJ 020/1, 15 October 1982.

70 "Good government looks difficult, but crucial", *The Times*, 13 October 1982.

extremism of right or left. Maybe the explanation lay in the fact that the art of compromise, "which they have to apply continually to the formulation of policy by coalition governments", made Italian political leaders particularly apt at proposing reasonable and acceptable solutions for the more complicated international problems. Italy was therefore to play the role of "honest broker" which belonged to Britain in the past, although with a difference: while the United Kingdom was moving from a position of strength, the government of Rome was playing from a position of apparent weakness, without provoking the same suspicion or jealousy. The article highlighted how, apart from the natural Italian instinct for negotiation rather than conflict, a personal factor, i.e. Foreign Secretary Emilio Colombo, had given a new impetus to the external policy of the country. He also profited from the weakness of the Italian coalition government, boasting a freedom of action and initiative which his British and French opposite numbers could only envy. Italy had been increasingly active in the Middle East (managing to remain on good terms with all sides, including Gaddafi) and in Latin America. NATO and Europe remained the twin pillars on which Italian foreign policy had been based since the end of the 1940s: a strong united Europe was the essential corollary of a powerful American ally and Italy did not fear the loss of national sovereignty to get closer political cooperation and more European unity. According to Hargrove, that policy had a sociological and cultural explanation "in a country where the sovereignty of the individual – or of the family – is much greater than the sovereignty of the state".[71] The article had a positive reception in Rome. The *Corriere della Sera* welcomed the unexpectedly encouraging assessment on Italian foreign policy: despite the alleged offences, Italy was taken seriously when she could act seriously, playing a coherent and constructive role, adequate to her mediation skills.[72]

At the end of 1982, this sense of optimism was to come to a stop: Spadolini had to face a new government crisis in November which led to his definitive resignation. The crisis arose entirely outside Parliament, from a row between two Ministers, the DC Treasury Secretary Beniamino Andreatta and Formica, while Spadolini was visiting the United States. The British Embassy in Rome described this new crisis as like "watching a drunk on a tightrope: everyone knew that he would fall, but no-one knew when". Moreover, the *pentapartito*'s unity and effectiveness seemed irremediably damaged.[73]

---

71 "A leading world role despite its weakness", *The Times*, 13 October 1982.

72 Cianfanelli R., "Piace agli esperti di Londra la politica estera dell'Italia", *Corriere della Sera*, 15 October 1982.

73 TNA, FCO 33/5748, "Italian government crisis", Richardson to Wood, WRJ 014/2, 16 November 1982.

In order to form a new government, President Pertini gave a mandate to an old acquaintance of Palazzo Chigi: 74-year-old Amintore Fanfani. Fanfani had been DC Secretary and "the power behind the throne" when Italy signed the Treaty of Rome, and his career coincided with the life of the post-war Republic. Four times President of the Council between 1954 and 1963, Fanfani had been the architect, together with Aldo Moro, of the centre-left formula. His handling of Italy's growing economic difficulties aroused many doubts among British diplomats: he was the man of the post-war economic miracle, "a spender rather than a saver" and could find it distasteful to grapple with Italy's economic problems. But he was a pragmatist and could well want to be remembered as "the saviour of Italy".[74] A positive note came from the Ministry of Foreign Affairs: Emilio Colombo remained at the Farnesina, thus guaranteeing continuity to foreign policy.

As seen from London, the fifth Fanfani government was a backwards step for Italian politics, although it was to be a mere transition cabinet while waiting for new general elections. Yet, the primary concern for Britain lay in the weakness of the two main political parties in Italy and the likely repercussions on the West as a whole. In particular, in the unsettled state of Italian politics, the situation of the PCI was critical. The party was in decline, losing votes and a sense of purpose, and it lacked dynamic guidance, with Berlinguer looking "anything but a successful leader". Arculus acknowledge that, while he was not "obsessed with the PCI, as [his] US colleagues tend[ed] to be", it remained a formidable party in terms of "votes, discipline and disruptive ability":

> They brought down Cossiga, one of the best Prime Ministers Italy has produced in recent years. They gave Spadolini a soft ride first time round, but he rightly expects them to get tough between now and their party congress in February 1983. They need to heal internal divisions and to give an air of purpose and direction; opposing the present rather enfeebled administration or any similar coalition which succeeded it, would be one way. They aim to prove, whenever opportunity offers, that Italy is ungovernable while they are excluded from Government.[75]

The PCI's downward trend since 1979 had been confirmed by local election results and opinion polls; and its retreat into opposition, with the long-term aim of establishing a government of the left, had put it further away from power at the national level than at any time in the

74 TNA, PREM 19/1818, Tel No. 616, "Italian crisis: Fanfani", 1 December 1982.

75 TNA, FCO 30/5241, "Italy's Communists", Arculus R. to Pym F., 10 November 1982.

1970s. Although the party's freedom from corruption was an essential part of its appeal, PCI success in future would depend mainly on the failure of the Christian Democrats and to a lesser extent upon the fortunes of the Socialists. Yet it remained the largest Communist party in Western Europe and dominated the administration of all but one of Italy's seven largest cities.[76]

Another aspect to be taken into consideration was the relation between the PCI and the CPSU. Already in 1979, the Soviet invasion of Afghanistan had provoked direct criticism from the PCI. After Jaruzelski's imposition of military rule in Poland in December 1981, the PCI's condemnation stung the Kremlin into a series of bitter attacks on the PCI and its leadership. The Soviet Party could not accept Berlinguer in a TV programme describing the 1917 revolution as a "spent force". However, there had been some contacts with the USSR: Berlinguer knew that some militants, especially of the older generation, still regarded Moscow as their spiritual home, and that many more were unhappy to see Italy siding with the United States in any clash of interests between the superpowers. What had gone for good, however, was the acceptance by the PCI of a guiding role for the USSR or the CPSU. Yet Berlinguer refused – both privately and in public – to define the Polish case as a watershed for the PCI.[77]

Pressure from the party base, combined with a poor showing in elections, forced the leadership at the end of 1980 to produce a new objective, the so-called democratic alternative; this was meant to be an alliance of the left, excluding the Christian Democrats. As seen from London, it was not such a definite turnaround as it could appear: the democratic alternative was so precise that it could embrace genuinely left-wing figures in the DC. Nevertheless, the change of direction served its primary purpose, which was to reassure PCI supporters unhappy about the association with the establishment party which they held responsible for Italy's ills. Some PCI members saw the party's proper role as being to influence government policy through opposition, rather than adopting the strategy most likely to give it a share of power.

For British diplomacy, the key difference between the two strategies was that whereas the historic compromise in 1973 looked capable of achievement, the democratic alternative in 1982 looked "a pipe-dream". The reality facing Berlinguer since early 1980 was that no majority existed

[76] TNA, FCO 30/5241, "Italy's Communists", by Chancery of the British Embassy in Rome (mainly a work by Culshaw R.), 10 November 1982.

[77] For a detailed reconstruction of PCI-CPSU relations during the Polish crisis see Pons S., *Berlinguer e la fine del comunismo*, quoted, pp. 520-621.

in either the DC or the PSI for a policy of alliance with the PCI. As long as those two parties agreed to stick together, the only role for the PCI was opposition. Its aim had to be to detach the PSI from the coalition, but it looked like an impossible task, at least while Craxi remained Secretary. No form of Communist participation in government was likely in the immediate future. Therefore, British policy towards the PCI should be based on an assessment, however tentative, of whether that opposition would be permanent. Anyway, the party's size and role in opposition justified paying serious attention to it. This meant adopting a different attitude towards the Communists: it was in British interests to cultivate effective contacts so that the UK government was informed about PCI policies and had some chance of influencing it. The argument that such contacts 'legitimised' the PCI and thus helped its advance towards power should no longer prevail, as it did, for instance, on the occasion of Berlinguer's dreaded visit to the United Kingdom in 1978. Britain and other West Europeans had far less influence in this respect than the United States, and the Communist Party's legitimacy came from the 11 million Italians who voted for it. In short, the United Kingdom should "treat the PCI as if it were the same as any other Italian lay party while recognising that it was not".[78]

In fact, in 1982 and 1983, it was the state of Italy's Christian Democrats that worried the British most. The real short-term threat was not a Communist-led government, but rather a government not led by the DC. This was strictly related to a more general overview of Italian foreign policy and its links with the United Kingdom. Britain acknowledged it had far less influence on domestic Italian politics than the US and did not have to back one of the parties. Nevertheless, it was worth asking what sort of Italian government best served UK interests. One answer was that, provided Italy remained a staunch NATO ally and EC partner, it was mostly irrelevant to Britain what went on in the DC and the Italian government; after all, Italy's underlying foreign and security policy had since the war been remarkably unaffected by political upheavals in Rome. For Arculus, this was too simple a view. The Italian electorate could be more tolerant of corruption and inefficiency than were many of their European counterparts, but could, in the end, turn against the party which bore the major share of responsibility – the DC – unless the latter saw the risk in time and introduced necessary reforms. Severe economic collapse, for example, could bring in its wake irresistible demands for an end to

78 TNA, FCO 30/5241, "Italy's Communists", by Chancery of the British Embassy in Rome, 10 November 1982.

DC hegemony. The election of Ciriaco De Mita as the new Christian Democrat Secretary in May 1982 did not change the overall scenario: too many energies were spent on electing the Secretary, while little was heard of reforms, new policies or programmes.[79] Conversely, the US Department of State talked about "Christian Democrats resurgent" in Italy, describing De Mita as "a visionary": the difference of opinions between London and Washington on the issue could hardly be wider.[80]

For Arculus, an Italian government not dominated by the DC could contain risks for Britain and the West as a whole. The helpful policies of the DC Foreign Minister Colombo had been carried on under Spadolini's Republican-led administration, but Craxi's "maverick behaviour" during the Falklands crisis showed that "a bigger PSI share in foreign policy-making [could] be unwelcome". However, the Ambassador believed that the DC was likely to retain its commanding position in Italian politics and that this could well be the best result for British interests; but that the United Kingdom should also hope for a reduction of the corrupt practices and of the "arrogance of power" which had crept in during its thirty-five years of running Italy. In this regard, an improvement in British links with the DC as a party – and not merely as contact with its leader in their government capacity – was desirable, although the Italian Christian Democrats were not interested in the outside world, and their links were stronger with their German counterparts than with the Conservative Party. Consultations with other parties (including the PCI, but not the extreme left or the neo-fascist MSI) was welcome, but this should not be done as to imply a loss of faith in the DC, who would "continue to carry many of [Britain's] eggs in their basket".[81]

In this unpromising scenario for the two main Italian parties, the third contender, i.e. Craxi's Socialist Party, could take advantage of the situation to strengthen its position. British diplomacy did not favour the possibility of Craxi becoming Prime Minister: in particular, the blind opposition to the policy of the Thatcher government during the Falklands War marked the relationship between London and the PSI in the months to come. It is apparent that Ambassador Arculus did not favour Craxi and considered his party as a menace greater than the Communists, although it

79 TNA, FCO 33/5748, "Italy's Christian Democrats", Arculus R. to Pym F., 3 August 1982.

80 TNA, FCO 33/6659, "Italy: Christian Democrats resurgent", Bureau of Intelligence and Research, State Department of the United States of America, 10 February 1983.

81 TNA, FCO 33/5748, "Italy's Christian Democrats", Arculus R. to Pym F., 3 August 1982.

would not be correct to say that he had a negative bias against the Italian politician. In this regard, Arculus quoted a private conversation with Craxi about the PCI, which the Socialist Secretary defined as "rigid bureaucrats imprisoned in a sterile policy". The British Ambassador then reminded him of two anomalies of the Italian political scene. Firstly, that while the PCI was outside central government, it helped to form many left-wing governments in the provinces, and Communists ran most large cities. Secondly, on Parliamentary Commissions, DC and PCI members worked together much as Conservative and Labour members did in Britain, while the PSI was "notorious for absenteeism", and in that respect, the Socialists were bad colleagues. According to Arculus, Craxi had no answer.[82]

Here comes Bettino

In his valedictory remarks at the beginning of 1983, Arculus predicted that the forthcoming Italian elections would change little: the lay bloc was still "wishful thinking", the historic compromise unlikely to come back into play. Marginal changes were the likely result, together with a more unstable coalition.[83] The Ambassador's prediction proved to be wrong in every instance: the general election of June 1983 marked a watershed in Italy's political history. Bettino Craxi became Prime Minister, the first Socialist to be given the office in the history of the Italian Republic. His government would stay in power for three years, being the third longest-lasting cabinet since the war, and was followed by a second Craxi government: in total, the PSI Secretary was to be President of the Council for almost four years, until March 1987. This despite a somewhat disappointing electoral result: the Socialists gained only 11 per cent of the votes. But the DC performed even worse, losing 5 per cent of preferences and stopping at 33 per cent, while the "middle ground" strengthened – the PSI and the other three small parties of the *pentapartito* increased their share of the vote to 23.5 per cent. "Luck favour the persistent", *The Economist* commented: yet Craxi had to make some concessions to win Christian Democratic and Republican support, with an agreement to introduce the policies of economic restraint they favoured.[84]

In the spring of 1983, Arculus left Rome – and the diplomatic service – and was replaced by Tom Bridges. The new ambassador showed from the

---

82 TNA, FCO 30/5241, "Italy's Communists", Arculus R. to Pym F., 10 November 1982.

83 TNA, FCO 33/6663, "Italy: Annual review for 1982", by Arculus R., WRD 014/2, 20 January 1983.

84 "Veni, vidi...", *The Economist*, 6 August 1983.

beginning a more positive attitude towards Craxi. For Bridges, the Socialist Secretary was a reformer in a party whose origins were of the old-fashioned revolutionary variety. For years the party was strong on rhetoric but short on administrative competence, and in the 1960s it acquired a reputation for corruption not far short of the DC's. Craxi deserved credit for trying to change all this and now hoped that the PSI would eventually overtake the PCI as the main party of the left, on the analogy of Mitterrand. The PSI could hardly have been weaker when Craxi replaced De Martino in 1976. He had come a long way since then (the Ambassador quoted a 1982 opinion poll showing that Italians regarded Craxi as "the most powerful man in the country"). This was as much a matter of image as of achievement, but Spadolini's success showed how vital image could be to a minor party.

According to Bridges, three significant factors had contributed to Craxi's influence. Firstly, he subdued his many rivals in the party, packing the party leadership with his young supporters. Secondly, he gave the party a more modern programme, "social democrat rather than Marxist, Atlanticist in defence (PSI support for the double decision of 1979 was crucial), for efficiency in government and the management of the economy". He advocated expansion of the economy to attract business votes. Pertini's popularity also helped, although the two had never been close and Pertini's old-fashioned socialism was the antithesis of Craxi's. Thirdly, Craxi was determined to keep the PSI in the news. He exploited the party's indispensability to any centre-left government to the maximum. He was determined to cut the DC and PCI down to size and to create a third force under his leadership: "typically his abrasiveness and suspicious nature have alienated many in the smaller lay parties whose support he needs". All his decisions in foreign affairs – from his support for the dual track to attacks on Jaruzelski and the opposition to sanctions on Argentina during the Falklands War – were taken to show that he counted. The merits of each case mattered less than domestic political considerations.

However, the British Ambassador stressed how the previous year had not been favourable to Craxi: he failed to remove Spadolini in August 1982 and the PSI, after some corruption scandals, did less well in the June 1983 elections than they had hoped. The resulting political arithmetic would not make it easy to form a stable government. Many in the DC were bitterly anti-Craxi, and enemies in his own party had been vocal in the last month. But Craxi was approaching his presidency with characteristic drive and determination. It would be a highly personal administration. So was Spadolini's, but "whereas Spadolini inspired trust, Craxi arouse[d] fears of autocracy and presidentialism". He would need early successes and would be everywhere doing everything. As for his foreign policy, Bridges assessed that Craxi had little experience in this field. He could be found more of an Italian nationalist than expected; he would not be easy to deal with, and his sympathies lay with Mitterrand's Socialists and the German SPD, rather than with Britain ("he despised the Labour" and was equally critical of Thatcher's economic policies during the election campaign). Some feared Craxi would want to take grandiose foreign policy initiatives, but the British Ambassador thought he valued American support for him too much to stray far. In any case, for Bridges it was worth reminding that a healthy, moderate and successful PSI, able to take votes away from or impose its values on the PCI, was strongly in the interest of Italy's partners in NATO and the EEC.[85]

On 4 August, Craxi succeeded in forming his cabinet. Italy's forty-fourth post-war government was a five-party coalition comprising the Socialists, the Christian Democrats, Republicans, Social Democrats and Liberals. Peter Nichols reported that Craxi presented his government to the Parliament speaking "more as leader of a disparate coalition than as the country's first Socialist Prime Minister", and comment was divided between commending him for this and criticising an attitude seen to be too close to his predecessors.[86]

Craxi would mark the 1980s with his assertive leadership, aspirations for clearly defined internal reforms and for emphasising Italy's international role. In this context, Giulio Andreotti, "a supreme political tactician" in the British view, Foreign Minister between 1983 and 1989 (and again Prime Minister between 1989 and 1992, represented the continuity of Christian Democrat power.[87] Craxi's description by the Foreign Office is worth quoting:

> A tall, dominating figure, he looks older than his years. Fond of good living, and eloquent in private conversation, but spends too much of his time with close party colleagues, isolated from criticism. Held in respect by other PSI Deputies though not greatly loved; generally distrusted by other politicians. Something of a bully. […] But he chooses his words carefully and his salvoes are

---

85 TNA, FCO 33/6660, Rome Tel. No. 354, 27 July 1983.

86 "Craxi presents policies of a coalition leader rather than a Socialist", *The Times*, 11 August 1983.

87 Varsori A., "Bettino Craxi and Giulio Andreotti", in Jones E., Pasquino G., *The Oxford Handbook of Italian Politics*, Oxford University Press, Oxford 2015, pp. 378-393. See Andreotti's description in TNA, CAB 133/535, "Anglo-Italian summit, 26-27 January 1984", PMVF (84), General brief by the Foreign Office: Personality notes, 23 January 1984.

> never accidental. Scathing in his attacks on the inequalities and inefficiencies of Italian society, but less eloquent when forced to suggest remedies. [...] A clever self-publicist.[88]

As for the relations between Craxi and Thatcher, the two Prime Ministers met for the first time in September 1983. Thatcher later reported to the Cabinet that she had been impressed by the personality of Craxi.[89]

The new socialist leadership was not seen as a break with the past, but Craxi was presented as the man that Italy needed: a weak country like Italy required a strong man.[90] For British diplomacy, the first Craxi government appeared – at least on paper – as "one of the most impressive Italian administrations since the war". It contained three former Prime Ministers (Andreotti, Forlani and Spadolini), a party President and three of the five coalition party Secretaries. One consequence, however, was that seasoned ministers had to accept jobs of lesser rank, and some of them (like Colombo, offended of being offered to lead the Ministry of Agriculture) declined to serve. Whether this "Government of all the talents" would retain cohesion had to be an open question. In assessing Craxi's government overall, two factors stood out. The first was his own relative isolation: there was only one important post for the PSI (the Ministry of Labour). The British Ambassador reported a joke that the new Cabinet was actually "a DC-Republican Government which happened to have a socialist at its head" and Craxi could overestimate the power of his office. The second factor was the DC's disarray: the shock caused by the party's electoral defeat still ran deep, and internal tensions could weaken the Craxi government if they reflected among the Christian Democrat ministers. Despite these liabilities, Craxi also had two major assets. Firstly, that very DC weakness could guarantee him several quiet months (the Christian Democrats were in no shape to claim his post before their next Party Congress in summer 1984). Secondly, if Craxi fell, he could make life difficult for any successor, not least because PSI support was crucial in forming a Parliament majority. Behind all this lay "Italy's unresolved

88 TNA, CAB 133/535, "Anglo-Italian summit, 26-27 January 1984", PMVF (84), General brief by the Foreign Office: Personality notes, 23 January 1984.

89 TNA, CAB 128/76, Minutes of Full Cabinet – CC (83) 28th, 22 September 1983.

90 See "Bettino or Benito?", *The Economist*, 28 January 1984. On the analysis of Italy's image in foreign press in the 1980s see Lomellini V., Varsori A., "'Italian way of life': vizi e virtù dell'Italia degli anni '80 nella stampa internazionale", *Memoria e Ricerca*, Vol. 52, No. 2, 2016, pp. 261-282; Raponi D., "L'Italia vista dall'estero (1980-2010)", in Pons S., Roccucci A., Romero F., *L'Italia contemporanea dagli anni Ottanta a oggi, Vol. I Fine della Guerra fredda e globalizzazione*, Carocci, Roma 2014, pp. 393-412.

question – what to do about the Communists – and it [would] not go away".[91]

Craxi's appointment was also a further step in the march of socialism in southern Europe: while the northern countries of the Old Continent saw a strengthening of conservatism, it was now the turn of what *The Economist* labelled as "sunbelt socialism", with five Socialist-led governments in Italy, France, Spain, Greece and Portugal. Although the new Italian cabinet did not look very socialist "either in policy or in composition" (the PSI had only six of the 30 ministerial posts), the Socialist Party registered its best electoral result in 15 years. According to the weekly, there were essentially four reasons for this southern trend: a "justifiable itch for left-of-centre change"; a strong time-lag in the welfare state; a firm grasp on the centre; and the attractiveness of southern Socialist leaders.[92]

Craxi was to lead a country with lights and shadows, but after all in ferment.[93] *The Economist* dedicated a new survey to Italy in July 1983 titled *Eppur si muove* ("And yet it moves") and the comparison with the former investigation in 1978 was quite striking. Italy had survived the tormented 1970s, and its political and terrorist troubles had receded. The "kick-in-the-pants" that voters gave the ruling Christian Democratic party at the general election in June gave rise to hopes that the country could be about to get to grips with its underlying economic malaise – and in particular with its sprawling state sector. Moreover, "La dolce vita has returned, even if it is less vulgar, brash or frenetic than it was in the Fellinian 1960s". There were still many economic problems because Italy's economy was "like a racehorse labouring under a particularly heavy jockey" – the weight of public spending. The country was still too close to recession for comfort, but Italians had made a way to get the economy to expand by some 12 per cent between 1977 and 1980, making their country the fastest growing in Europe. One of the possible explanations (not immune to prejudices) for Italy's survival could be that it was a society with a cohesive set of values:

> Italians have too long been governed by outsiders – the Spanish, the French and the Austrians – to have much faith in those that lord it over them, or the motives from which they claim to act.

---

91 TNA, FCO 33/6661, Rome Tel. No. 361, 8 August 1983.

92 "Sunbelt socialism", *The Economist*, 13 August 1983, pp. 11-12.

93 Gervasoni M., *Storia d'Italia negli anni Ottanta. Quando eravamo moderni*, Marsilio, Venezia 2010; Caviglia D., Labbate S. (eds.), *Al governo del cambiamento. L'Italia di Craxi tra rinnovamento e obiettivi mancati*, Rubbettino, Soveria Mannelli 2014.

> But because they are accustomed to misrule from the top, the Italians have a fierce set of strictly personal loyalties. What is acceptable within the family is socially acceptable. [...]
> One of the strongest Italian social values is the commitment to democracy. This may sound strange to say about a country which was ruled by Fascism for 21 years and which now has western Europe's largest Communist party. Yet democracy is only an extension of Italy's renaissance-descended, every-man-a-party individualism. [...] The fact that Italian individualism is combined with respect for the individualism of others gives Italy some kind of stability. [...] For all its apparent tranquillity, change is now taking place in Italian democracy beneath the surface that could allow the country to get to grips with its awful, although still overcomeable, economic problems.[94]

British diplomats partially shared this assessment of Italy's economy. Although the statistics recorded a deterioration of the country's economic condition during 1983, with industrial production falling by 5 per cent, a rise in unemployment and inflation still twice the EC average, the position was probably not quite as bad as the figures suggested. Italy did not have a worrying deficit on its current account, her reserves were substantial, and there had recently been a modest recovery in the industrial North. A reviving world economy – and a weaker dollar – could help Italy to solve her problems effectively.[95] The International Economic Department of the Foreign Office wondered how Italians had managed "to perform so creditably, for instance in comparison to the United Kingdom, despite the apparent inappropriateness of their policies". Perhaps the submerged economy held the key to much of Britain's difficulty; her unique industrial structure, based on medium and small-scale industry employing "appropriate technologies", could explain Italy's ability to back economic trends. The British lack of understanding meant that it was particularly difficult to judge whether Italy could surprise the UK again or whether the deterioration in fundamental economic aggregates had advanced "beyond the point of no return".[96]

As for Craxi, his performance in the first months as Prime Minister was rather disappointing for the British, showing few signs of the "purposeful and aggressive reforming style" expected by many. The approval of the budget in the Parliament had been obtained at the cost of a more modest cut in public sector borrowing than envisaged, while the coalition had

---

94 "*Eppur si muove* – A survey of Italy", *The Economist*, 23 July 1983.

95 TNA, FCO 33/7428, "Italy: annual review for 1983", by Bridges, 9 January 1984.

96 TNA, FCO 33/6661, "Italia Vostra", Chrimes N. to Collins A., WRJ 014/1, 25 August 1983.

found it difficult to maintain its unity because of the great divergence of objectives of its part. In particular, the rivalry over foreign policy between Craxi, Spadolini and Andreotti was marked. But the balance of forces inside this legislature gave the leader of the Socialist Party a rather strong position and, hopefully, Craxi would even make a start on the reforms the country so badly needed.[97]

A surge of optimism came from Ambassador Bridges, who gave a very positive assessment of Italy in 1983. Nevertheless, the "tremendous changes" which had been taking place in Italy had been imperfectly understood in Britain. There was a tendency to think of Italy as the country of the immediate post-war years, without seeing her "considerable economic achievements". Bridges also invited Britain to do more business in Italy, "particularly political and commercial business". Britain should "pay more attention to Italy in our thinking as well as in our acts", and would find it rewarding to do so.[98]

97 TNA, FCO 33/7428, "Italy: annual review for 1983", by Bridges T., 9 January 1984.

98 TNA, FCO 33/6661, "Italia Vostra", Bridges T. to Howe J., Diplomatic Report No. 137/83, WRD 014/1, 4 August 1983.

Conclusion

This volume has offered a historical appraisal of the political and economic crisis which affected Britain and Italy in the years following 1976 and the strategies adopted by the two countries to recover from it and gain a stronger international position. It has also analysed the reciprocal images and perceptions of the two countries and how they affected Anglo-Italian relations from the mid 1970s to the early 1980s. This book offers a comparative study, without being restricted to a mere study of the bilateral relations between Italy and the United Kingdom. Using a comparative perspective, this work reveals the obvious differences, but also the many unexpected similarities between two countries which are seemingly poles apart, highlighting political and economic overlaps and a common path out of their crises.

In the years which are the subject of this analysis, it is possible to identify three turning points for the British and Italian political and economic scene alike. The first watershed is 1976, when this investigation begins. For both countries, it epitomised the weakness of their economic system and the inability of the governments in London and Rome to deal with the effects of a crisis which had affected the West as a whole. In Italy, economic and political strains mingled: 1976 saw the most controversial general elections in Italy since the foundation of the Republic, when the Communist "overtaking" seemed a concrete and dreaded possibility. It was also the moment when the Western powers tried to work out a common strategy in order to counter the Italian Communist "threat", solve the country's endemic political instability and set the basis for an adequate economic recovery. As for Britain, 1976 marked the end of an illusion. The IMF loan (the largest ever requested to the Fund) put an official seal on the country's economic decline, which had already emerged in the previous years. The IMF crisis has become part of British political memory: twenty years after the Suez crisis marked a loss of political power, the United Kingdom experienced the weakening of its economic status. In the meantime, the internal political scene lacked the necessary unity to cope with the financial and social emergency, with sharp divisions inside the Labour Party in government.

The second defining moment is 1979, although with differing results for Italy and the United Kingdom. The "winter of discontent" brought the question of British decline back into the limelight – further strengthened, a few months later, by the publication of the Henderson despatch. In this scenario, the general election of May 1979 saw the victory of the Conservative Party under the leadership of Margaret Thatcher. The new path of Thatcherism would mark British history for the following eighteen years, yet the first years of the Thatcher government did not prove to be successful, and the United Kingdom struggled to rebuild a strong international image. Conversely, Italy was set on full realignment with the major Western powers. The immediate entry into the EMS was a fundamental signal that allegiance to the European ideal had never been under discussion, regardless of the country's precarious economic situation and the internal divisions it could create; on the other hand, by accepting the deployment of "Euromissiles" Italy confirmed her loyalty to the Atlantic Alliance. Moreover, the elections of 1979 marked the end of national solidarity and paved the way for the new political formula of *pentapartito*.

Finally, the last turning point – and the ideal conclusion of this analysis – is 1983. In Britain, the victory in the Falklands War of the previous year gave a new voice to British ambitions and swept away the uncertainties about Thatcher's political future. In 1982 the polls indicated that Thatcher was the most unpopular Prime Minister ever, but the "Falklands effect" gave her a new image. In the general election of June 1983, the Conservative Party had its most decisive victory, a success that would have been inconceivable only 14 months earlier. This electoral triumph gave the Tory government a new impetus to pursue the most distinctive features of Thatcherite policy. As regards Italy, the 1983 elections brought a Socialist to Palazzo Chigi[1] for the first time since the foundation of the Republic. Bettino Craxi would mark the whole decade with his firm leadership, aspirations for internal reforms and emphasis on Italy's international role.

As it has emerged from this analysis, despite the many differences, from the mid 1970s Britain and Italy showed many similarities. The most apparent was a critical economic situation. In the broader context of the European and international crisis of the "golden age" of economic growth in the 1970s, the Italian and the British malaises seemed acuter than those of other Western countries: the United Kingdom and Italy were perceived as the two "sick men" of Europe. As showed by many US documents, British and Italian economic problems, although originating from different situations and political scenarios, had many points in common and could

1 Palazzo Chigi was the official residence of the Italian Minister of Foreign Affairs from 1922; in 1961 it became the residence of the Italian President of the Council in Rome.

be treated jointly. London and Rome shared a path of decline that was steady and seemingly irreversible, although with different degrees and starting point. In the case of Italy, decline took the place of the economic "miracle" of the 1950s and 1960s; for Britain, it was a decay from the greatest industrial and trade power of the late 19th century.

Moreover, until the end of the 1970s, there was another and less obvious similarity: Italy and the United Kingdom shared a common scene of political instability, with due differences. It was nothing new for Italy, generally regarded as endemically unstable and whose party system made coalition governments the general rule. After the 1976 general election, the third government under the lead of Giulio Andreotti inaugurated the era of "national solidarity": the new cabinet was formed only by Christian Democrats, while the PCI and the PSI, although not part of the majority coalition, agreed not to cause its downfall. Nevertheless, by 1978 the intra-party solidarity, which had been strengthened by the kidnapping and murder of DC President Aldo Moro, began to founder. Italy seemed to have returned once more to the political uncertainty which characterised much of the 1970s, after two and a half years of relative stability under Andreotti's premiership. In January 1979, the Communist withdrawal from the majority caused the longest period of government crisis in Italian history since the war, which was only resolved seven months later with the formation of the government led by Francesco Cossiga. Many cabinets continued to follow one another, even after the adoption of the *pentapartito* formula: in the years which are the object of this analysis, from 1976 to 1983, Italy had eleven governments and seven Prime Ministers.

In the British case, the difficulties of the two Labour cabinets led by Harold Wilson and Jim Callaghan in securing a substantial majority in Parliament were quite unusual, although not a total novelty in UK history. Hung parliaments (occurring when no party has won a majority of seats in the House of Commons) and minority governments have been the exception rather than the rule in twentieth century Britain. Since the end of the First World War, only three general elections had been followed by minority governments, and all of them were led by the Labour Party (in 1924, 1929 and 1974). In the October 1974 election, Labour under Wilson won a minuscule majority in seats and a higher vote share than the Tories. Nevertheless, by the time Wilson resigned and Callaghan became the new Prime Minister, this majority was whittled away through by-election losses and defections. In March 1977, the Callaghan government lost its majority and faced likely defeat on a motion of no confidence: to prevent this vote, the Prime Minister negotiated an agreement with the

Liberal Party led by David Steel. Although the "Lib-Lab pact" sustained the minority government through nearly a year and a half, it was also the embodiment of Labour's political failure.[2] Moreover, beyond these political difficulties, the "winter of discontent" of 1978-1979, with its rash of strikes in crucial public services, spread the image of a country on the edge of ungovernability. The fact that the Callaghan government was the first to be defeated on an issue of confidence since MacDonald's minority Labour government in 1924 (it was the first government in 55 years to have no control over the decision to dissolve) reveals a lot about the degree of political uncertainty in the United Kingdom.

This work has also analysed a further and previously unexplored element in Anglo-Italian relations in the Cold War, that is to say, the perceptions and reciprocal attitudes which emerge not only from diplomatic documents but also from an examination of the press, in order to understand the role played by public opinion and the influence of the media. In this game of mirrors of mutual images, British policy towards Italy was based on three primary evaluations. First, as seen from London, the main dangers to Italian democracy came from law and order and political instability, and only secondarily from the "Communist threat". One indicator of the evolution of British policy towards Italy can be found in the "Country assessment sheets", prepared on a three-year basis. If in 1974 the main threat to British and Western interests was a "collapse of the Italian economy leading to the demise of democratic government", in 1977 what concerned the UK most was the "collapse of law and order and/or of the Italian economy". Moreover, the possibility of Communist participation in the government was fraught with dangers for the Alliance.[3] In 1980, the situation was still different. The first – and most remote – threat was a serious economic decline or disintegration of law and order, which could cause the collapse of democracy. There was also continuing uncertainty about the future role and influence of the PCI, although it had undertaken to work within the democratic framework and had taken an independent line from Moscow. The third threat was that further pressure from the left for a reduction in

2 See Brazier R., *Constitutional Practice: The Foundations of British Government*, Oxford University Press, Oxford 1999, pp. 30-51; Hazell R., Paun A. (eds.), *Making minority government work. Hung parliaments and the challenges for Westminster and Whitehall*, Institute for Government, London 2009.

3 TNA, FCO 33/2496, "Country assessment sheet: Italy", June 1974; TNA, FCO 33/3209, "Country assessment sheet: Italy. British interests and objectives", 12 July 1977.

Italy's links with the USA and its support for NATO could lead to a serious weakening of the Alliance.[4]

Law and order were of paramount importance in a country considered by the Foreign Office as endemically inclined to the use of violence for political ends ("one could surely trace some of its origins back to the Middle Ages and Renaissance, if not to Roman times").[5] As for political instability, in the words of Ambassador Ronald Arculus, "Italy survives despite not because of its governments".[6] The "Communist threat" became a less critical issue for Britain from 1978, although there were differences between the more anti-Communist Foreign Office and the British Embassy in Rome, and also within the same Villa Wolkonsky.[7] This approach also caused some tensions between London and Washington, like in January 1978 when different evaluations emerged about the way to solve the Italian crisis. Britain was a major part in the Western strategy for Italy's "concerted stabilisation"[8] yet she adopted a lower profile in comparison with the other "big three" – the United States, the German Federal Republic and France. Indeed, this "softer" attitude originated from internal causes: the 1976 Italian general elections, and in particular, the question of Communist participation in Italy's government, were perceived as a potentially divisive issue for the already divided Labour Party.[9] Moreover, economic difficulties made the Callaghan government less likely to be at the forefront in formulating firm stabilisation measures for another country. However, it must be pointed out that in the summer of 1976, despite a common path of crisis with Rome, the British government did not adopt a softer approach on the economic conditions to be applied to Italy, but only on the political requests. This is quite surprising if one thinks that, only a few months later, Britain would be another victim of "conditionality" to obtain the IMF loan.

4 TNA, FCO 33/4446, "Country assessment paper: Italy", (no date) 1980.

5 TNA, TNA, FCO 33/4594, "Terrorism in Italy", Gladstone D. to Arculus R., WRJ 051/3, 15 September 1980.

6 TNA, FCO 33/4594, "Terrorism in Italy", despatch (051/4) by Arculus R., WRJ 051/3, 8 August 1980.

7 Villa Wolkonsky is the residence of the British Ambassador in Rome.

8 Cominelli L., quoted.

9 See Michael Palliser's remark: "There were two main strands. [...] One important aspect was what reaction would be politically feasible within the Labour Party [...]. The second aspect was to assess what was in the UK's overall interest taking this in the widest sense". In TNA, FCO 33/2942, "Italy", by Fergusson E., WRJ 011/1, 19 May 1976.

The second strand of British policy towards Rome was that Italy's value as a European partner increased for Britain as the years passed by, becoming an asset more important than the Italian role inside the Atlantic Alliance. If we look once again at the "Country assessment sheets", in 1974 and 1977 the judgement was basically the same: Italy's importance to the UK derived principally from her membership of NATO and the EEC.[10] However, in 1980, the most important aspect of Anglo-Italian relations was the common membership of the EEC. Although there were inevitably areas of disagreement, Italy and Britain shared views about an open economic system.[11] By January 1984, the Foreign Office reported that after France and Germany, Italy was the most important to Britain among the Community partners.[12]

However, this policy was in contrast with the third and final feature of British policy towards Italy: the United Kingdom often adopted a "patronising" attitude with the government in Rome. There was the British tendency to downgrade Italy's role, an assessment that originated from economic, political and almost anthropological considerations. In this context, personalities mattered: in particular, we can see the different approaches of the British Ambassadors who were posted in Rome from 1976 to 1983. While Alan Campbell was an uncommon interpreter of Italian politics and society and Tom Bridges was able to understand the complexities of "Italian exceptionalism", Ronald Arculus was less well-disposed towards Italy, which he defined as "in many respects a sick society".[13]

As for Italy's attitude toward Britain, we can identify two main themes. First, Italian policy was based on an acute awareness of the similarities of the economic problems which London and Rome had to face, a theme often raised by the Italians but rarely shared by the British. Secondly, the Community aspect was essential in Italy's relations with Britain. The EEC dimension had always been a privileged context for consolidating Anglo-Italian relations, and the opportunity of creating an "alternative axis" between London and Rome as a counterpart to the Franco-German partnership also emerged in the late 1970s and early 1980s. Nevertheless,

10 TNA, FCO 33/2496, "Country assessment sheet: Italy", June 1974; TNA, FCO 33/3209, "Country assessment sheet: Italy. British interests and objectives", 12 July 1977.

11 TNA, FCO 33/4446, "Country assessment paper: Italy", (no date) 1980.

12 TNA, CAB 133/535, "Anglo-Italian summit, 26-27 January 1984", PMVF (84), General brief by the Foreign Office, 20 January 1984.

13 TNA, FCO 33/4897, "Italy: Annual Review for 1980", 7 January 1981.

the results were quite disappointing for Italy: the negotiations for the EMS showed that the Italians placed too much faith in the alliance with the British. Also in 1980, despite an important mediating role for a positive outcome of the British requests on budget contribution, Italy was left outside of a trilateral meeting between Britain, France and West Germany, proving Italy's minor role in the elaboration of Community policies.

In conclusion, by 1983, the two "sick men" of Europe looked to be on their way to recovery. Though "healing" was still to be completed, the prospects were encouraging. In Britain, with their majority secure, the Tories continued a programme of radical reform. The 1983-1984 period can be considered the zenith of Thatcher's power.[14] As for British foreign policy, Thatcher eventually reached a successful conclusion to the British Budgetary Question in June 1984, on the occasion of the Fontainebleau European Council, and showed progress in relations with the Soviet Union. The special relationship with Washington was further strengthened when Ronald Reagan was confirmed for a second term in November 1984. On the domestic side, with the opposition reduced to parliamentary impotence, the distinctive features of Thatcherite policy emerged, in particular privatisation. Since it seemed unlikely that a Labour government could reverse the policy of denationalisation, from 1983 onwards privatisation was pursued with new ambition and energy. North Sea oil was finally giving a return: its revenue from 1983 to 1987 totalled 41.6 billion pounds – in 1975, it had been 25 million pounds. This allowed the new Chancellor of the Exchequer, Nigel Lawson, to pay off public debts and make further reductions in direct taxation. Also, the City of London was transformed by deregulation of financial services (the so-called "Big Bang") in 1986. The deregulation of the City also had implications for the kind of economy that could be possible in Britain: an economy based on service rather than industry suddenly began to seem plausible. Above all, the success of the City seemed to sweep away the question of national decline.[15]

In the meantime, the image of a new Italy, active and dynamic, began to spread after the coming to power of Bettino Craxi in 1983, epitomised by the slogan "*Milano da bere*" ("Milan to drink"), from the advertising campaign from the bitter liqueur Amaro Ramazzotti in 1985. The commercial caught the euphoric atmosphere of those years, showing a mixture of glamour and tradition and a city offering endless opportunities.

---

14 Garnett M., Mabon S., Smith R., *British Foreign Policy since 1945*, Routledge, Abingdon 2018, pp. 208-209.

15 Vinen R., quoted, pp. 181-191.

Milan was the Prime Minister's birthplace and his electoral stronghold and was going to replace the country's capital, Rome, becoming the centre of power for the PSI hegemony during the Craxi leadership. While a new generation of businessmen emerged – the *condottieri* of Italian finance and industry, as they were labelled by the foreign press – the economy showed positive signs, with inflation decreasing to 4-5 % by the end of the 1980s.[16] Italy seemed to have overcome the gloomy 1970s and was rapidly modernising, while adopting a more effective foreign policy in the Mediterranean and towards the United States, epitomised by the "Sigonella affair" in 1985.[17] Craxi also aspired to confirming Italy's leading international role in the European context; the Italian Presidency in the first semester of 1985 would focus on the ambitious goal of convening an inter-governmental conference (ICG), which would lead to the signing of the Single European Act (SEA). In spite of Thatcher's fierce opposition, and with the support of Mitterrand and Kohl, the decision was taken at the Milan European Council.[18]

In February 1987, *Newsweek* dedicated its cover to Gianni Agnelli and the "miracle makers" of Italy's economy, under the headline "It is a good time to be Italian".[19] Still in 1987, Craxi could state that Italy had overtaken Britain in terms of nominal GDP: an overtaking less dreaded than the Communist one in 1976, but with a deeper impact on British national pride. It was immediately and hotly disputed by Nigel Lawson, but the OECD figures for that year confirmed the overtaking: in 1986

16 Among them, Gianni Agnelli, Silvio Berlusconi, Carlo De Benedetti and Raul Gardini.

17 In the military base of Sigonella, in Sicily, the Italian government resisted the US attempt to capture the Palestinian hijackers of the cruise ship *Achille Lauro* without Rome's consent and against the rules of Italian jurisdiction. On the episode, see Gerlini M., *Il dirottamento dell'Achille Lauro e i suoi inattesi e sorprendenti risvolti*, Mondadori, Milano 2016; and the volume published by the Fondazione Craxi, *Bettino Craxi. La notte di Sigonella. Documenti e discorsi sull'evento che restituì l'orgoglio all'Italia*, Mondadori, Milano 2015. For an analysis of Italy's foreign policy in the 1980s see Varsori A., "Italy's foreign policy in the 1980s: from enthusiasm to disillusion", in Varsori A., Zaccaria B. (eds.), quoted, pp. 95-124.

18 Some scholars have portrayed the Milan European Council as an outstanding Italian diplomatic achievement, when the Italian presidency was able to defeat the opposition of the British delegation. However, the efforts of Craxi and Foreign Minister Andreotti would have been to no avail without French and German support. For these different interpretations see Mammarella G., "Il Consiglio Europeo di Milano del giugno 1985", in Di Nolfo E. (ed.), quoted, pp. 189-210; Varsori A., "The relaunching of Europe in the mid-1980s", in Patel K. K., Weisbrode K. (eds.), *European integration and the Atlantic Community in the 1980s*, Cambridge University Press, Cambridge 2013, pp. 226-242.

19 *Newsweek*, 16 February 1987.

Italy had a GDP of 599.8 billion dollars, compared to the UK's 547.4 billion dollars.[20]

Obviously, not everything "in the Italian garden [was] lovely", to quote the words of Ambassador Alan Campbell.[21] The inefficiencies of the political system and the civil service continued, the backwardness of the south persisted, while the widespread corruption and bribery system would lead to the *Tangentopoli* scandal and the demise of the so-called "First Republic" in the early 1990s. As for Britain, while the "Thatcher's revolution" showed the first creaking signs ("Black Monday" in October 1987 saw the largest recorded fall in stock-market prices ever recorded), the apparent successes began the processes that ultimately undermined the Prime Minister's leadership.

But despite the drawbacks, Britain and Italy were no longer the two sick men of Europe and 1983 seemed the beginning of a new Renaissance for both – or, at least, of the image of it.

---

20 See Ginsborg P., *Italy and its discontent. Family, civil society, state 1980-2001*, Palgrave Macmillan, Basingstoke 2003, p. 6.

21 TNA, FCO 33/3568, "The Italian scene in 1978" – HM's Ambassador at Rome to the Secretary of State for FCO (Campbell to Owen), WRJ 014/2, 20 July 1978.

Italy had a GDP of 798.8 billion dollars, compared to the UK's 847.4 billion dollars.[illegible]

Obviously, not "everything" in the Italian garden was lovely, to quote the words of Ambassador Alan Campbell:[illegible] the inefficiencies of the political system and the civil service continued, the backwardness of the south persisted, while the widespread corruption and bribery system would lead to the *Tangentopoli* scandal and the demise of the so-called "First Republic" in the early 1990s. As for Britain, while the "Thatcherite revolution" showed the first troubling signs ("Black Monday" in October 1987 saw the largest recorded fall in stock-market prices ever recorded), the apparent successes began the processes that ultimately undermined the Prime Minister's leadership.

But despite the drawbacks, Britain and Italy were no longer the two sick men of Europe and 1985 seemed the beginning of a new Renaissance for both—or, at least, of the image of it.

[illegible] See Ginsborg P., *Italy and its discontents: Family, Civil Society, State, 1980-2001*, Palgrave Macmillan, Basingstoke, 2003, p. 4.

[illegible] TNA, FCO 33/5868, "The Italian scene in 1978", HM's Ambassador at Rome to the Secretary of State for FCO (Campbell to Owen), WRI 014/1, 20 July 1978.

Sources and Bibliography

Archival Sources

Italy

Archivio Storico della Presidenza della Repubblica, Rome

Ufficio per gli Affari Diplomatici (1955-1992)

United Kingdom

The National Archives, Kew, London

Prime Minister's Office: Correspondence and Papers, 1974-1979 (PREM 16)

Records of the Prime Minister's Office: Correspondence and Papers, 1979-1997 (PREM 19)

Cabinet: Minutes (CAB 128)

Cabinet: Memoranda (CAB 129)

Cabinet: Miscellaneous Committees: Minutes and Papers (CAB 130)

Cabinet Office: Commonwealth and International Conferences and Ministerial Visits to and from the UK: Minutes and Papers (CAB 133)

Foreign Office and Foreign and Commonwealth Office: European Economic Organisations Department and successors: Registered Files (FCO 30)

Foreign Office, Western Department and Foreign and Commonwealth Office, Western European Department: Registered Files (FCO 33)

Foreign and Commonwealth Office and predecessors: Planning Staff and Commonwealth Policy and Planning Department: Registered Files (FCO 49)

Foreign and Commonwealth Office and predecessors: Research Department: Registered Files (FCO 51)

Labour History Archive and Study Centre, Manchester

Labour Party: International Department

Labour Party: National Executive Committee Minutes

Eric Heffer Papers

Conservative Party Archive, Oxford

Conservative Central Office
Conservative Research Department: International Democrat Union

Thatcher Archive

CCOPR 544

United States

Gerald R. Ford Presidential Library, Ann Arbor, Michigan
Arthur Burns Papers
Council of Economic Adviser Records, 1974-77
National Security Adviser: International economic affairs staff, 1975-6
National Security Adviser: NSC Europe Canada and Ocean affairs staff
Office of Economic Affairs: L. William Seidman

Press

Avanti!
Corriere della Sera
Financial Times
Il Sole 24 Ore
L'Espresso
L'Unità
La Stampa
Mondoperaio
Socialist Commentary
The Economist
The Times

Books, Articles, Essays

Aga Rossi E., *L'Italia nella sconfitta: politica interna e situazione internazionale durante la seconda guerra mondiale*, Edizioni Scientifiche Italiane, Napoli 1985.

Aldous R., *Reagan and Thatcher: The Difficult Relationship*, Arrow, London 2013.

Alford B.W.E., *British Economic Performance, 1945-1975*, Macmillan, Basingstoke 1988.

Bagnato B., "L'Italia vista da Palazzo Farnese: la missione di Gilles Martinet (1981-1984)", in Di Nolfo E. (ed.), *La politica estera italiana negli anni ottanta*, Marsilio, Venezia 2007, pp. 231-289.

Baldoli C., *Exporting fascism: Italian fascists and Britain's Italians in the 1930s*, Berg, Oxford 2003.

Barbagallo F., "Il PCI dal sequestro di Moro alla morte di Berlinguer", in De Rosa G., Monina G. (eds.), *L'Italia Repubblicana nella crisi degli anni Settanta. Sistema politico e istituzioni, Vol. 4*, Rubbettino, Soveria Mannelli 2003, pp. 79-130.

Barca L., *Cronache dall'interno del vertice del PCI Vol. 3: La crisi del PCI e l'effetto domino*, Rubbettino, Napoli 2005.

Bartlett C., *'The special relationship': a political history of Anglo-American relations since 1945*, Longman, London 1992.

Basosi D., Bernardini G., "The Puerto Rico Summit of 1976 and the End of Eurocommunism", in Nuti L. (ed.), *The Crisis of Détente in Europe. From Helsinki to Gorbachev*, 1975-1985, Routledge, London 2009, pp. 256-267.

Beckett A., *When the lights went out*, Faber&Faber, London 2009.

Benn T., *Conflicts of Interest: Diaries 1977-80*, Arrow, London 1991.

Bentivoglio G., "'Our sole commitment is to negotiate; no more, no less': the Conservative Party and Britain's entry into the EEC", in Bonfreschi L., Orsina G., Varsori A. (eds.), *European Political Parties and the European Integration Process, 1945-1992*, Peter Lang, Brussels 2015, pp. 195-211.

Bentivoglio G., "Redefining immigration through citizenship? Britain and the case of the 1981 Nationality Act", in Calandri E., Paoli S., Varsori A. (eds.), *Peoples and Borders: Seventy Years of Migration in Europe, from Europe, to Europe (1945-2015)*, Nomos, Brussels 2017, pp. 183-201.

Bentivoglio G., "Violenza endemica o eterodiretta? Il terrorismo italiano degli anni Settanta e Ottanta visto da Londra", in Lomellini V. (ed.), *Il mondo della guerra fredda e l'Italia degli anni di piombo. Una regia internazionale per il terrorismo?*, Le Monnier, Firenze 2017, pp. 205-224.

Bentivoglio G., *La relazione necessaria. La Gran Bretagna del Governo Heath e gli Stati Uniti (1970-74)*, FrancoAngeli, Milano 2011.

Bentivoglio G., Varsori A. (eds.), *Realtà e immagine della politica estera italiana*, FrancoAngeli, Milano 2017.

Benyon J., *Scarman and After. Essays Reflecting on Lord Scarman's Report, the riots and their aftermath*, Pergamon, Oxford 1984.

Beresford D., *Ten Men Dead: The Story of the 1981 Irish Hunger Strike*, Atlantic Monthly Press, New York 1997.

Bernardini G., "Stability and socialist autonomy: the Spd, the Psi and the Italian political crisis of the 1970s", *Journal of European Integration History*, No. 1, 2009, pp. 95-114.

Bernardini G., "The Federal Republic of Germany and the resistible rise of the 'historic compromise' in Italy (1974-1978)", in Varsori A., Migani G., *Europe in the International Arena during the 1970s*, Peter Lang, Brussels 2011, pp. 317-338.

Berrettini M., *La Gran Bretagna e l'antifascismo italiano. Diplomazia clandestina, intelligence, operazioni speciali (1940-1943)*, Le Lettere, Firenze 2010.

Berrington H., "Change in British Politics: An Introduction", in Berrington H. (ed.), *Change in British politics*, Frank Cass, London 1983, pp. 1-24.

Borsani D., *La "special relationship" anglo-americana e la guerra delle Falkland (1982)*, Le Lettere, Firenze 2016.

Bosco V., *L'amministrazione Nixon e l'Italia. Tra distensione e crisi mediterranea*, Eurilink, Roma 2009.

Boyce G.D., *The Falklands War*, Palgrave Macmillan, Basingstoke 2005.

Brazier R., *Constitutional Practice: The Foundations of British Government*, Oxford University Press, Oxford 1999.

Britton A., *Macroeconomic Policy in Britain, 1974-1987*, Cambridge University Press, Cambridge 1994.

Burk K., Cairncross A., *Goodbye, Great Britain: The 1976 IMF Crisis*, Yale University Press, New Haven 1992.

Butler D., Kavanagh D., *The British general election of 1979*, Macmillan, Basingstoke 1980.

Caines E., *Heath and Thatcher in Opposition*, Palgrave Macmillan, London 2017.

Caligaris L., "Western peacekeeping in Lebanon: lessons of MLF", *Survival*, No. 6, 1984, pp. 262-268.

Campbell A., *Colleagues and friends*, Michael Russell, Salisbury 1988.

Campbell J., *Margaret Thatcher – volumes 1 and 2*, Jonathan Cape, London 2000 and 2007.

Camps M., *Britain and the European community: 1955-1963*, Princeton University Press, Princeton 1964.

Caviglia D., Labbate S. (eds.), *Al governo del cambiamento. L'Italia di Craxi tra rinnovamento e obiettivi mancati*, Rubbettino, Soveria Mannelli 2014.

Cawkell M., Hunt R., *The History of the Falkland Islands*, Anthony Nelson, London 2001.

Chaney E., *The Evolution of the Grand Tour: Anglo-Italian Cultural Relations since the Renaissance*, Frank Cass, London 1998.

Chipman J., *NATO's Southern Allies: Internal and External Challenges*, Routledge, London 2004.

Ciarrapico A., "Rapporti Est-Ovest 1977-79. La vicenda degli euromissili", *Rivista di Studi Politici Internazionali*, Vol. 69, No. 3, 2002, pp. 363-380.

Coates K., "What went wrong?", in *Id.* (ed.), *What went wrong: explaining the fall of the Labour government*, Spokesman Books, Nottingham 2008.

Coffey P., *European Monetary System: Past, Present, and Future*, Martinus Nijhoff, Dordrecht 1984.

Colarizi S., Gervasoni M., *La cruna dell'ago. Craxi, il partito socialista e la crisi della Repubblica*, Laterza, Roma-Bari 2005.

Collana di testi diplomatici. Vol. 13 Roberto Ducci, Ministero degli Affari Esteri – Ufficio Studi, Roma 1989.

Cominelli L., *L'Italia sotto tutela. Stati Uniti, Europa e crisi italiana degli anni Settanta*, Le Monnier, Firenze 2014.

Conroy H., *Callaghan*, Haus Publishing, London 2006.

Craveri P., *La Repubblica dal 1958 al 1992*, TEA, Torino 1996.

Cronin J., *New Labour's Pasts. The Labour Party and its discontents*, Longman, Harlow 2004.

Curini L., Martelli P., *I partiti nella Prima Repubblica. Maggioranze e governi dalla Costituente a Tangentopoli*, Carocci, Roma 2009.

Daddow O., *Harold Wilson and European integration: Britain's second application to join the EEC*, Frank Cass, London 2003.

Davidson J.W., *America's Allies and War*, Palgrave Macmillan, Basingstoke 2011.

de Leonardis M., *La 'diplomazia atlantica' e la soluzione del problema di Trieste (1952-1954)*, Edizioni Scientifiche Italiane, Napoli 1992.

de Leonardis M., *La Gran Bretagna e la Resistenza italiana (1943-1945)*, Edizioni Scientifiche Italiane, Napoli 1988.

De Rosa G., "Il Governo Spadolini di fronte alle 'quattro emergenze'", *Civiltà Cattolica*, quaderno 3146, 1981, pp. 191-199.

Deighton A., "Britain and the Three Interlocking Circles", in Varsori A. (ed.), *Europe 1945-1990s – The end of an era?*, Palgrave Macmillan, Basingstoke 1995, pp. 155-169.

Deighton A., Milward A.S. (eds.), *Widening, Deepening and Acceleration: the European Economic Community 1957-63*, Peter Lang, Brussels 1999.

Del Pero M., "The United States and the crises in Southern Europe", in Varsori A., Migani G. (eds.), *Europe in the international arena during the 1970s*, Peter Lang, Brussels 2011, pp. 301-316.

Del Pero M., Gavìn V., Guirao F., Varsori A. (eds.), *Democrazie. L'Europa meridionale e la fine delle dittature*, Le Monnier, Firenze 2010.

Del Pero M., *L'alleato scomodo. Gli Usa e la DC negli anni del centrismo (1948-1955)*, Carocci, Roma 2001.

Dell E., "Britain and the Origins of the European Monetary System", *Contemporary European History*, No. 1, 1994, pp. 1-60.

Devoto F.J., *Storia degli italiani in Argentina*, Donzelli, Roma 2007.

Di Donato M., "The Cold War and Socialist Identity: The Socialist International and the Italian 'Communist Question' in the 1970s", *Contemporary European History*, Vol. 24, No. 2, 2015, pp. 193-211.

Di Donato M., *I comunisti italiani e la sinistra europea*, Carocci, Roma 2015.

Di Donato M., Portolani R.D., "Il Foreign Office e la stampa italiana", in Taviani E., Vacca G. (eds.), *Gli intellettuali nella crisi della Repubblica (1968-1980)*, Viella, Roma 2016, pp. 333-352.

Di Martino P., Vasta M. (eds.) *Ricchi per caso. La parabola dello sviluppo economico italiano*, Il Mulino, Bologna 2017.

Dumbrell J., *A Special Relationship: Anglo-American Relations from the Cold War to Iraq*, Palgrave Macmillan, Basingstoke 2006.

Elliott P., Schlesinger P., "Eurocommunism: their word or ours?", in Childs D. (ed.), *The Changing Face of Western Communism*, Routledge, London 1980, pp. 37-73.

Elliott P., Schlesinger P., "Studying 'Eurocommunism', on unfolding ideology", *The Sociological Review*, 27, 1979, pp. 55-81.

Ellwood D.W., *L'alleato nemico. La politica dell'occupazione anglo-americana in Italia (1943-1946)*, Feltrinelli, Milano 1977.

Evangelista M., "Atomic ambivalence: Italy's evolving attitude towards nuclear weapons", in Verbeek B., Giacomello G. (eds.), *Italy's foreign policy in the twenty-first century: the new assertiveness of an aspiring middle power*, Lexington Books, Lanham, 2011, pp. 115-134.

Falciola L., *Il Movimento del 1977 in Italia*, Carocci, Roma 2015.

Farrell-Vinay G., "Lo specchio europeo. L'Italia vista dalla stampa britannica", in Giovagnoli A., Pons S. (eds.), *L'Italia repubblicana nella crisi degli anni Settanta. Tra guerra fredda e distensione, Vol. 1*, Rubbettino, Soveria Mannelli 2003, pp. 479-498.

Favretto I., *The Long Search for a 'Third Way': the British Labour Party and the Italian Left since 1945*, Palgrave Macmillan, Basingstoke 2003.

Felice E., *Ascesa e declino. Storia economica dell'Italia*, Il Mulino, Bologna 2015.

Filippone Thaulero G., *La Gran Bretagna e l'Italia dalla conferenza di Mosca a Potsdam (1943-1945)*, Edizioni di Storia e Letteratura, Roma 1979.

Filo della Torre P., *Thatcher la bambola di ferro*, Rizzoli, Milano 1983.

Fiore M., *Anglo-Italian relations in the Middle East, 1922-1940*, Ashgate, Farnham 2010.

Folly M., "Britain and the Issue of Italian Membership of NATO, 1948-49", *Review of International Studies*, Vol. 13, 1987, pp. 177-196.

Fondazione Craxi, *Bettino Craxi. La notte di Sigonella. Documenti e discorsi sull'evento che restituì l'orgoglio all'Italia*, Mondadori, Milano 2015.

Fornasier R., "The DC and the PCI in the Seventies: A Complex Relationship Supervised by the United States", *Bulletin of Italian Politics*, Vol. 4, No. 2, 2012, pp. 209-229.

Freedman L., *The official history of the Falklands campaign*, Vol. 1. *The origins of the Falklands War* and Vol. 2. *War and diplomacy*, Routledge, London 2005.

Galli G., *I partiti politici italiani (1943-2004)*, Rizzoli, Milano 2004.

Garnett M., Mabon S., Smith R., *British Foreign Policy since 1945*, Routledge, London 2018.

Garthoff R.L., *Détente and confrontation. American-Soviet Relations from Nixon to Reagan*, the Brookings Institutions, Washington 1985.

Gat M., *Britain and Italy, 1943-1949: The Decline of British Influence*, Sussex Academic Press, Brighton 1996.

Gentiloni Silveri U., *L'Italia sospesa. La crisi degli anni Settanta vista da Washington*, Einaudi, Torino 2009.

Gentiloni Silveri U., "Gli anni Settanta nel giudizio degli Stati Uniti: 'Un ponte verso l'ignoto'", in Giovagnoli A., Pons S. (eds.), *L'Italia repubblicana nella crisi degli anni Settanta. Tra guerra fredda e distensione, Vol. 1*, Rubbettino, Soveria Mannelli 2003, pp. 89-122.

George S., *An awkward partner. Britain in the European Community*, Oxford University Press, Oxford 1990.

Gerlini M., *Il dirottamento dell'Achille Lauro e i suoi inattesi e sorprendenti risvolti*, Mondadori, Milano 2016.

Gervasoni M., *Storia d'Italia negli anni Ottanta. Quando eravamo moderni*, Marsilio, Venezia 2010.

Gilbert M., "Il governo e la politica dell'Italia repubblicana", in Woolf S. (ed.), *L'Italia repubblicana vista da fuori (1945-2000)*, Il Mulino, Bologna 2007, pp. 85-127.

Ginsborg P., *A History of Contemporary Italy. Society and Politics, 1943-1988*, Penguin, London 1990.

Ginsborg P., *Italy and its discontent. Family, civil society, state 1980-2001*, Palgrave Macmillan, Basingstoke 2003.

Giovagnoli A., Pons S. (eds.), *L'Italia repubblicana nella crisi degli anni Settanta. Tra guerra fredda e distensione, Vol. 1*, Rubbettino, Soveria Mannelli 2003.

Goebel J., *The Struggle for the Falkland Islands: A Study in Legal and Diplomatic History*, Yale University Press, New Haven 1982.

González M.A., *The genesis of the Falklands (Malvinas) conflict. Argentina, Britain and the failed negotiations of the 1960s*, Palgrave Macmillan, Basingstoke 2013.

Gowland D., *Britain and the European Union*, Taylor & Francis, Abingdon 2016.

Gowland D., Turner A., *Reluctant Europeans: Britain and European Integration 1945-1998*, Routledge, London 1999.

Greenwood S., "Helping to Open the Door? Britain in the Last Decade of the Cold War", in Njølstad O. (ed.), *The Last Decade of the Cold War. From Conflict Escalation to Conflict Transformation*, Frank Cass, London 2004.

Gualtieri R., "The Italian Political system and Détente (1963-1981)", *Journal of Modern Italian Studies*, Vol. 9, No. 4, 2004, pp. 428-429.

Guarna L., *Richard Nixon e i partiti politici italiani*, Mondadori, Milano 2015.

Hajek A., "Memories on the Move: The Italian Student Movement of 1977 between Local, National and Global Memories of Protest", in Beyen M., Deseure B. (eds.), *Local Memories in a Nationalizing and Globalizing World*, Palgrave Macmillan, London 2015, pp. 258-276.

Harmon M., *The British Labour Government and the 1976 IMF Crisis*, Macmillan, Basingstoke 1997.

Hastings M., Jenkins S., *The battle for the Falklands*, Pan Books, London 2010.

Hazell R., Paun A. (eds.), *Making minority government work. Hung parliaments and the challenges for Westminster and Whitehall*, Institute for Government, London 2009.

Hennessey T., *Hunger Strike: Margaret Thatcher's Battle with the IRA, 1980-1981*, Irish Academic Press, Kildare 2013.

Heurtebize F., *Le péril rouge. Washington face à l'eurocommunisme*, PUF, Paris 2014.

Hickson K., *The IMF Crisis of 1976 and British Politics*, I.B. Tauris, London, 2005.

Hine D., "The Italian Socialist Party under Craxi: surviving but not reviving", in Lange P., Tarrow S. (eds.), Special issue on "Italy in transition", *West European Politics*, Vol. 2, No. 3, October 1979, pp. 133-148.

Hirowatari K., *Britain and European Monetary Cooperation, 1964/1979*, AIAA, Reston 2015.

Istituto Affari Internazionali, *L'Italia nella politica Internazionale (1979-1980)*, Edizioni di Comunità, Roma 1981.

"Italy-Malta: Agreement on the neutrality of Malta", *International Legal Materials*, Vol. 21, No. 2, 1982, pp. 396-398.

James H., *Making the European Monetary Union*, Belknap Press, Cambridge 2012.

Jenkins R., *A Life at the Centre*, Macmillan, London 1994.

Jenkins R., *Europe's Present Challenge and Future Opportunity* (first Jean Monnet Lecture), European University Institute, Florence, 27 October 1977.

Johansson K.M., "The alliance of European Christian democracy and conservatism: convergence through networking", in Kaiser W., Starie P., *Transnational European Union: Towards a Common Political Space*, Routledge, London 2005, pp. 131-149.

Kaiser W., *Using Europe, abusing the Europeans: Britain and European integration, 1945-63*, Palgrave Macmillan, Basingstoke 1996.

Katz S., Russell L.E., *Armies in Lebanon 1982-84*, Bloomsbury, London 2012.

Kelly S., *Cold War in the Desert: Britain, the US and the Italian Colonies, 1945-52*, Palgrave Macmillan, Basingstoke 2000.

Kirkup J., *The Lib-Lab Pact: A Parliamentary Agreement, 1977-78*, Springer, New York 2016.

Kitson M., "Failure followed by success or success followed by failure? A re-examination of British economic growth since 1949", in Floud R., Johnson P., *The Cambridge Economic History of Modern Britain, Vol. III: Structural Change and Growth, 1939-2000*, Cambridge University Press, Cambridge 2004, pp. 27-56.

Lagorio L., *L'ultima sfida. Gli euromissili*, Loggia de' Lanzi, Firenze 1998.

Lamb R., *Mussolini and the British*, John Murray, London 1997.

Lange P., "Preface", in Lange P., Tarrow S. (eds.), Special issue on "Italy in transition", *West European Politics*, Vol. 2, No. 3, October 1979, pp. 1-5.

Lange P., Tarrow S. (eds.), Special issue on "Italy in transition", *West European Politics*, Vol. 2, No. 3, October 1979.

Lawson N., *The View from No. 11: Memoirs of a Tory Radical*, Bantam, London 1992.

Leffler M.P., Westad O.A. (eds.), *The Cambridge History of the Cold War, Vol. III Endings*, Cambridge University Press, Cambridge 2010.

Leonardi R., Wertman D., *Italian Christian Democracy: the politics of dominance*, Springer, New York 1989.

Levi A., "Eurocommunism: myth or reality?", in Filo della Torre P., Mortimer E., Story J. (eds.), *Eurocommunism: myth or reality?*, Penguin Books, London 1979, p. 9-34.

Lipsey D., *In the Corridors of Power: An Autobiography*, Biteback Publishing, London 2012.

Lomellini V., Varsori A., "'Italian way of life': vizi e virtù dell'Italia degli anni '80 nella stampa internazionale", *Memoria e Ricerca*, Vol. 52, 2/2016, pp. 261-282.

Lubitz R., *The Italian Economic Crises of the 1970s*, International Finance Discussion Papers, No. 120, June 1978.

Ludlow N.P., "In search of a balance: Italy, Britain and the dream of another European axis?", in Craveri P., Varsori A. (eds.), *L'Italia nella costruzione europea. Un bilancio storico (1957-2007)*, FrancoAngeli, Milano 2009, pp. 67-78.

Ludlow N.P., *Dealing with Britain: the Six and the First UK Application to the EEC*, Cambridge University Press, Cambridge 1997.

Ludlow P., *The Making of the European Monetary System*, Butterworth, London 1982.

Macaluso E., *50 anni nel PCI*, Rubbettino, Soveria Mannelli 2003.

Mammarella G., "Il Consiglio Europeo di Milano del giugno 1985", in Di Nolfo E. (ed.), *La politica estera italiana negli anni ottanta*, Marsilio, Venezia 2007, pp. 189-210.

Margiocco M., *Stati Uniti e PCI 1943-1980*, Laterza, Roma-Bari 1981.

Marr A., *A history of modern Britain*, Pan Books, Basingstoke 2008.

Martin L.L., "Institutions and Cooperation: Sanctions during the Falkland Islands Conflict", *International Security*, Vol. 16, No. 4 (Spring, 1992), pp. 143-178.

Martin Lopez T., *The Winter of Discontent: Myth, Memory, History*, Liverpool University Press, Liverpool 2014.

Mechi L., "'Fra solidarietà europea e vincoli di sangue'. L'Italia e la crisi delle Falkland/Malvinas", *Annali della Fondazione Ugo La Malfa*, Vol. XVI, 2001, pp. 139-173.

Mechi L., Chiampan A., "Des intérêts difficilement conciliables: l'Italie, l'Europe et la crise des Falkland (avril-juin 1982)", *Guerres mondiales et conflits contemporains*, 245, 2012, pp. 115-132.

Micheletta L., *Italia e Gran Bretagna nel primo dopoguerra: le relazioni diplomatiche tra Roma e Londra dal 1919 al 1922*, Jouvence, Roma 1999.

Mistry K., *The United States, Italy and the Origins of the Cold War: Waging Political Warfare 1945-1950*, Cambridge University Press, Cambridge 2014.

Moore C., *Margaret Thatcher: The Authorized Biography – Vol. 1 and 2*, Penguin, London 2014 and 2016.

Mourlon-Druol E., *A Europe made of money. The emergence of the European Monetary System*, Cornell University Press, Ithaca 2012.

Mourlon-Druol E., Romero F. (eds.), *International Summitry and Global Governance. The Rise of the G7 and the European Council, 1974-1991*, Routledge, London 2014.

Napolitano G., *The Italian Road to Socialism. An interview by Eric Hobsbawm with Giorgio Napolitano of the Italian Communist Party*, Journeyman Press, London 1977.

Needham D., *UK Monetary Policy from Devaluation to Thatcher, 1967-82*, Palgrave Macmillan, London 2014.

Neri Gualdesi M., "Under a Multinational Mantle: Italy's Participation in the G7 (1975-76)", in Varsori A., Zaccaria B., *Italy in the International System from Détente to the End of the Cold War*, Palgrave Macmillan, London 2017, pp. 69-94.

Nichols P., "On the Italian Crisis", *Foreign Affairs*, Vol. 54, No. 3, April 1976, pp. 511-526.

Nichols P., *Italia, Italia*, Fontana Press, New York 1975.

Nichols P., *La scelta italiana*, Garzanti, Milano 1977.

Njølstad O. (ed.), *The Last Decade of the Cold War. From Conflict Escalation to Conflict Transformation*, Frank Cass, London 2004.

Nuti L., "Italy, the British application and the January debacle", in Griffiths R., Ward S. (eds.), *Courting the Common Market: the first attempt to enlarge the European Community 1960-63*, Lothian Foundation Press, London 1996, pp. 101-119.

Nuti L., "The Nuclear Debate in Italian Politics in the Late 1970s and the Early 1980s", in Nuti L., Bozo F., Rey M.-P., Rother B. (eds.), *The Euromissile Crisis and the End of the Cold War*, Stanford University Press, Stanford 2015, pp. 231-250.

Nuti L., Bozo F., Rey M.-P., Rother B. (eds.), *The Euromissile Crisis and the End of the Cold War*, Stanford University Press, Stanford 2015.

Nuti L., *Gli Stati Uniti e l'apertura a sinistra. Importanza e limiti della presenza americana in Italia*, Laterza, Roma-Bari 1999.

Nuti L., *La sfida nucleare*, Il Mulino, Bologna 2007.

OECD Economic Surveys. Italy 1976, Organization for Economic Co-operation and Development, Paris 1976.

Owen D., "Communism, Socialism, and Democracy", *The Washington Quarterly*, Vol. 1, No. 2, 1978, pp. 4-15.

Parr H., *Britain's policy towards the European Community. Harold Wilson and Britain's world role, 1964-1970*, Routledge, London 2006.

Parsons M., *The Falklands War*, Sutton, Stroud (Gloucestershire) 2000.

Pasquino G., "Italian Christian Democracy: a party for all season?", in Lange P., Tarrow S. (eds.), Special issue on "Italy in transition", *West European Politics*, Vol. 2, No. 3, October 1979, p. 88-109.

Pedaliu E., *Britain, Italy and the origins of the Cold War*, Palgrave Macmillan, Basingstoke 2003.

Piffer T., *Gli Alleati e la Resistenza italiana*, Il Mulino, Bologna 2010.

Poggiolini I., *Alle origini dell'Europa allargata. La Gran Bretagna e l'adesione alla CEE (1972-1973)*, Unicopli, Milano 2004.

Pons S., "Il socialismo europeo, la sinistra italiana e la crisi del comunismo", in Colarizi S., Craveri P., Pons S., Quagliariello G. (eds.), *Gli anni Ottanta come storia*, Rubbettino, Soveria Mannelli 2004, pp. 215-230.

Pons S., "The rise and fall of Eurocommunism", in Leffler M., Westad O. (eds.), *The Cambridge History of the Cold War*, Cambridge University Press, Cambridge 2010, pp. 45-65.

Pons S., *Berlinguer e la fine del comunismo*, Einaudi, Torino 2006.

Pons S., *The Global Revolution. A History of International Communism 1917-1991*, Oxford University Press, Oxford 2014.

Pope R., *The British economy since 1914: a study in decline?*, Longman, London 1998.

Raponi D., "L'Italia vista dall'estero (1980-2010)", in Pons S., Roccucci A., Romero F., *L'Italia contemporanea dagli anni Ottanta a oggi. Vol. I Fine della Guerra fredda e globalizzazione*, Carocci, Roma 2014, pp. 393-412.

Report of the Seventy-Fifth Annual Conference of the Labour Party, Labour Party, London 1976.

Reynolds D., *Britannia Overruled. British Policy and World Power in the Twentieth Century*, Longman, Harlow 2000.

Ritter C., "The double life of the Italian suit", in Cinotto S. (ed.), *Making Italian America: Consumer Culture and the Production of Ethnic Identities*, Fordham University Press, New York 2014, pp. 195-206.

Rizas S., *The rise of the Left in Southern Europe: Anglo-American responses*, Pickening&Chatto, London 2012.

Rizzo A., *La frontiera dell'Eurocomunismo*, Laterza, Roma-Bari 1977.

Roberts R., *When Britain went bust. The 1976 IMF crisis*, OMFIF Press, London 2016.

Sassoon D., "Eurocommunism, the Labour Party and the EEC", *The Political Quarterly*, Vol. 50, No. 1, January 1979, pp. 86-99.

Savignoni D., "The Internal Dissenter: Italy", in Stavridis S., Hill C. (eds.), *Domestic Sources of Foreign Policy: West European Reactions to the Falklands Conflict*, Berg, Oxford 1996, pp. 114-131.

Scoppola P., "Una crisi politica e istituzionale", in De Rosa G., Monina G. (eds.), *L'Italia Repubblicana nella crisi degli anni Settanta, Vol. 4 Sistema politico e istituzioni*, Rubbettino, Soveria Mannelli 2003, pp. 17-40.

Shavit Y., Westerbeek K., "Educational Stratification in Italy: Reforms, Expansion, and Equality of Opportunity", *European Sociological Review*, Vol. 14, No. 1, 1998, pp. 33-47.

Shepherd J., "The Fall of the Callaghan Government, 1979", in Heppell T., Theakston K. (eds.), *How Labour Governments Fall*, Palgrave Macmillan, Basingstoke 2013, pp. 113-140.

Shepherd J., *Crisis? What crisis? The Callaghan government and the British "winter of discontent"*, Manchester University Press, Manchester 2013.

Spaventa L., "Italy Joins the EMS: A Political History", *Johns Hopkins University Bologna Center Occasional Paper*, No. 32, 1980, pp. 67-93.

Statler J., "The European Monetary System: From Conception to Birth", *International Affairs*, No. 2, 1979, pp. 206-225.

Stoddart K., "Creating the 'Seamless Robe of Deterrence': Great Britain's Role in NATO's INF Debate", in Nuti L., Bozo F., Rey M.-P., Rother B. (eds.), *The Euromissile Crisis and the End of the Cold War*, Stanford University Press, Stanford 2015, pp. 176-195.

Story J., "The launching of the EMS: An Analysis of Change in Foreign Economic Policy", *Political Studies*, 3, 1988, pp. 397-412.

Strange I.J., *The Falkland Islands*, David & Charles, London 1983.

Tarrow S., "Aspetti della crisi italiana: note introduttive", in Graziano L., Tarrow S. (eds.), *La crisi italiana*, Einaudi, Torino 1979, pp. 3-40.

Tarrow S., "Italy: Crisis, Crises or Transition?", in Lange P., Tarrow S. (eds.), Special issue on "Italy in transition", *West European Politics*, Vol. 2, No. 3, October 1979, pp. 166-186.

Thatcher M., *The Downing Street years*, HarperCollins, London 1993.

The Brixton Disorders 10-12 April 1981, Report of an Inquiry by the Rt. Hon. The Lord Scarman, Cmnd. 8427, HMSO, 1981.

Theakston K. (ed.), *British Foreign Secretaries since 1974*, Routledge, London 2004.

Treharne S.-A., *Reagan and Thatcher's Special Relationship*, Edinburgh University Press, Edinburgh 2015.

Turner M.J., *Britain's International Role, 1970-1991*, Palgrave Macmillan, Basingstoke 2010.

Valiani L., *I governi Spadolini e la lotta al terrorismo*, Edizioni de La Voce Repubblicana, Roma 1983.

Varsori A., *Gli alleati e l'emigrazione democratica antifascista (1940-1943)*, Sansoni, Firenze 1982.

Varsori A., *Il diverso declino di due potenze coloniali: gli eventi di Mogadiscio del gennaio 1948 e i rapporti anglo-italiani*, Elengraf, Roma 1981.

Varsori A., *La Cenerentola d'Europa? L'Italia e l'integrazione europea dal 1947 ad oggi*, Rubbettino, Soveria Mannelli 2010.

Varsori A., "Great Britain and Italy 1945-1956: The Partnership between a Great Power and a Minor Power?", *Diplomacy and Statecraft*, Vol. 2, 1992, pp. 188-228.

Varsori A., "La Gran Bretagna e le elezioni politiche italiane del 18 aprile 1948", *Storia Contemporanea*, Vol. 13, No. 1, 1982, pp. 5-71.

Varsori A., "Puerto Rico (1976): le potenze occidentali e il problema comunista in Italia", *Ventunesimo Secolo*, 2008, pp. 89-121.

Varsori A., "The relaunching of Europe in the mid-1980s", in Patel K.K., Weisbrode K. (eds.), *European integration and the Atlantic Community in the 1980s*, Cambridge University Press, Cambridge 2013, pp. 226-242.

Varsori A., "Italy's foreign policy in the 1980s: from enthusiasm to disillusion", in Varsori A., Zaccaria B. (eds.), *Italy in the International System from Détente to the End of the Cold War. The Underrated Ally*, Palgrave Macmillan, London 2017, pp. 95-124.

Varsori A., Migani G. (eds.), *Europe in the International Arena during the 1970s*, Peter Lang, Brussels 2011.

Varsori A., Zaccaria B. (eds.), *Italy in the International System from Détente to the End of the Cold War. The Underrated Ally*, Palgrave Macmillan, London 2017.

Vinen R., *Thatcher's Britain. The Politics and Social Upheaval of the 1980s*, Simon&Schuster, London 2009.

Wall S., *A stranger in Europe. Britain and the EU from Thatcher to Blair*, Oxford University Press, Oxford 2008.

Walsh J.I., *European Monetary Integration & Domestic Politics: Britain, France, and Italy*, Lynne Rienner, Boulder 2000.

Wass D., *Decline to Fall: The Making of British Macro-Economic Policy and the 1976 IMF Crisis*, Oxford University Press, Oxford 2008.

Whitehead P., *The writing on the wall*, Michael Joseph, London 1985.

Whittam J.R., "Drawing the Line: Britain and the Emergence of the Trieste Question, January 1941-May 1945", *The English Historical Review*, Vol. 106, No. 419, 1991, pp. 346-370.

Wilson H., "The impact of Eurocommunism on the Western alliance", *Labour & Trade Union Press Service of the Labour Committee for Transatlantic Understanding*, Vol. 11, No. 9, November 1977.

XIV Congresso del Partito Comunista Italiano. Atti e Risoluzioni, Editori Riuniti, Roma 1975.

Young H., *This blessed plot*, The Overlook Press, New York 1998.

Young J., *A Conservative interpretation of the Italian crisis*, The Monday Club, London 1979.

Zavoli S., *La notte della Repubblica*, Nuova Eri-Mondadori, Roma, 1992.

Index

H

I

J

Q

R

S

EUROCLIO – Published Books

N° 103 – *Alcide De Gasperi: European Founding Father*. Daniela Preda, 2018.

N° 102 – *Détente and Beyond. Anglo-Romanian Relations in the Aviation Industry (1966-1993)*. Mauro Elli, 2018.

N° 101 – *Experts and Expertise in Science and Technology in Europe since the 1960s Organized civil Society, Democracy and Political Decision-making*. Christine Bouneau, David Burigana (eds.), 2018.

N° 100 – *Jean Monnet et l'économie*. Gérard Bossuat (dir.), 2018.

N° 99 – *The History of the European Monetary Union. Comparing Strategies amidst Prospects for Integration and National Resistance.* Daniela Preda, 2017.

N° 98 – *The European Union Approach Towards Western Sahara*. Marco Balboni and Giuliana Laschi, 2016.

N° 97 – *Europe between Imperial Decline and Quest for Integration. Pro-European Groups and the French, Belgian and British Empires (1947-1957)*. Laura Kottos, 2016.

N° 96 – *Réinventer la diplomatie. Sociabilités, réseaux et pratiques diplomatiques en Europe depuis 1919 / Reshaping Diplomacy. Networks, Practices and Dynamics of Socialization in European Diplomacy since 1919.* Vincent Genin, Matthieu Osmont and Thomas Raineau (eds.), 2016.

N° 95 – *Sometimes Speaking with a Single Voice. The European Community as an International Actor, 1969-1979.* Lorenzo Ferrari, 2016.

N° 94 – *Competition Law Challenges in the Next Decade*. Sofia Oliveira Pais (ed.), 2016.

N° 93 – *The Borders of Schengen*. Alice Cunha, Marta Silva, Rui Frederico (eds.), 2015.

N° 92 – *Que dire à l'Espagne ? De l'isolement franquiste à la démocratie européiste, la France au dé i, 1957-1979*. Pablo Martin-Pañeda, 2015.

N° 91 – *Francis Delaisi, du dreyfusisme à « l'Europe nouvelle »*. Éric Bussière, Olivier Dard, Geneviève Duchenne (dir.), 2015.

N° 90 – *European Parties and the European Integration Process, 1945-1992.* Lucia Bonfreschi, Giovanni Orsina, Antonio Varsori (eds.), 2015

N° 89 – *Européanisation et démocratisation des États baltes dans la période de préadhésion à l'UE. Le rôle de la conditionnalité politique des organisations européennes.* Anne-Sylvie Pigeonnier, 2015.

N° 88 – *Le Continent basket. L'Europe et le basket-ball au XXe siècle.* Fabien Archambault, Loïc Artiaga, Gérard Bosc (dir.), 2015.

N° 87 – *The Convention on the Future of Europe. How States Behave in a New Institutional Context of Negotiation.* Francesco Marchi, 2015.

N° 86 – *Christian Democrat Internationalism. Its Action in Europe and Worldwide from post World War II until the 1990s. Volume III. The European People's Party Continental and Social Cooperation.* Jean-Dominique Durand (ed.), 2014.

N° 85 – *Pela Paz! For Peace! Pour la paix ! (1849-1939).* Maria Manuela Tavares Ribeiro, Maria Fernanda Rollo, Isabel Maria Freitas Valente, Alice Cunha (eds.), 2014.

N° 84 – *Economic Crisis and New Nationalisms. German Political Economy as Perceived by European Partners.* Antonio Varsori, Monika Poettinger (eds.), 2014.

N° 83 – *European Constitutionalism. Historical and Contemporary Perspectives.* Alexandre Dupeyrix, Gérard Raulet (eds.), 2014.

N° 82 – *Cross-Border Cooperation Structures in Europe. Learning from the Past, Looking to the Future.* Luis Domínguez, Iva Pires (eds.), 2014.

N° 81 – *The European Community and the World. A Historical Perspective.* Giuliana Laschi (ed.), 2014.

N° 80 – *Christian Democrat Internationalism. Its Action in Europe and Worldwide from Post World War II until the 1990s. Volume II: The Development (1945-1979). The Role of Parties, Movements, People.* Jean-Dominique Durand (ed.), 2013.

N° 79 – *Christian Democrat Internationalism. Its Action in Europe and Worldwide from Post World War II until the 1990s. Volume I: The Origins.* Jean-Dominique Durand (ed.), 2013.

N° 78 – *Investment Banking History. National and Comparative Issues (19th-21st centuries).* Hubert Bonin & Carlo Brambilla (eds.), 2013.

N° 77 – *Citizenship and Solidarity in the European Union. From the Charter of Fundamental Rights to the Crisis, the State of the Art.* Mariana Canotilho, Pedro Madeira Froufe & Alessandra Silveira (eds.), 2013.

N° 76– *The OSCE: Soft Security for a Hard World. Competing Theories for Understanding the OSCE.* Roberto Dominguez (ed.), 2013.

Euroclio European Network

together with the SEGEI Network

Coordination : Chaire Jean Monnet d'histoire de l'Europe contemporaine (Cehec)
Collège Erasme, 1, place Blaise-Pascal, B-1348 Louvain-la-Neuve

Germany
- Jürgen Elvert
- Wilfried Loth

Belgium
- Julie Cailleau
- Jocelyne Collonval
- Yves Conrad
- Gaëlle Courtois
- Pascal Deloge
- Geneviève Duchenne
- Vincent Dujardin
- Michel Dumoulin
- Roch Hannecart
- Pierre-Yves Plasman
- Béatrice Roeh
- Corine Schröder
- Caroline Suzor
- Pierre Tilly
- Arthe Van Laer
- Jérôme Wilson
- Natacha Wittorski

Spain
- Enrique Moradiellos
- Mercedes Samaniego Boneu

France
- Françoise Berger
- Marie-Thérèse Bitsch
- Gérard Bossuat
- Éric Bussière
- Jean-François Eck
- Catherine Horel
- Philippe Mioche
- Marine Moguen-Toursel
- Sylvain Schirmann
- Matthieu Trouvé
- Laurent Warlouzet
- Emilie Willaert

Hungary
- Gergely Fejérdy

Italy
- David Burigana
- Elena Calandri
- Eleonora Guasconi
- Luciano Segreto
- Antonio Varsori

Luxemburg
- Charles Barthel
- Etienne Deschamps
- Jean-Marie Kreins
- René Leboutte
- Robert Philippart
- Corine Schröder
- Gilbert Trausch

The Netherlands
- Anjo Harryvan
- Jan W. Brouwer
- Jan van der Herst

Poland
- Józef Laptos
- Zdzisiaw Mach

Switzerland
- Antoine Fleury
- Lubor Jilek